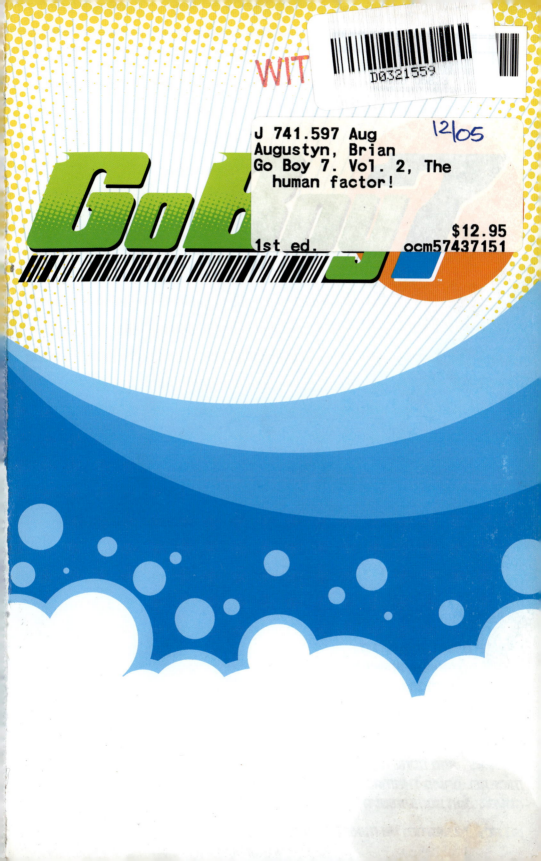

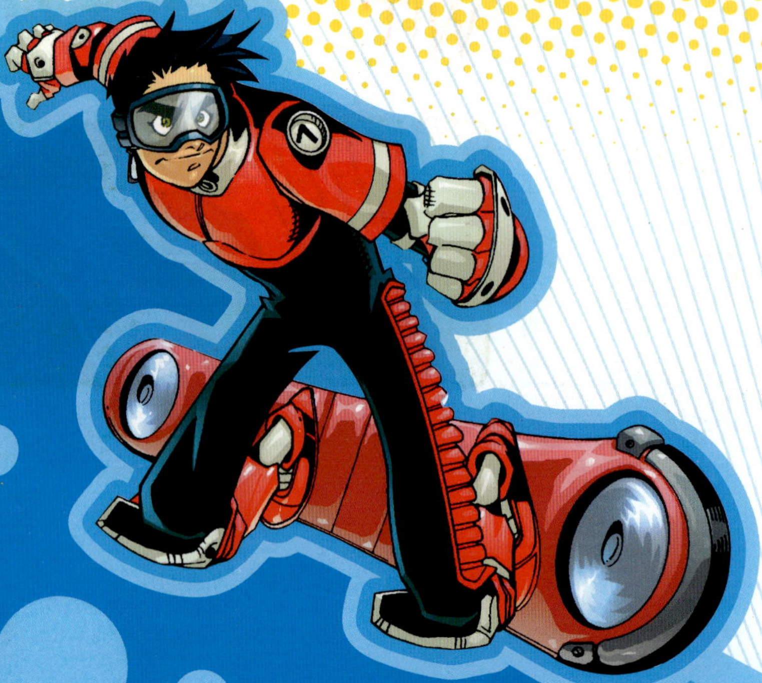

SCRIPT BRIAN AUGUSTYN
PENCILS JON SOMMARIVA
AND TODD DEMONG
INKS KRIS JUSTICE, AND VINCE RUSSELL
COLORS DAN JACKSON, DARRIN MOORE,
JON SOMMARIVA, AND DAVE NESTELLE
LETTERS SNO CONE AND
MICHAEL DAVID THOMAS
COVER JON SOMMARIVA

GO BOY 7 CREATED BY MIKE RICHARDSON

THE HUMAN FACTOR!

GoBoy 7™

ROCKET™ COMICS

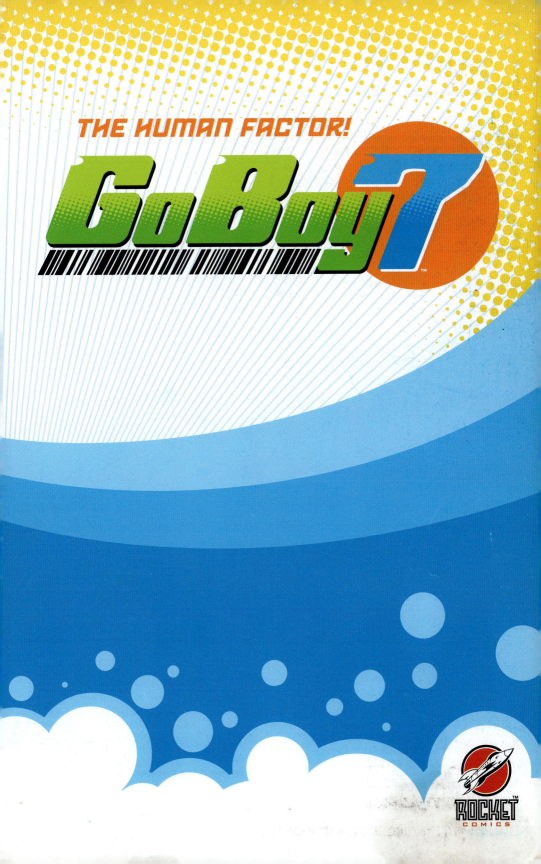

PUBLISHER MIKE RICHARDSON
EDITOR DAVE LAND
ASSISTANT EDITOR KATIE MOODY
COLLECTION DESIGNER DARIN FABRICK

THIS BOOK COLLECTS ISSUES 5 THROUGH 8 OF
THE DARK HORSE COMIC-BOOK SERIES GO BOY 7

DARK HORSE BOOKS
A DIVISION OF DARK HORSE COMICS, INC.
10956 SE MAIN STREET MILWAUKIE, OR 97222

WWW.ROCKETCOMICS.NET WWW.DARKHORSE.COM

TO FIND A COMICS SHOP IN YOUR AREA CALL
THE COMIC SHOP LOCATOR SERVICE TOLL-FREE AT (888) 266-4226

FIRST EDITION: SEPTEMBER 2004
ISBN: 1-59307-264-3
10 9 8 7 6 5 4 3 2 1
PRINTED IN CHINA

TO ROSEMARY ROJO
1956-2004

THANKS FOR BEING MY TEACHER,
ADVISOR, FRIEND, AND INSPIRATION.
BUT, ABOVE ALL ELSE, THANKS FOR
BEING THE GREATEST MUM.

LOVE YOU FOREVER,
JON

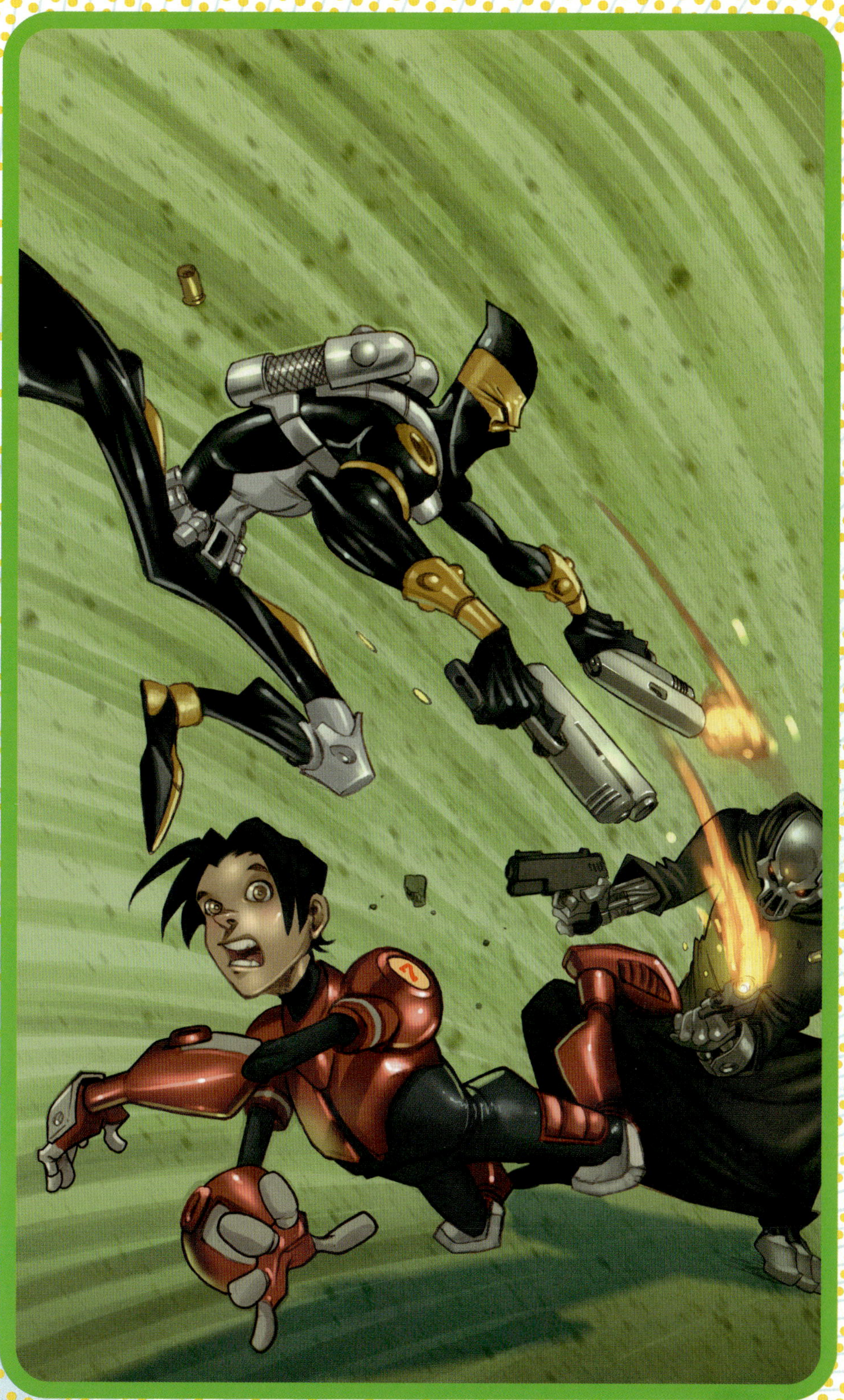

"THE HUMAN FACTOR"

SCRIPT BRIAN AUGUSTYN

PENCILS JON SOMMARIVA

INKS KRIS JUSTICE

COLORS DAN JACKSON

LETTERS SNO CONE

COVER FRANCISCO RUIZ VELASCO

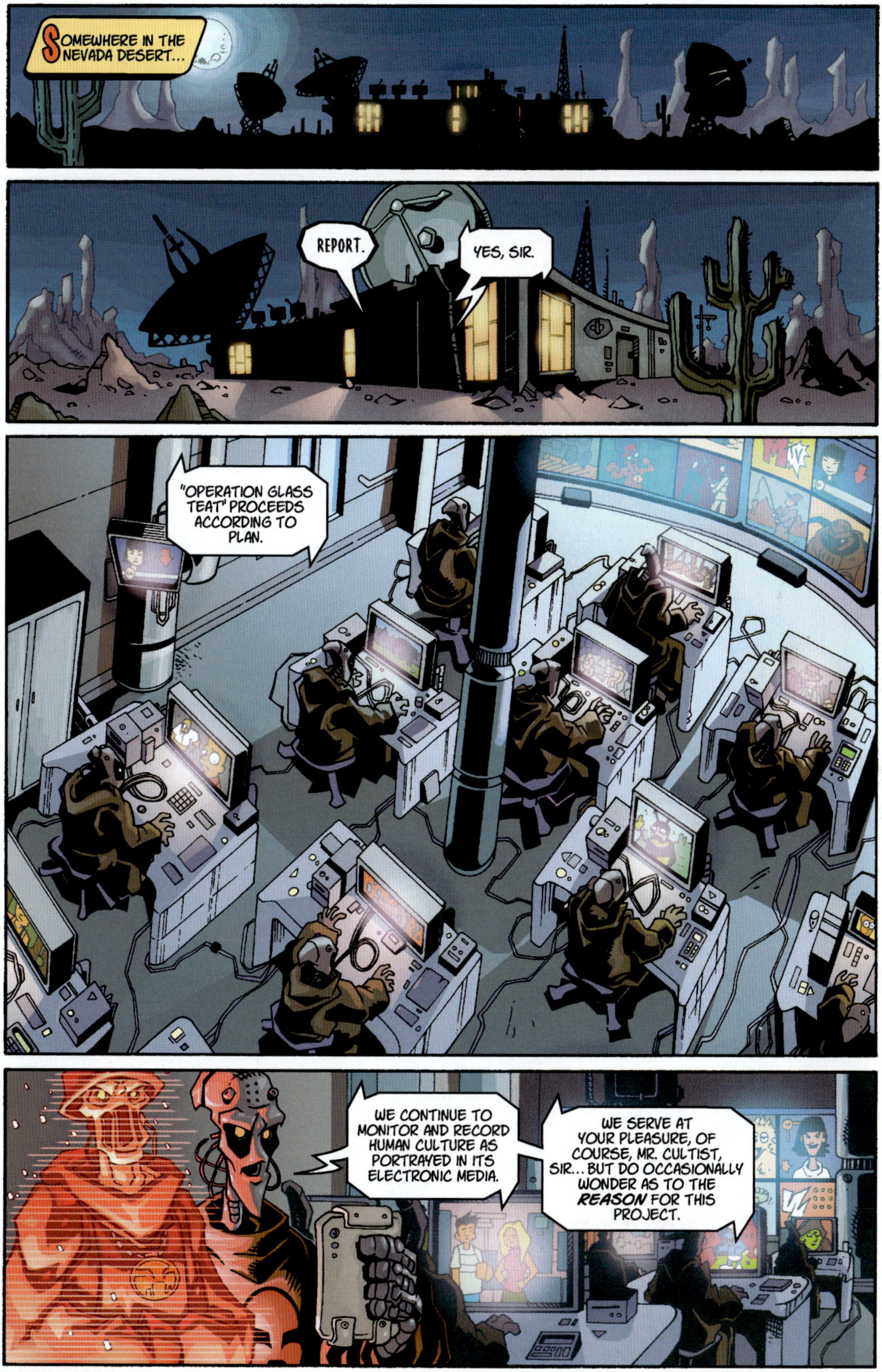
SOMEWHERE IN THE NEVADA DESERT...
REPORT.
YES, SIR.
"OPERATION GLASS TEAT" PROCEEDS ACCORDING TO PLAN.
WE CONTINUE TO MONITOR AND RECORD HUMAN CULTURE AS PORTRAYED IN ITS ELECTRONIC MEDIA.
WE SERVE AT YOUR PLEASURE, OF COURSE, MR. CULTIST, SIR... BUT DO OCCASIONALLY WONDER AS TO THE REASON FOR THIS PROJECT.

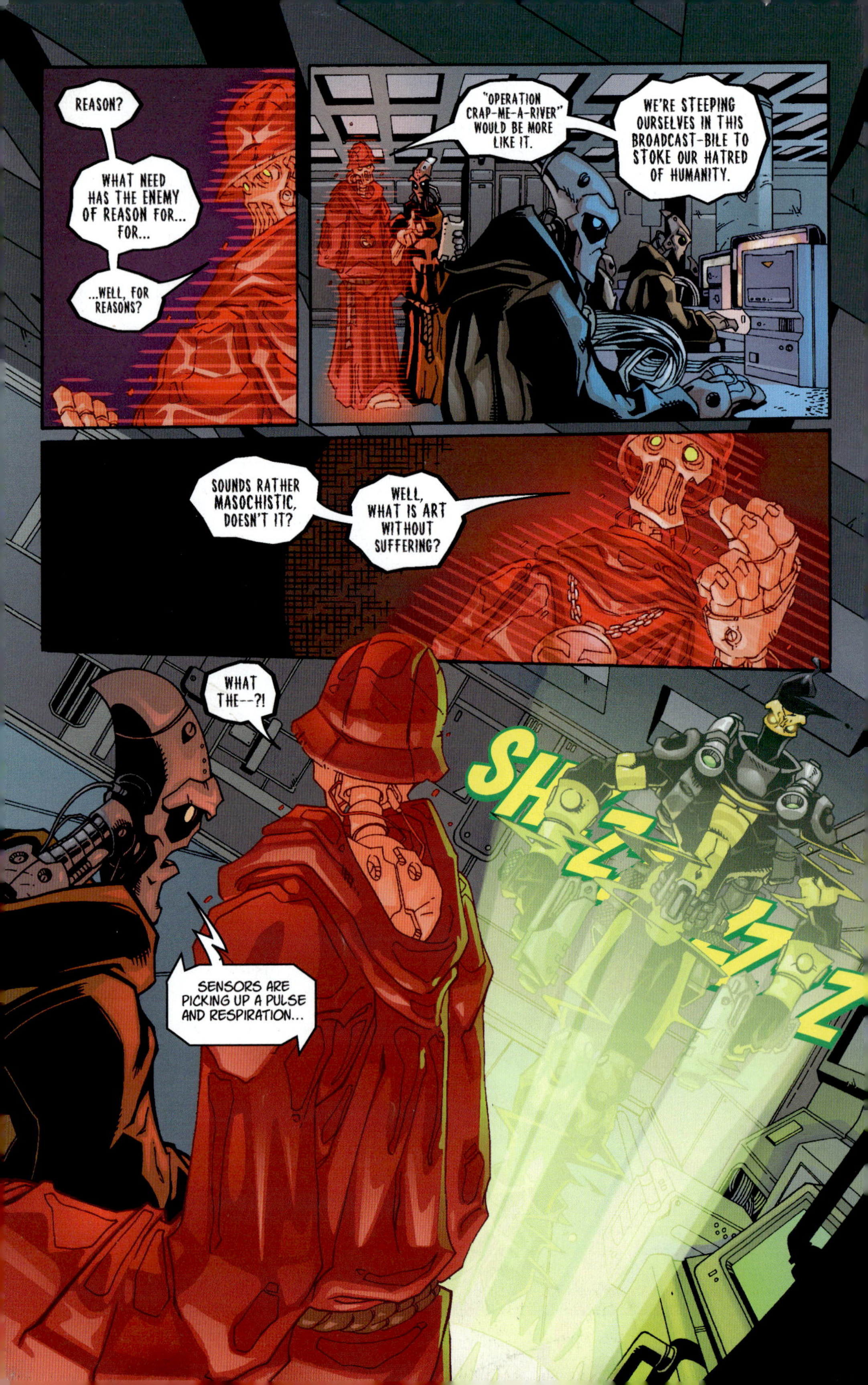
REASON?
WHAT NEED HAS THE ENEMY OF REASON FOR... FOR...
...WELL, FOR REASONS?
"OPERATION CRAP-ME-A-RIVER" WOULD BE MORE LIKE IT.
WE'RE STEEPING OURSELVES IN THIS BROADCAST-BILE TO STOKE OUR HATRED OF HUMANITY.
SOUNDS RATHER MASOCHISTIC, DOESN'T IT?
WELL, WHAT IS ART WITHOUT SUFFERING?
WHAT THE--?!
SENSORS ARE PICKING UP A PULSE AND RESPIRATION...

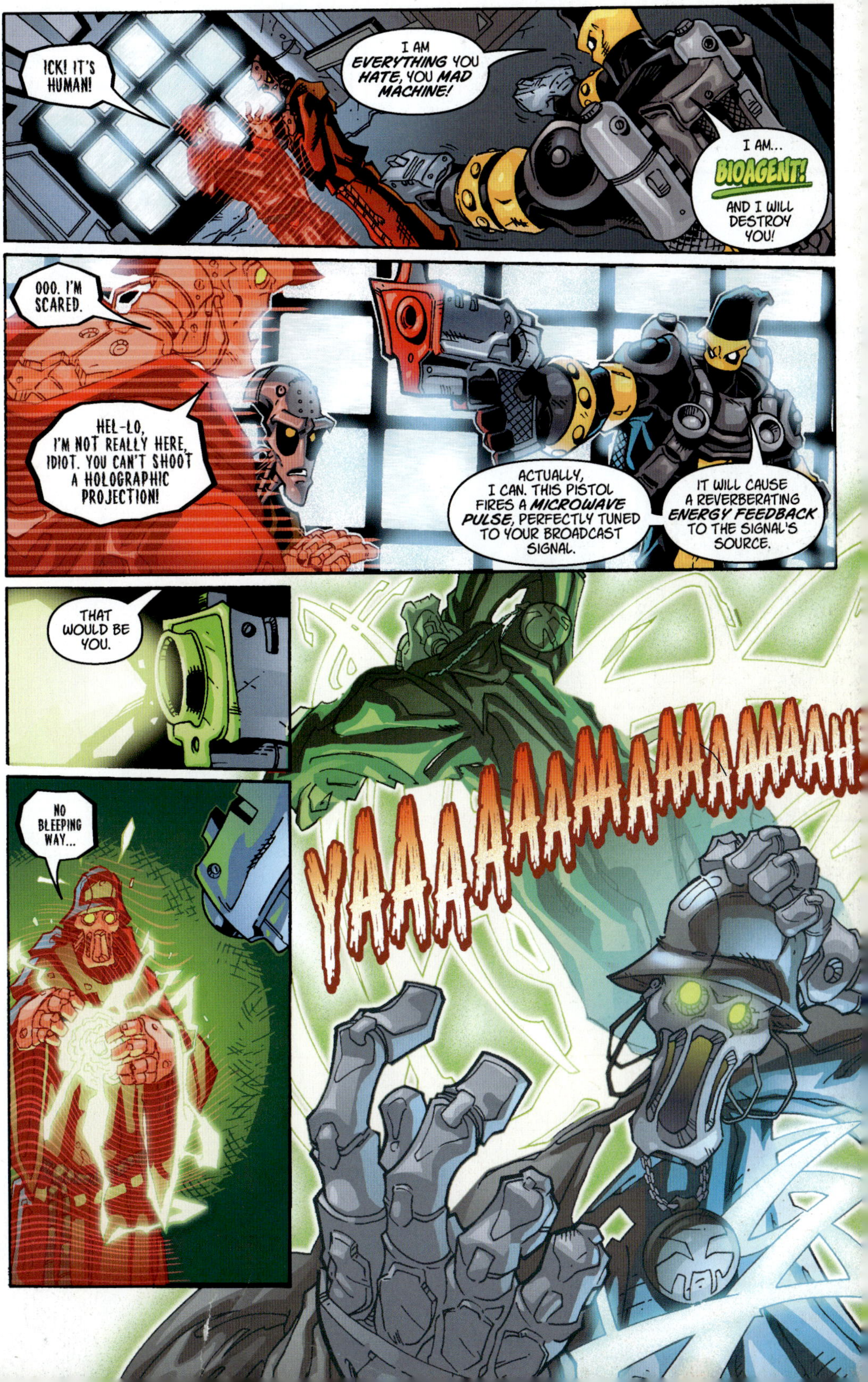
ICK! IT'S HUMAN!
I AM EVERYTHING YOU HATE, YOU MAD MACHINE!
I AM... BIOAGENT! AND I WILL DESTROY YOU!
OOO. I'M SCARED.
HEL-LO, I'M NOT REALLY HERE, IDIOT. YOU CAN'T SHOOT A HOLOGRAPHIC PROJECTION!
ACTUALLY, I CAN. THIS PISTOL FIRES A MICROWAVE PULSE, PERFECTLY TUNED TO YOUR BROADCAST SIGNAL.
IT WILL CAUSE A REVERBERATING ENERGY FEEDBACK TO THE SIGNAL'S SOURCE.
THAT WOULD BE YOU.
NO BLEEPING WAY...
YAAAAAAAAAAAAAAAAAH

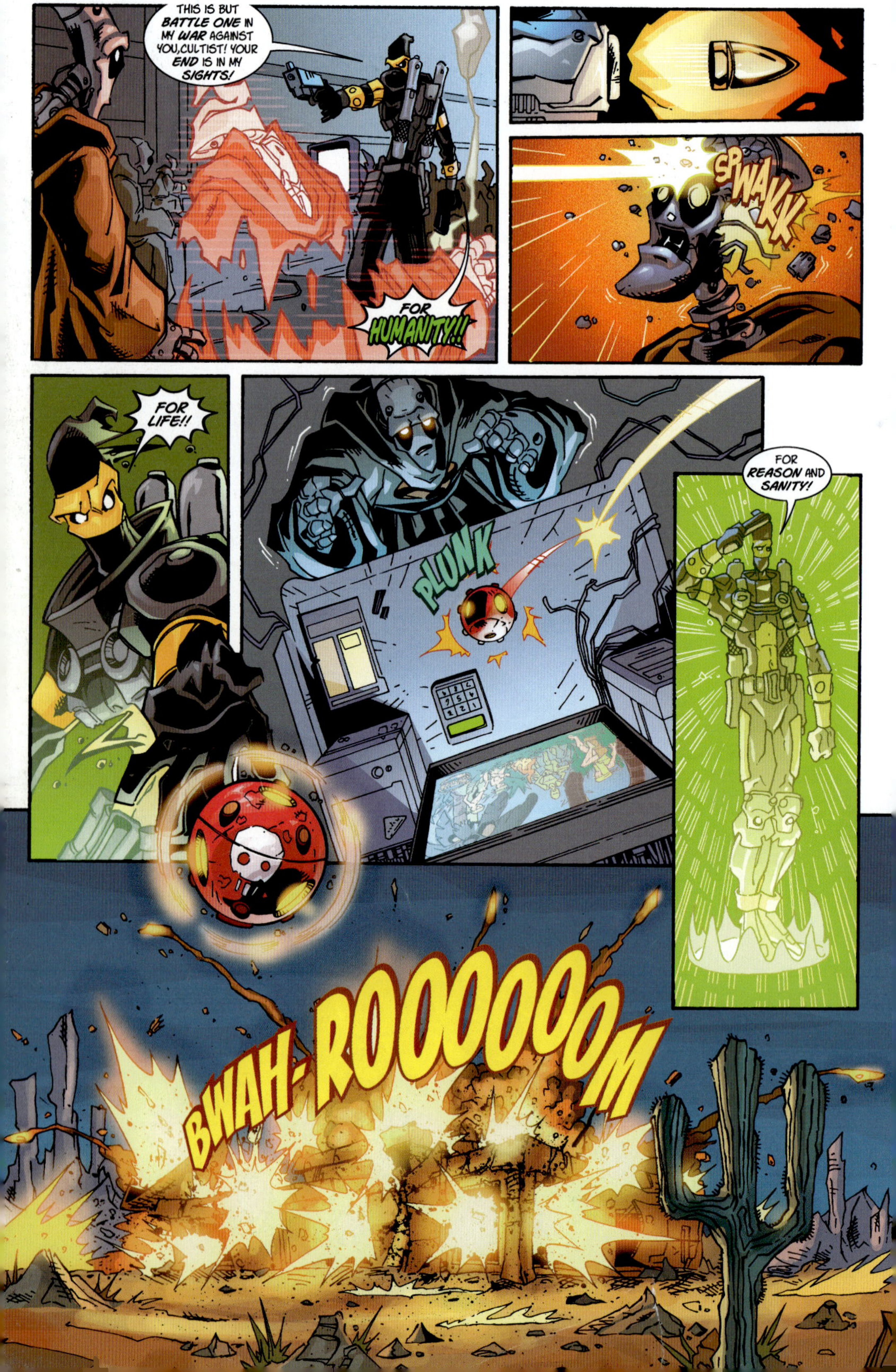
THIS IS BUT BATTLE ONE IN MY WAR AGAINST YOU, CULTIST! YOUR END IS IN MY SIGHTS!
FOR HUMANITY!!
SPWAKK
FOR LIFE!!
PLUNK
FOR REASON AND SANITY!
BWAH-ROOOOOOM

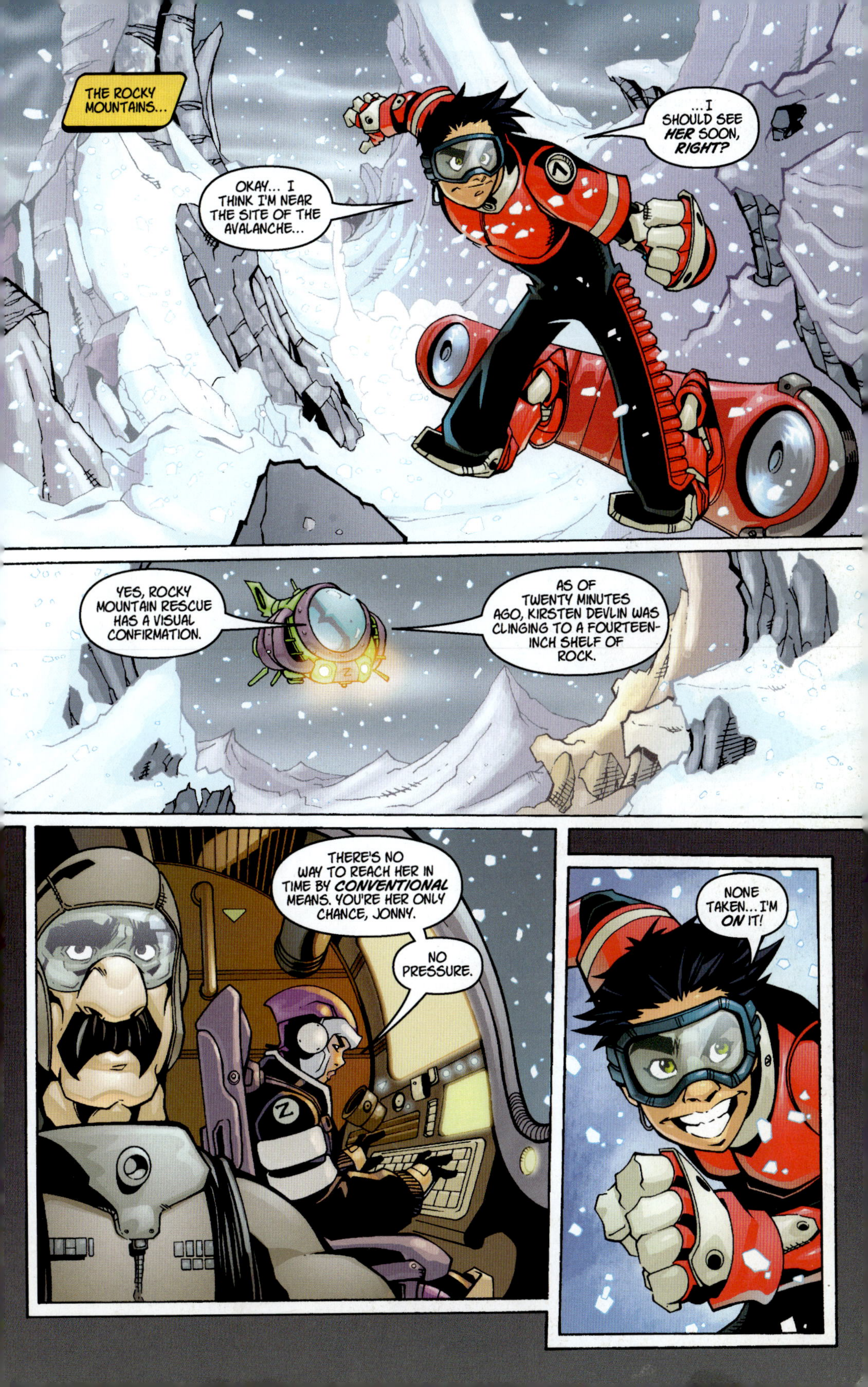
THE ROCKY MOUNTAINS...
OKAY... I THINK I'M NEAR THE SITE OF THE AVALANCHE...
...I SHOULD SEE HER SOON, RIGHT?
YES, ROCKY MOUNTAIN RESCUE HAS A VISUAL CONFIRMATION.
AS OF TWENTY MINUTES AGO, KIRSTEN DEVLIN WAS CLINGING TO A FOURTEEN-INCH SHELF OF ROCK.
THERE'S NO WAY TO REACH HER IN TIME BY CONVENTIONAL MEANS. YOU'RE HER ONLY CHANCE, JONNY.
NO PRESSURE.
NONE TAKEN... I'M ON IT!

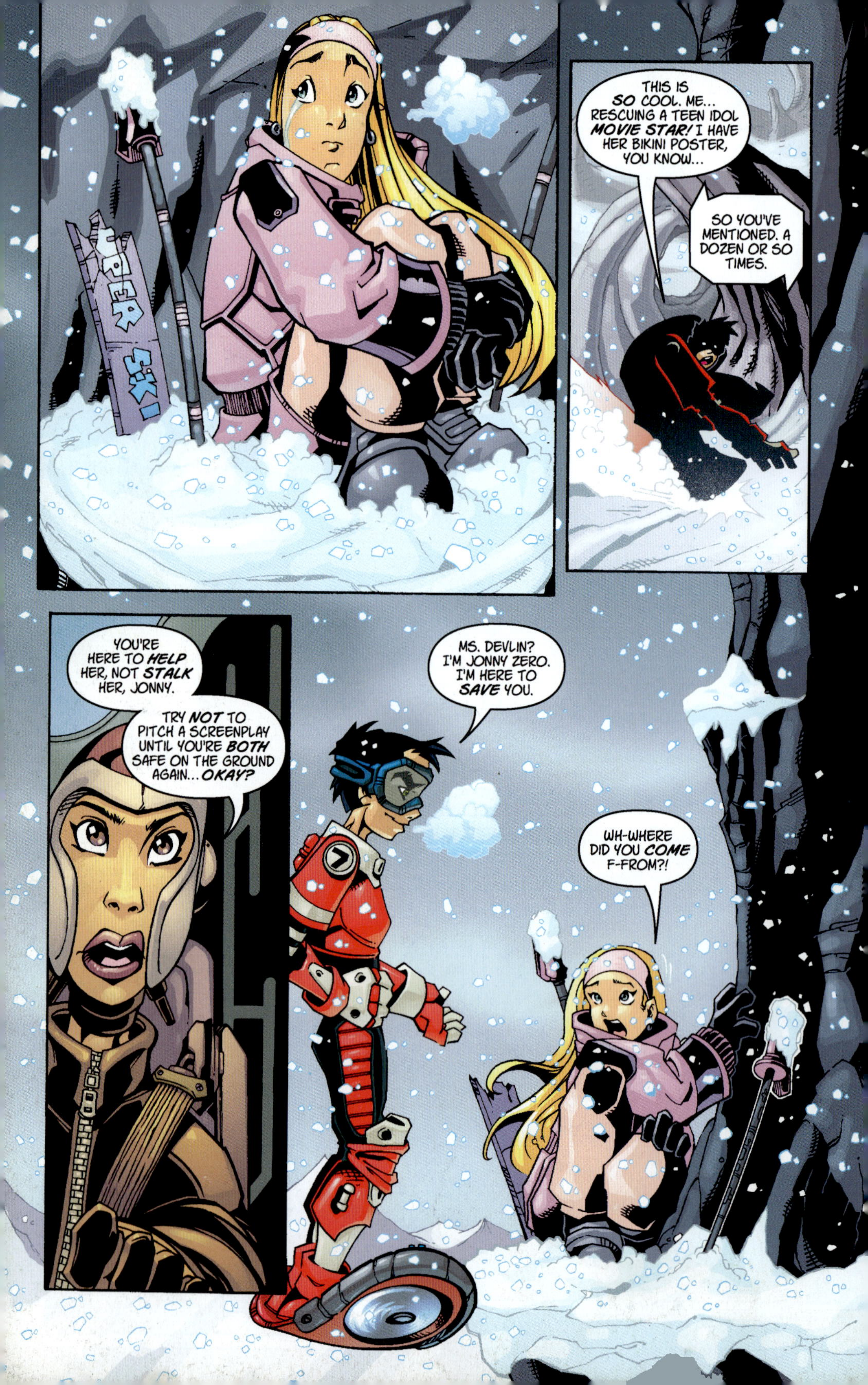

PER SKI
THIS IS SO COOL. ME... RESCUING A TEEN IDOL MOVIE STAR! I HAVE HER BIKINI POSTER, YOU KNOW...
SO YOU'VE MENTIONED. A DOZEN OR SO TIMES.
YOU'RE HERE TO HELP HER, NOT STALK HER, JONNY.
TRY NOT TO PITCH A SCREENPLAY UNTIL YOU'RE BOTH SAFE ON THE GROUND AGAIN... OKAY?
MS. DEVLIN? I'M JONNY ZERO. I'M HERE TO SAVE YOU.
WH-WHERE DID YOU COME F-FROM?!

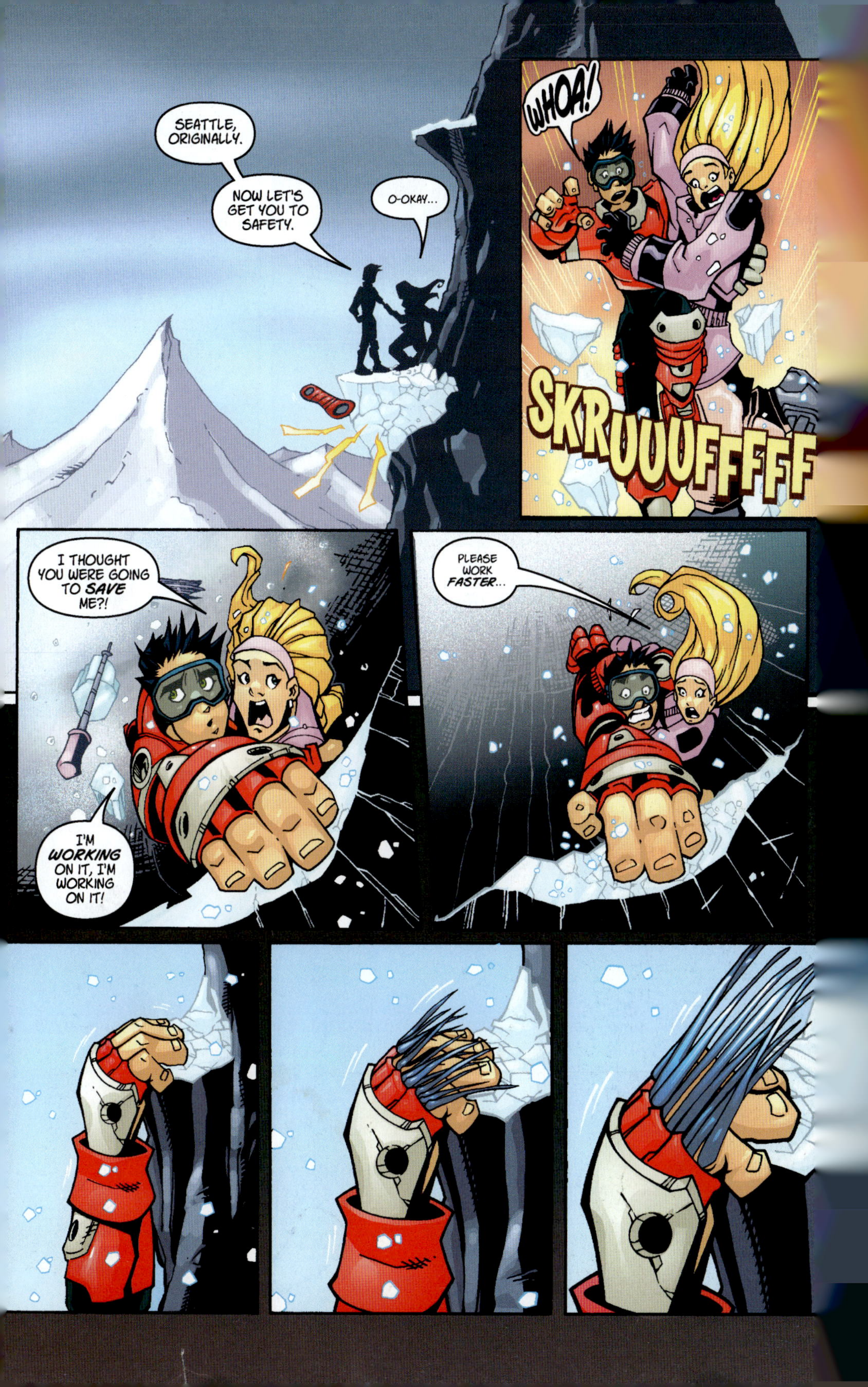

SEATTLE, ORIGINALLY.
NOW LET'S GET YOU TO SAFETY.
O-OKAY...
WHOA!
SKRUUUUFFFFF
I THOUGHT YOU WERE GOING TO *SAVE* ME?!
I'M *WORKING* ON IT, I'M WORKING ON IT!
PLEASE WORK *FASTER*...

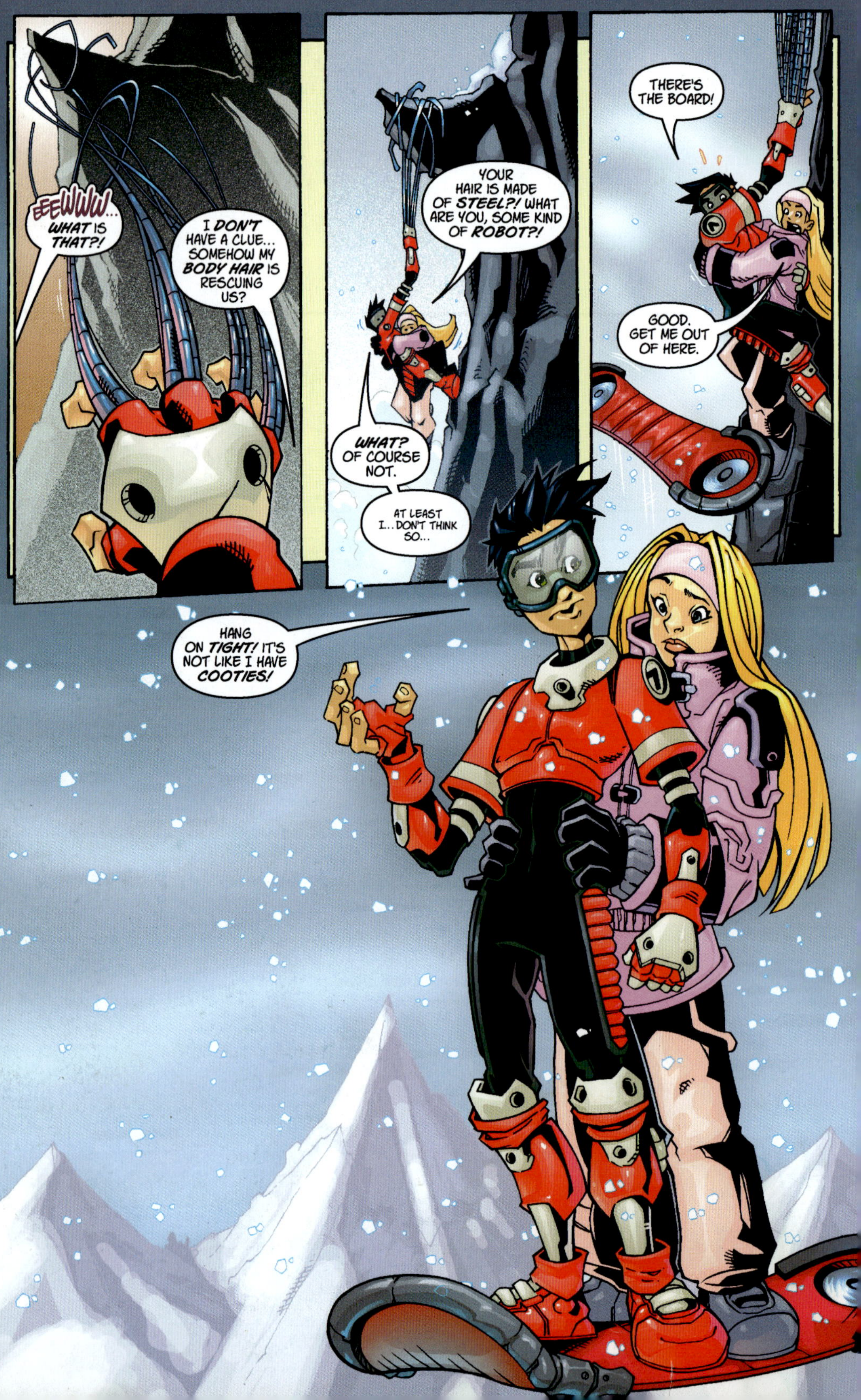
EEEWWW... WHAT IS THAT?!
I DON'T HAVE A CLUE... SOMEHOW MY BODY HAIR IS RESCUING US?
YOUR HAIR IS MADE OF STEEL?! WHAT ARE YOU, SOME KIND OF ROBOT?!
WHAT? OF COURSE NOT.
AT LEAST I...DON'T THINK SO...
THERE'S THE BOARD!
GOOD. GET ME OUT OF HERE.
HANG ON TIGHT! IT'S NOT LIKE I HAVE COOTIES!

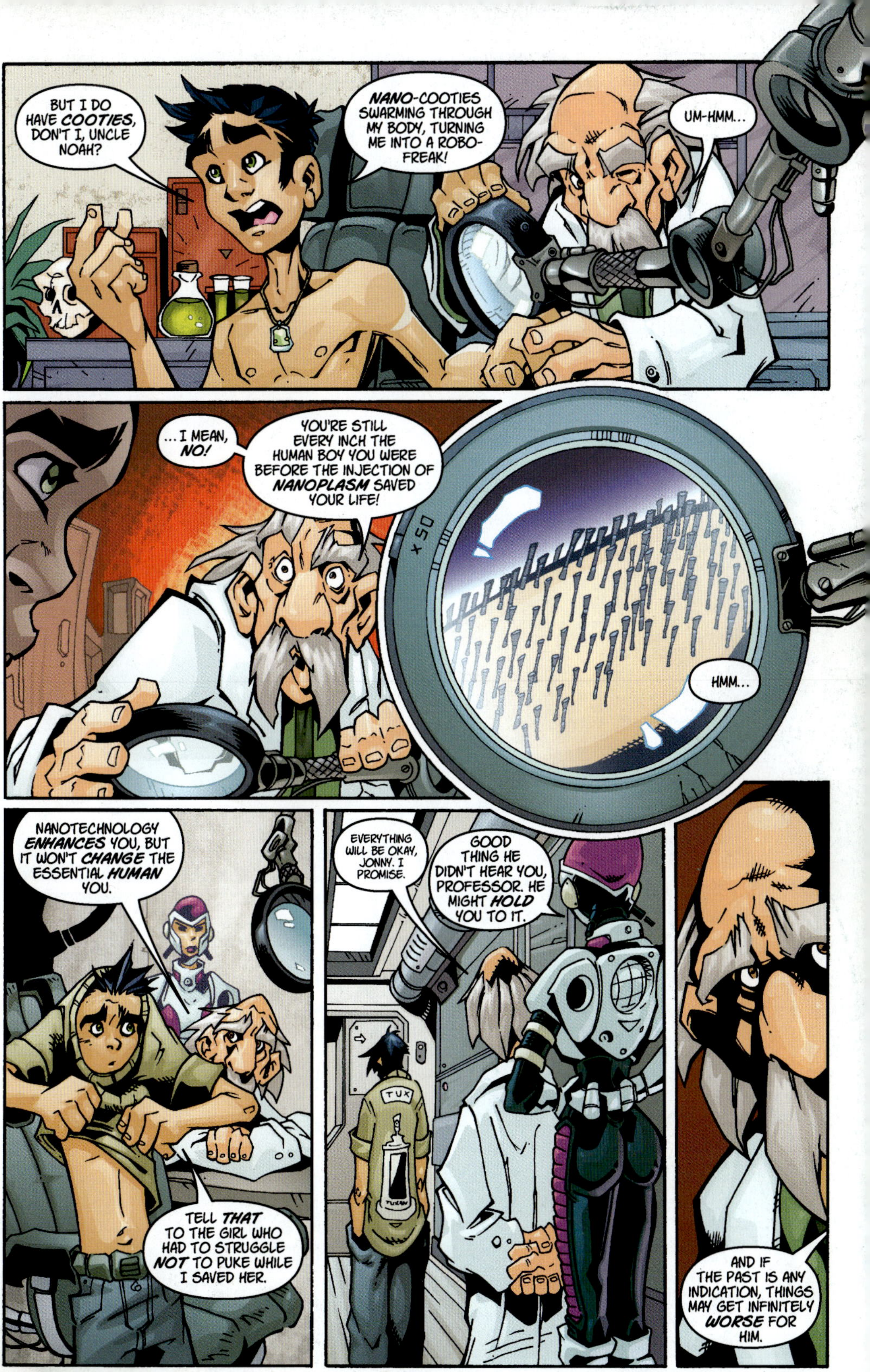

BUT I DO HAVE COOTIES, DON'T I, UNCLE NOAH?
NANO-COOTIES SWARMING THROUGH MY BODY, TURNING ME INTO A ROBO-FREAK!
UM-HMM...
...I MEAN, NO!
YOU'RE STILL EVERY INCH THE HUMAN BOY YOU WERE BEFORE THE INJECTION OF NANOPLASM SAVED YOUR LIFE!
x50
HMM...
NANOTECHNOLOGY ENHANCES YOU, BUT IT WON'T CHANGE THE ESSENTIAL HUMAN YOU.
TELL THAT TO THE GIRL WHO HAD TO STRUGGLE NOT TO PUKE WHILE I SAVED HER.
EVERYTHING WILL BE OKAY, JONNY. I PROMISE.
GOOD THING HE DIDN'T HEAR YOU, PROFESSOR. HE MIGHT HOLD YOU TO IT.
TUX
AND IF THE PAST IS ANY INDICATION, THINGS MAY GET INFINITELY WORSE FOR HIM.

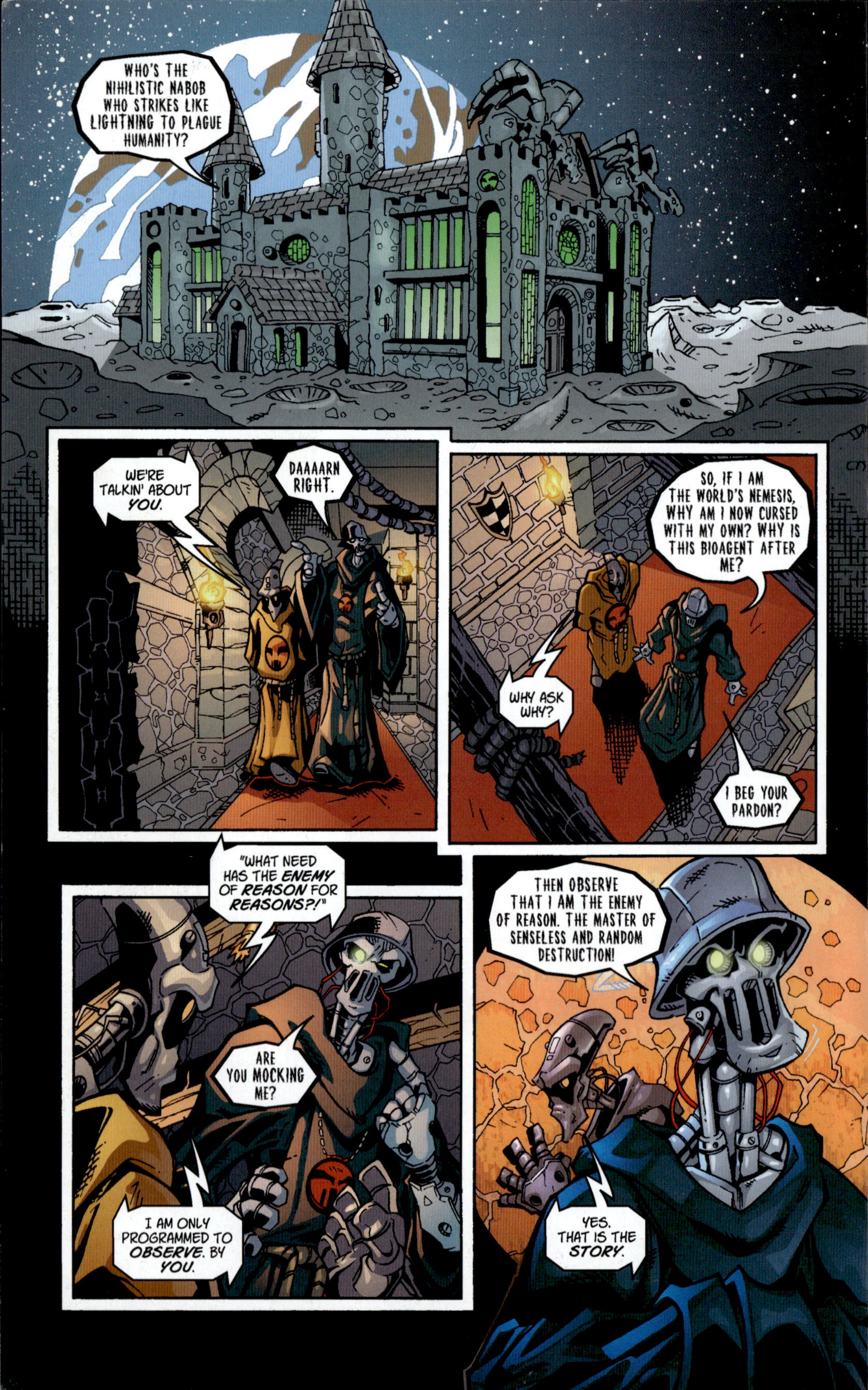
WHO'S THE NIHILISTIC NABOB WHO STRIKES LIKE LIGHTNING TO PLAGUE HUMANITY?
WE'RE TALKIN' ABOUT YOU.
DAAAARN RIGHT.
SO, IF I AM THE WORLD'S NEMESIS, WHY AM I NOW CURSED WITH MY OWN? WHY IS THIS BIOAGENT AFTER ME?
WHY ASK WHY?
I BEG YOUR PARDON?
"WHAT NEED HAS THE ENEMY OF REASON FOR REASONS?!"
ARE YOU MOCKING ME?
I AM ONLY PROGRAMMED TO OBSERVE. BY YOU.
THEN OBSERVE THAT I AM THE ENEMY OF REASON. THE MASTER OF SENSELESS AND RANDOM DESTRUCTION!
YES. THAT IS THE STORY.

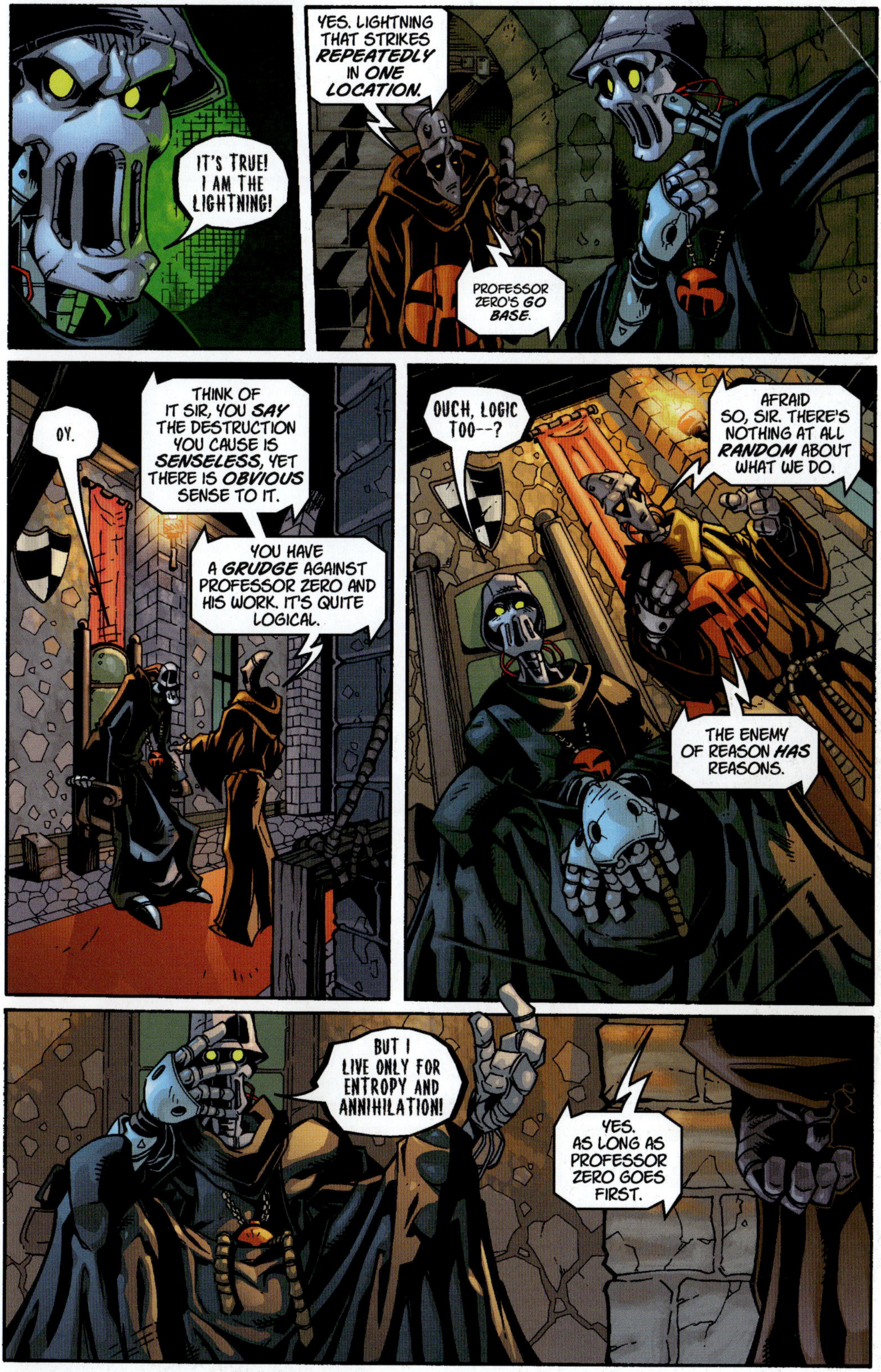
IT'S TRUE! I AM THE LIGHTNING!
YES. LIGHTNING THAT STRIKES REPEATEDLY IN ONE LOCATION.
PROFESSOR ZERO'S GO BASE.
OY.
THINK OF IT SIR, YOU SAY THE DESTRUCTION YOU CAUSE IS SENSELESS, YET THERE IS OBVIOUS SENSE TO IT.
YOU HAVE A GRUDGE AGAINST PROFESSOR ZERO AND HIS WORK. IT'S QUITE LOGICAL.
OUCH, LOGIC TOO--?
AFRAID SO, SIR. THERE'S NOTHING AT ALL RANDOM ABOUT WHAT WE DO.
THE ENEMY OF REASON HAS REASONS.
BUT I LIVE ONLY FOR ENTROPY AND ANNIHILATION!
YES. AS LONG AS PROFESSOR ZERO GOES FIRST.

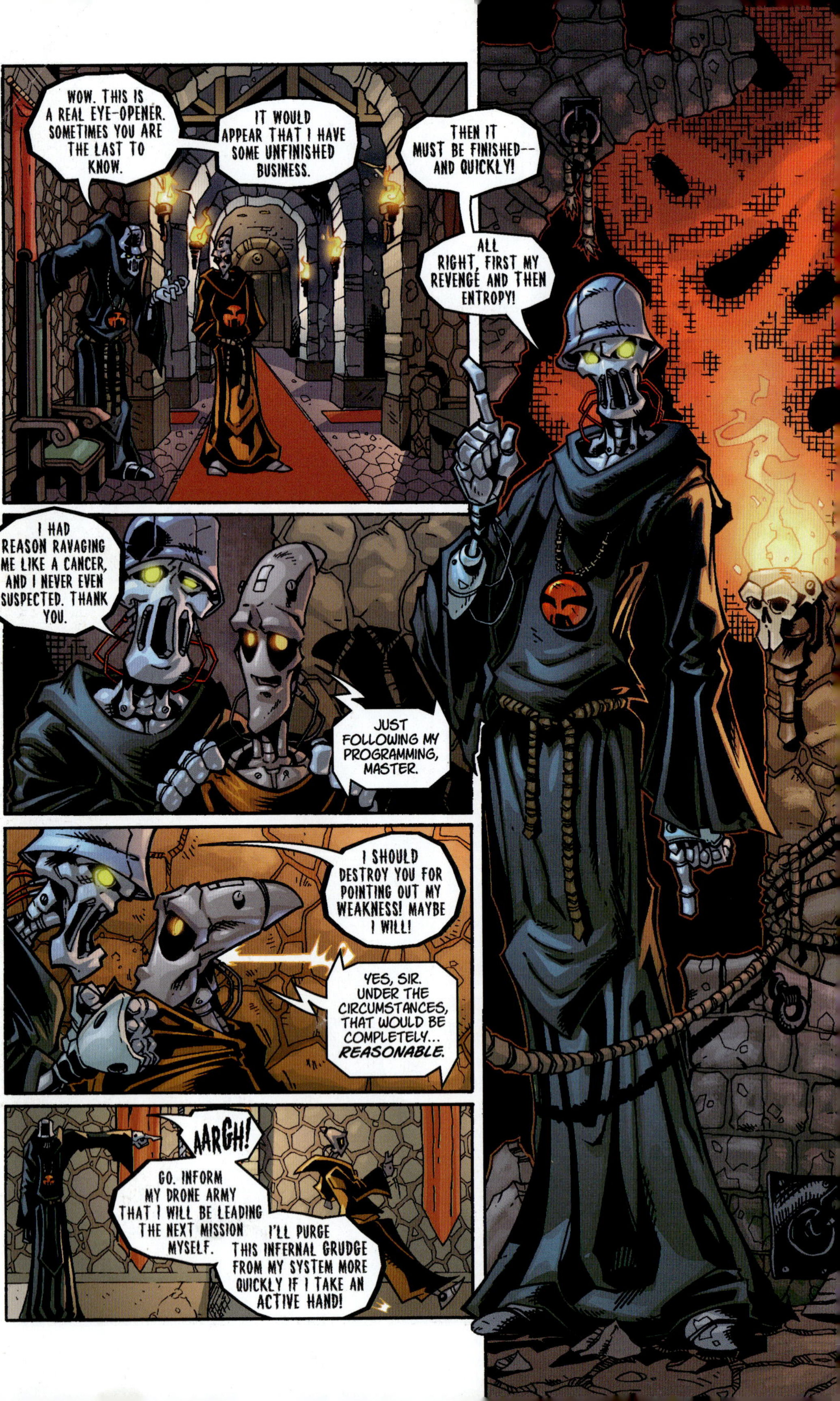
WOW. THIS IS A REAL EYE-OPENER. SOMETIMES YOU ARE THE LAST TO KNOW.
IT WOULD APPEAR THAT I HAVE SOME UNFINISHED BUSINESS.
THEN IT MUST BE FINISHED-- AND QUICKLY!
ALL RIGHT, FIRST MY REVENGE AND THEN ENTROPY!
I HAD REASON RAVAGING ME LIKE A CANCER, AND I NEVER EVEN SUSPECTED. THANK YOU.
JUST FOLLOWING MY PROGRAMMING, MASTER.
I SHOULD DESTROY YOU FOR POINTING OUT MY WEAKNESS! MAYBE I WILL!
YES, SIR. UNDER THE CIRCUMSTANCES, THAT WOULD BE COMPLETELY... *REASONABLE*.
AARGH!
GO. INFORM MY DRONE ARMY THAT I WILL BE LEADING THE NEXT MISSION MYSELF.
I'LL PURGE THIS INFERNAL GRUDGE FROM MY SYSTEM MORE QUICKLY IF I TAKE AN ACTIVE HAND!

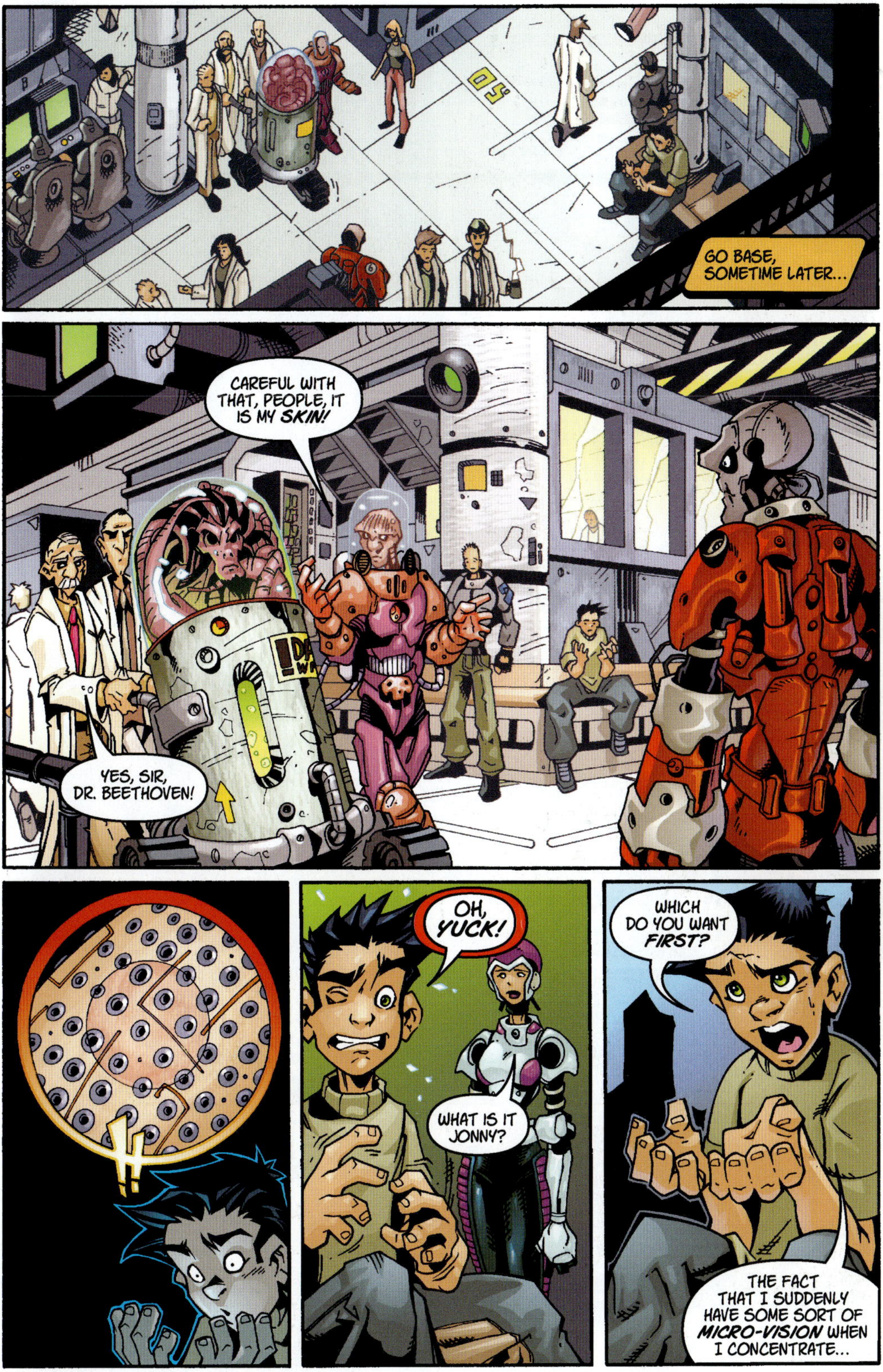
GO BASE, SOMETIME LATER...
CAREFUL WITH THAT, PEOPLE, IT IS MY SKIN!
YES, SIR, DR. BEETHOVEN!
OH, YUCK!
WHAT IS IT JONNY?
WHICH DO YOU WANT FIRST?
THE FACT THAT I SUDDENLY HAVE SOME SORT OF MICRO-VISION WHEN I CONCENTRATE...

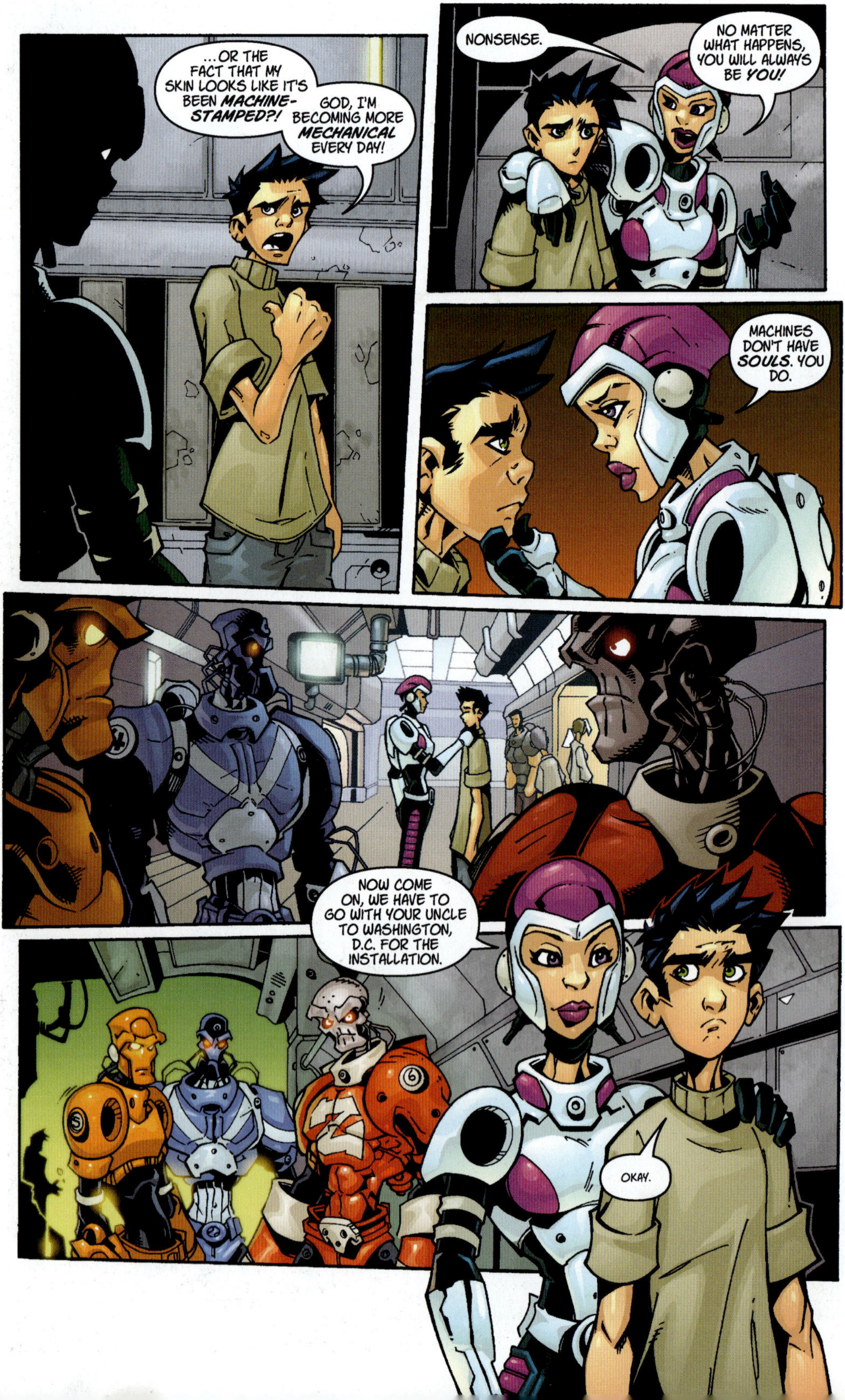
...OR THE FACT THAT MY SKIN LOOKS LIKE IT'S BEEN *MACHINE-STAMPED?!*
GOD, I'M BECOMING MORE *MECHANICAL* EVERY DAY!
NONSENSE.
NO MATTER WHAT HAPPENS, YOU WILL ALWAYS BE *YOU!*
MACHINES DON'T HAVE *SOULS*. YOU DO.
NOW COME ON, WE HAVE TO GO WITH YOUR UNCLE TO WASHINGTON, D.C. FOR THE INSTALLATION.
OKAY.

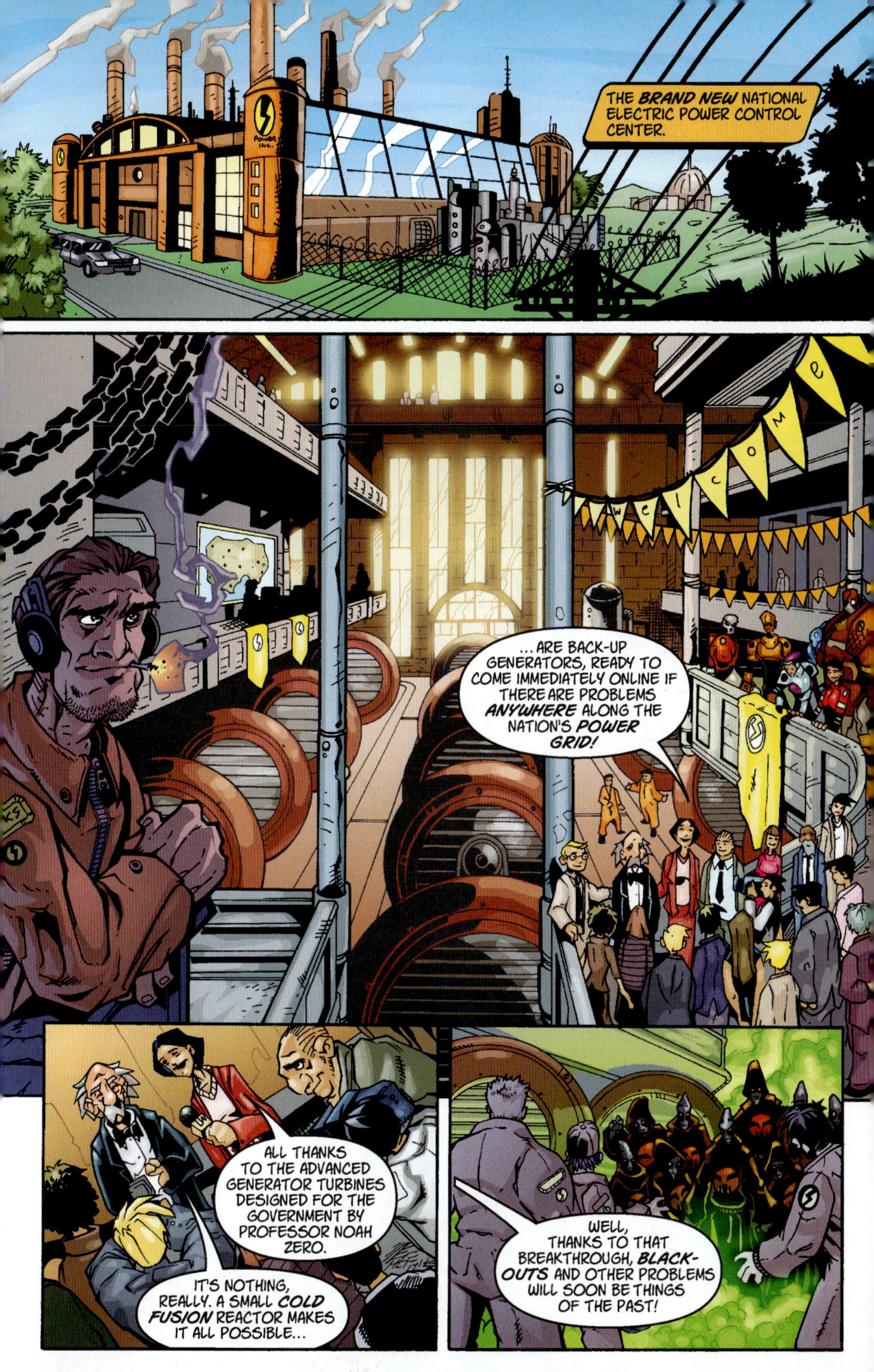

THE BRAND NEW NATIONAL ELECTRIC POWER CONTROL CENTER.
POWER INC.
WELCOME
...ARE BACK-UP GENERATORS, READY TO COME IMMEDIATELY ONLINE IF THERE ARE PROBLEMS ANYWHERE ALONG THE NATION'S POWER GRID!
ALL THANKS TO THE ADVANCED GENERATOR TURBINES DESIGNED FOR THE GOVERNMENT BY PROFESSOR NOAH ZERO.
IT'S NOTHING, REALLY. A SMALL COLD FUSION REACTOR MAKES IT ALL POSSIBLE...
WELL, THANKS TO THAT BREAKTHROUGH, BLACK-OUTS AND OTHER PROBLEMS WILL SOON BE THINGS OF THE PAST!

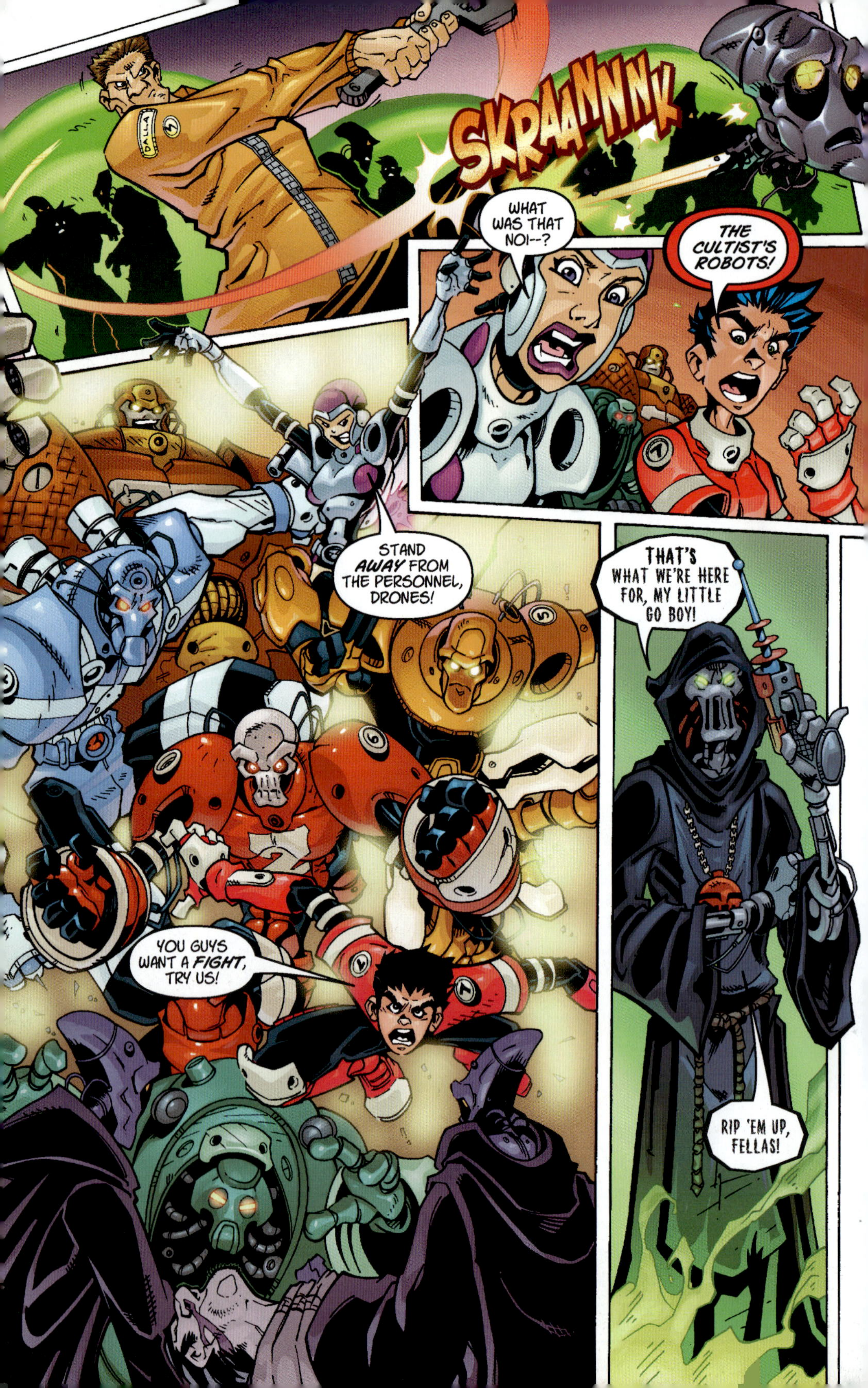
SKRAANNNK
WHAT WAS THAT NOI--?
THE CULTIST'S ROBOTS!
STAND AWAY FROM THE PERSONNEL, DRONES!
YOU GUYS WANT A FIGHT, TRY US!
THAT'S WHAT WE'RE HERE FOR, MY LITTLE GO BOY!
RIP 'EM UP, FELLAS!

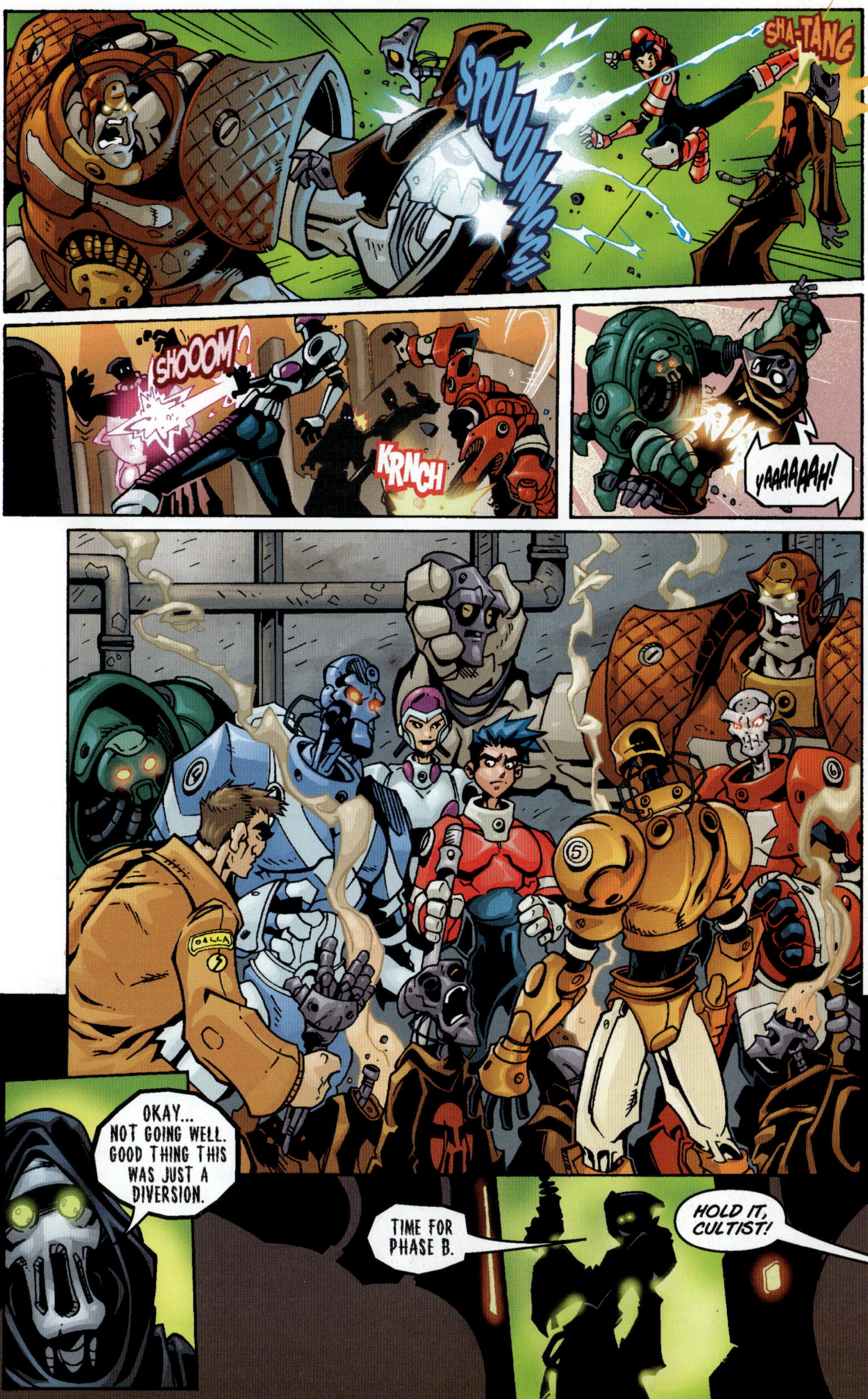

SPUUUNNCH
SHA-TANG
SHOOOM
KRNCH
YAAAAAAH!
OKAY... NOT GOING WELL. GOOD THING THIS WAS JUST A DIVERSION.
TIME FOR PHASE B.
HOLD IT, CULTIST!

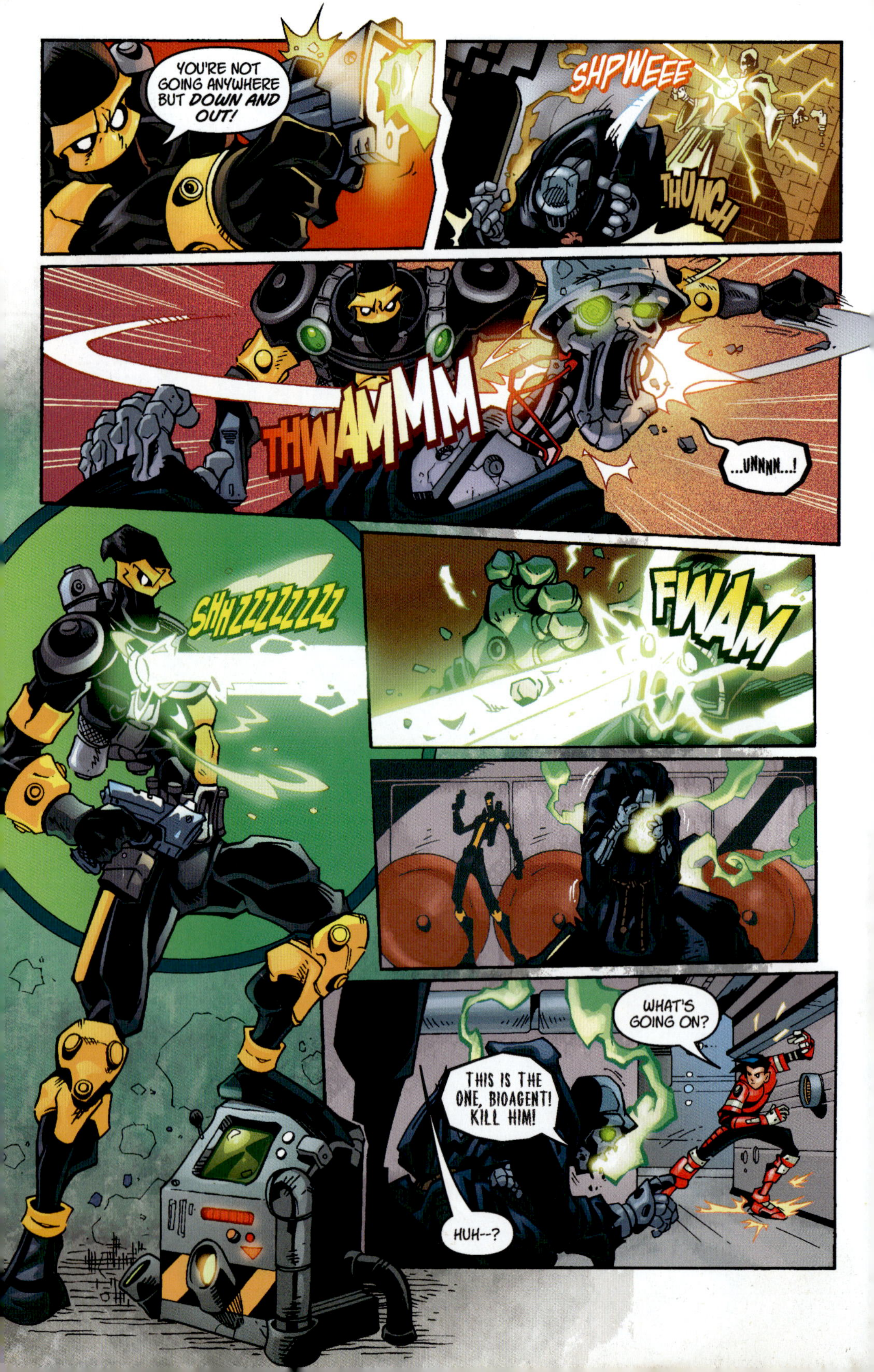
YOU'RE NOT GOING ANYWHERE BUT DOWN AND OUT!
SHPWEEE
THUNCH
THWAMMM
...UNNNN...!
SHHZZZZZZZZ
FWAM
WHAT'S GOING ON?
THIS IS THE ONE, BIOAGENT! KILL HIM!
HUH--?

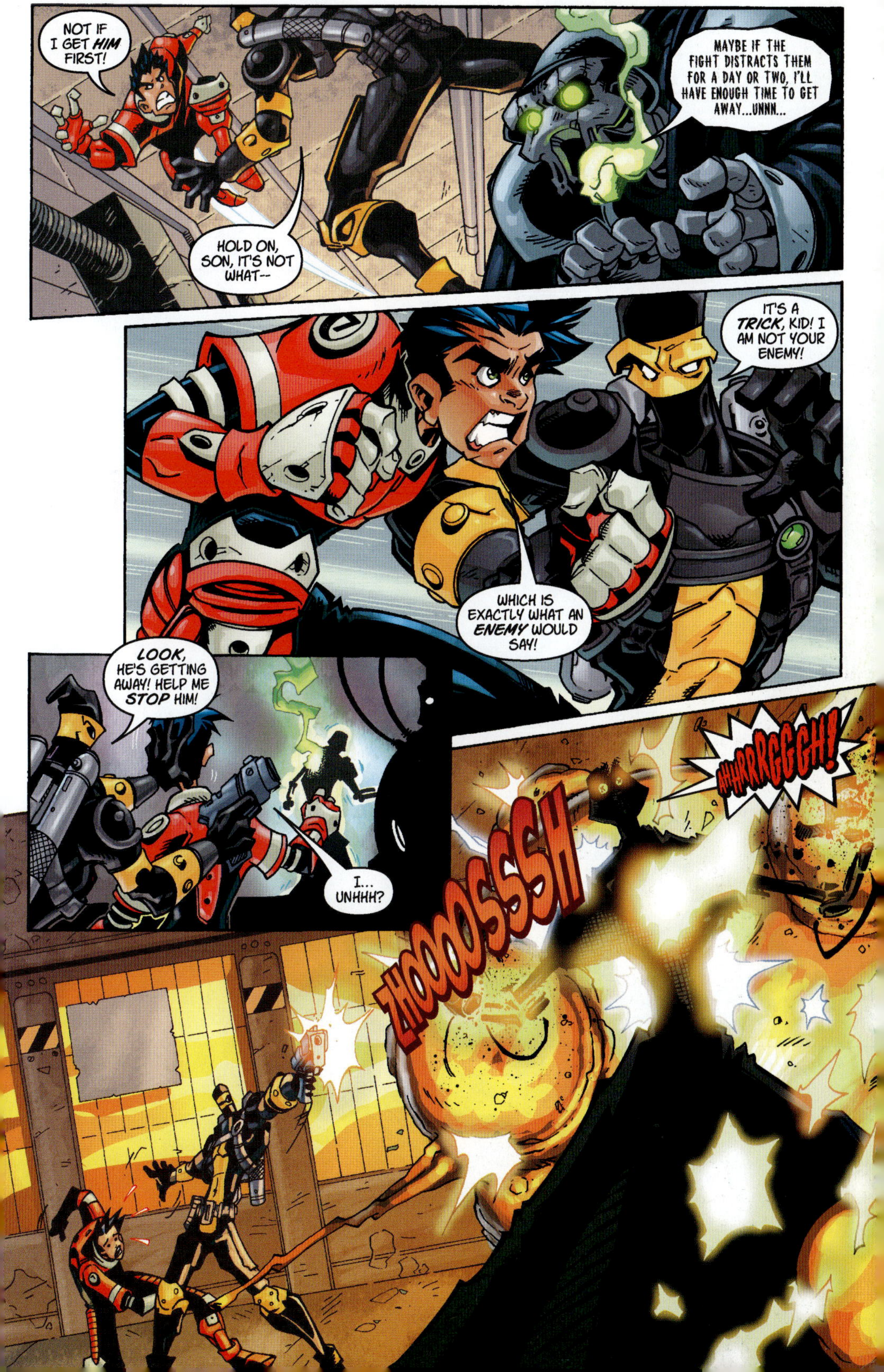
NOT IF I GET HIM FIRST!
MAYBE IF THE FIGHT DISTRACTS THEM FOR A DAY OR TWO, I'LL HAVE ENOUGH TIME TO GET AWAY...UNNN...
HOLD ON, SON, IT'S NOT WHAT--
IT'S A TRICK, KID! I AM NOT YOUR ENEMY!
WHICH IS EXACTLY WHAT AN ENEMY WOULD SAY!
LOOK, HE'S GETTING AWAY! HELP ME STOP HIM!
I... UNHHH?
AHHRRRGGGH!
ZHOOOOSSSSH

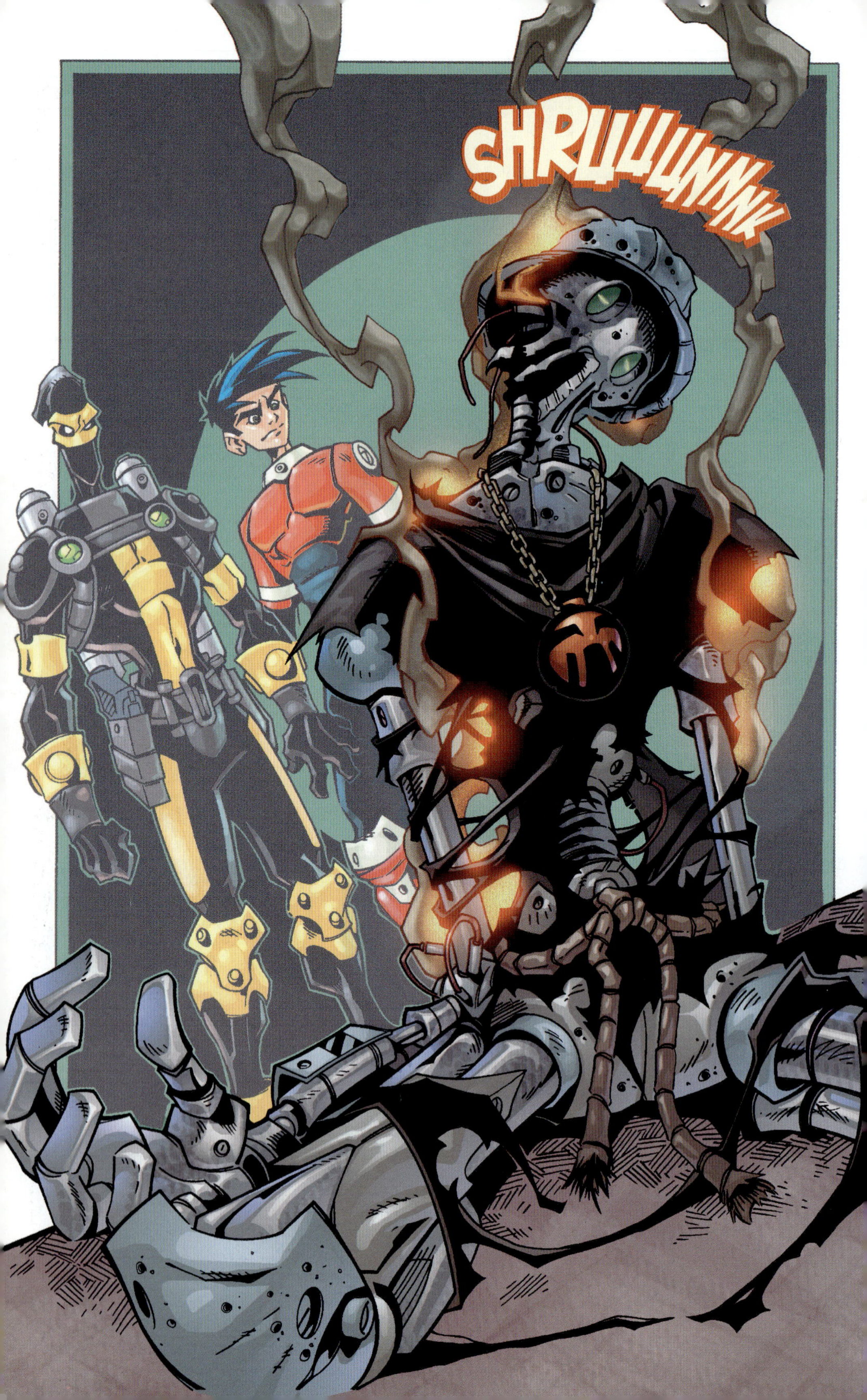
SHRUUUNNNK

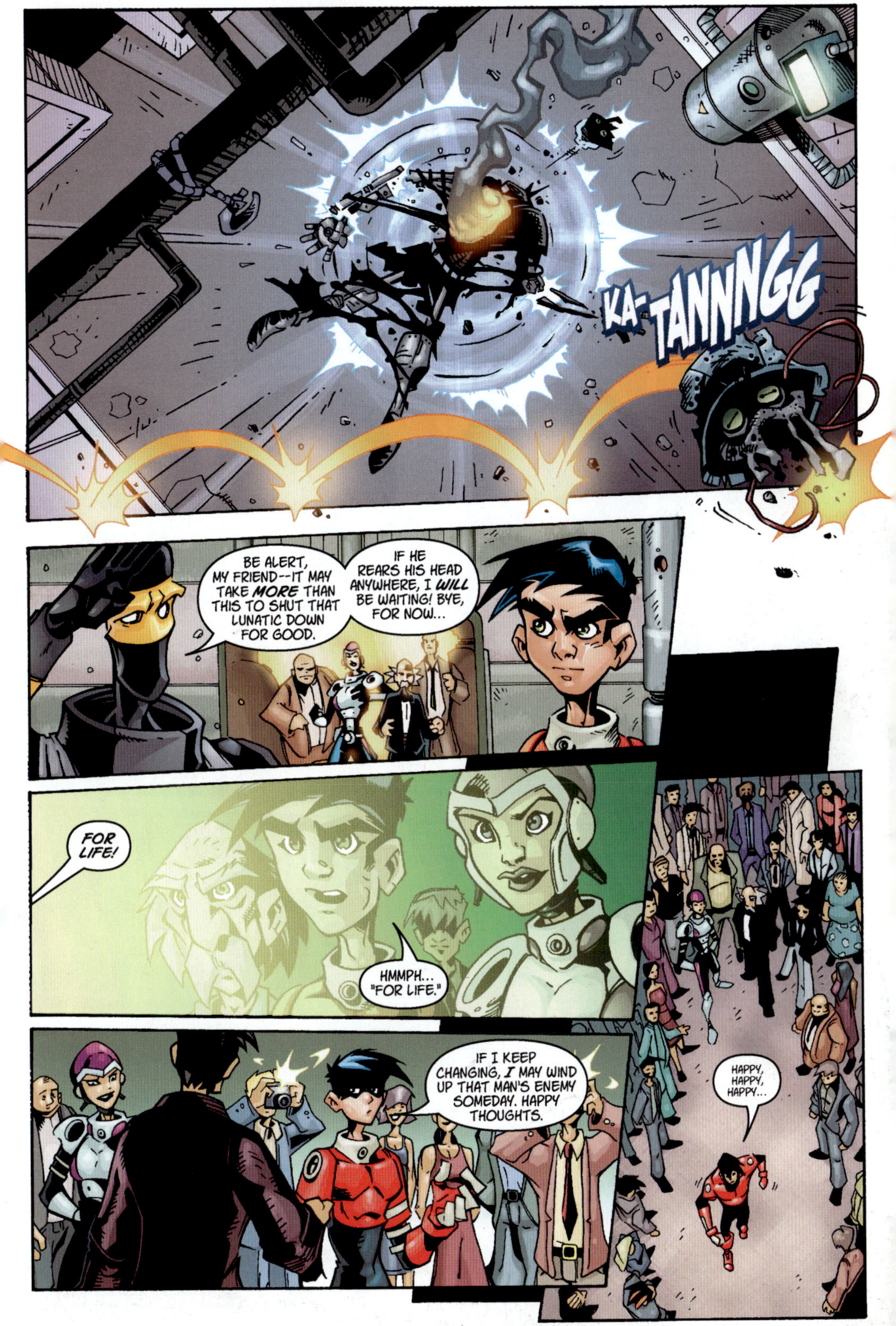
KA-TANNNGG
BE ALERT, MY FRIEND--IT MAY TAKE MORE THAN THIS TO SHUT THAT LUNATIC DOWN FOR GOOD.
IF HE REARS HIS HEAD ANYWHERE, I WILL BE WAITING! BYE, FOR NOW...
FOR LIFE!
HMMPH... "FOR LIFE."
IF I KEEP CHANGING, I MAY WIND UP THAT MAN'S ENEMY SOMEDAY. HAPPY THOUGHTS.
HAPPY, HAPPY, HAPPY...

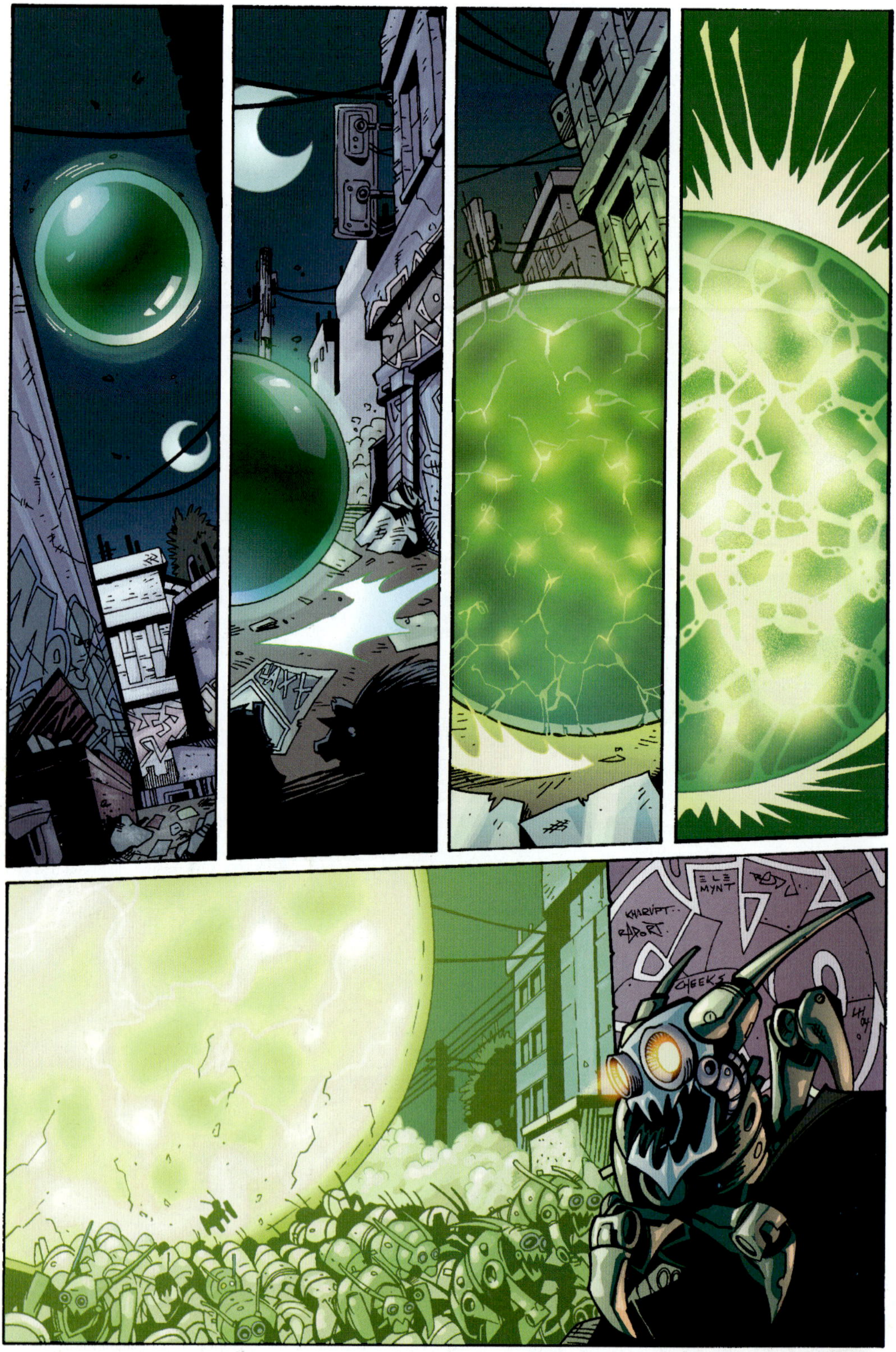
ELE MYNT
KHARUPT
RADORT
CHEEKS

NEXT: **PHASE B!**

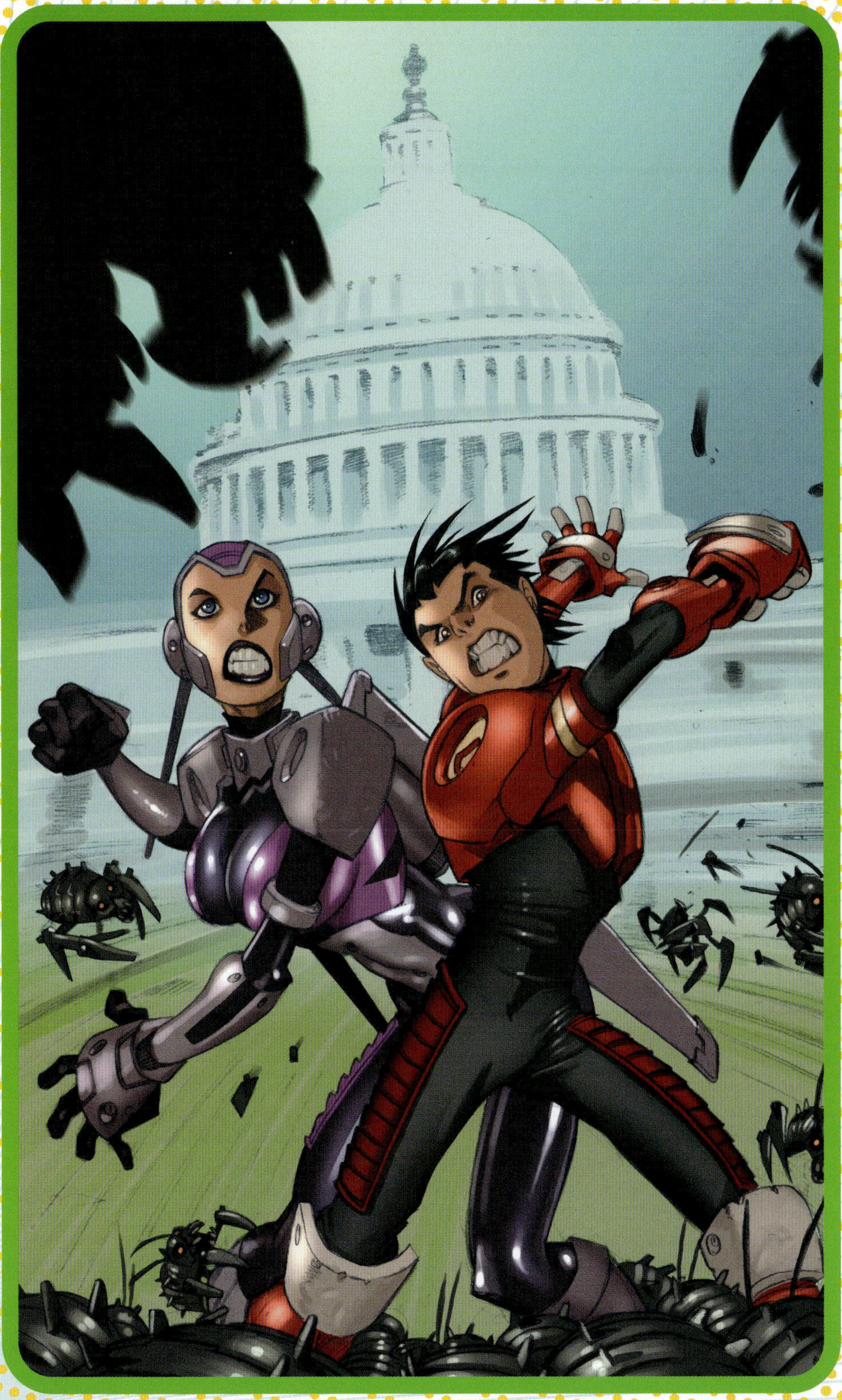

"POLITICAL MACHINERY"

SCRIPT BRIAN AUGUSTYN

PENCILS JON SOMMARIVA

COLORS DARRIN MOORE
AND JON SOMMARIVA

LETTERS MICHAEL DAVID THOMAS

COVER FRANCISCO RUIZ VELASCO

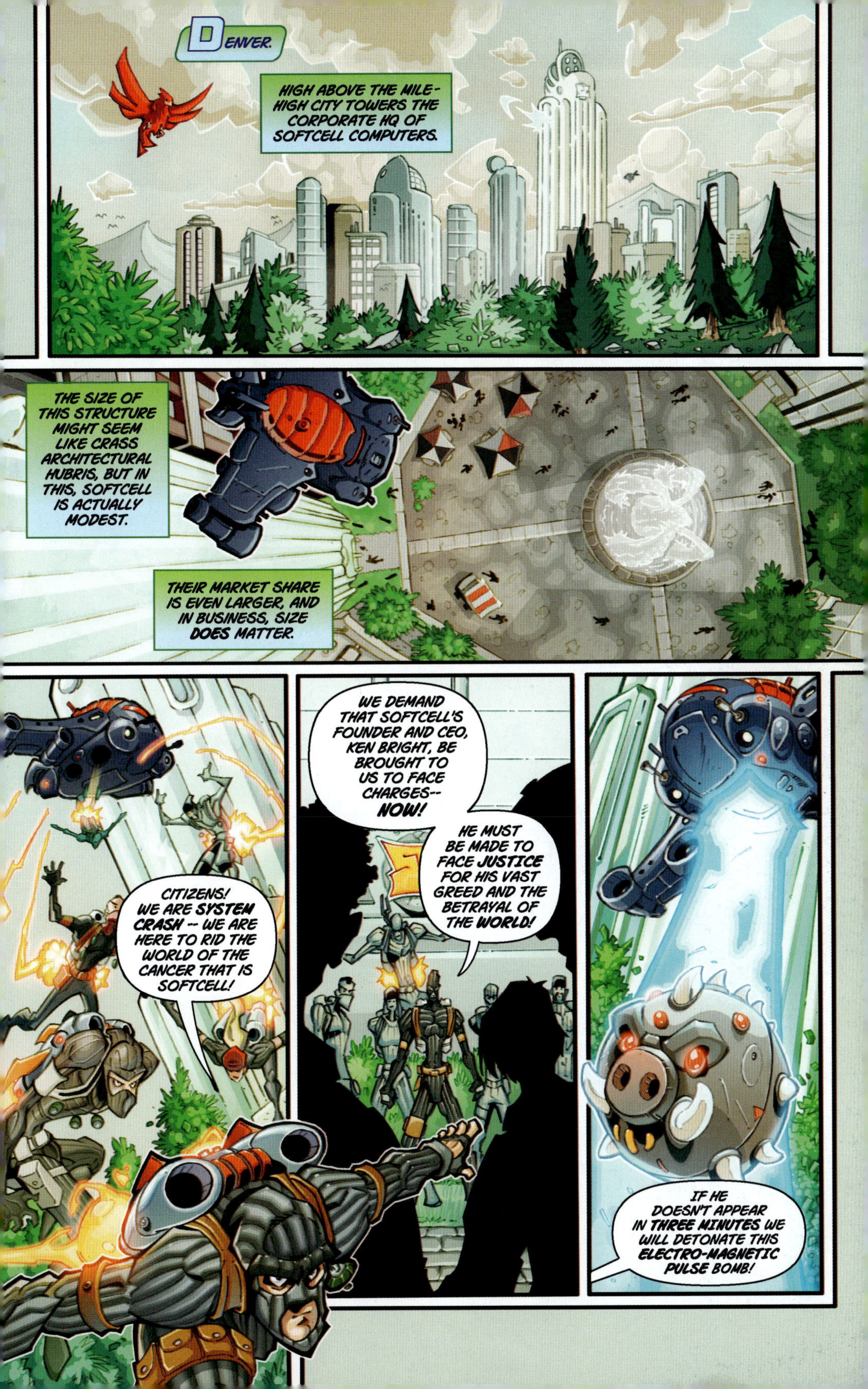
DENVER.
HIGH ABOVE THE MILE-HIGH CITY TOWERS THE CORPORATE HQ OF SOFTCELL COMPUTERS.
THE SIZE OF THIS STRUCTURE MIGHT SEEM LIKE CRASS ARCHITECTURAL HUBRIS, BUT IN THIS, SOFTCELL IS ACTUALLY MODEST.
THEIR MARKET SHARE IS EVEN LARGER, AND IN BUSINESS, SIZE DOES MATTER.
CITIZENS! WE ARE SYSTEM CRASH -- WE ARE HERE TO RID THE WORLD OF THE CANCER THAT IS SOFTCELL!
WE DEMAND THAT SOFTCELL'S FOUNDER AND CEO, KEN BRIGHT, BE BROUGHT TO US TO FACE CHARGES-- NOW!
HE MUST BE MADE TO FACE JUSTICE FOR HIS VAST GREED AND THE BETRAYAL OF THE WORLD!
IF HE DOESN'T APPEAR IN THREE MINUTES WE WILL DETONATE THIS ELECTRO-MAGNETIC PULSE BOMB!

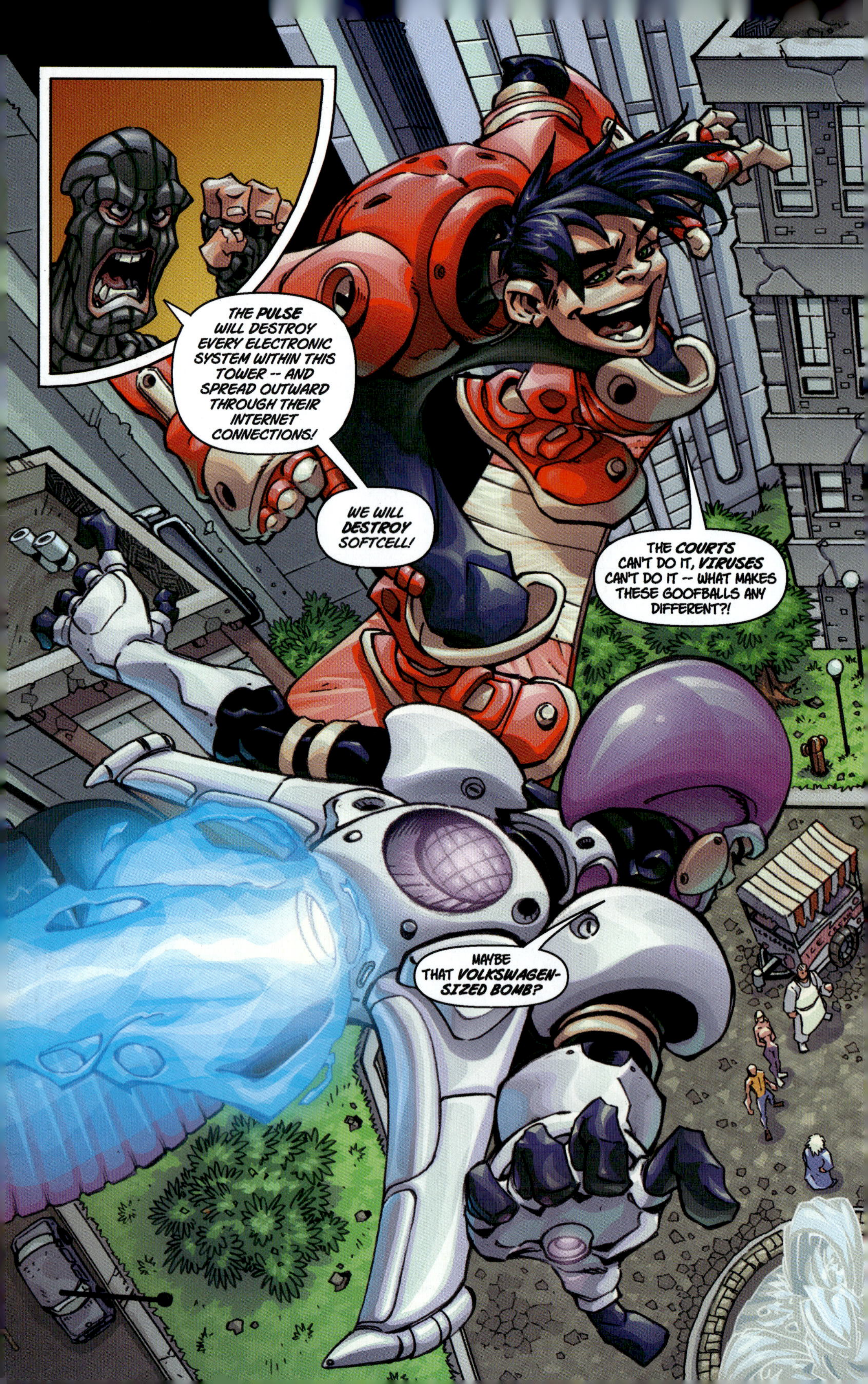
THE PULSE WILL DESTROY EVERY ELECTRONIC SYSTEM WITHIN THIS TOWER -- AND SPREAD OUTWARD THROUGH THEIR INTERNET CONNECTIONS!
WE WILL DESTROY SOFTCELL!
THE COURTS CAN'T DO IT, VIRUSES CAN'T DO IT -- WHAT MAKES THESE GOOFBALLS ANY DIFFERENT?!
MAYBE THAT VOLKSWAGEN-SIZED BOMB?

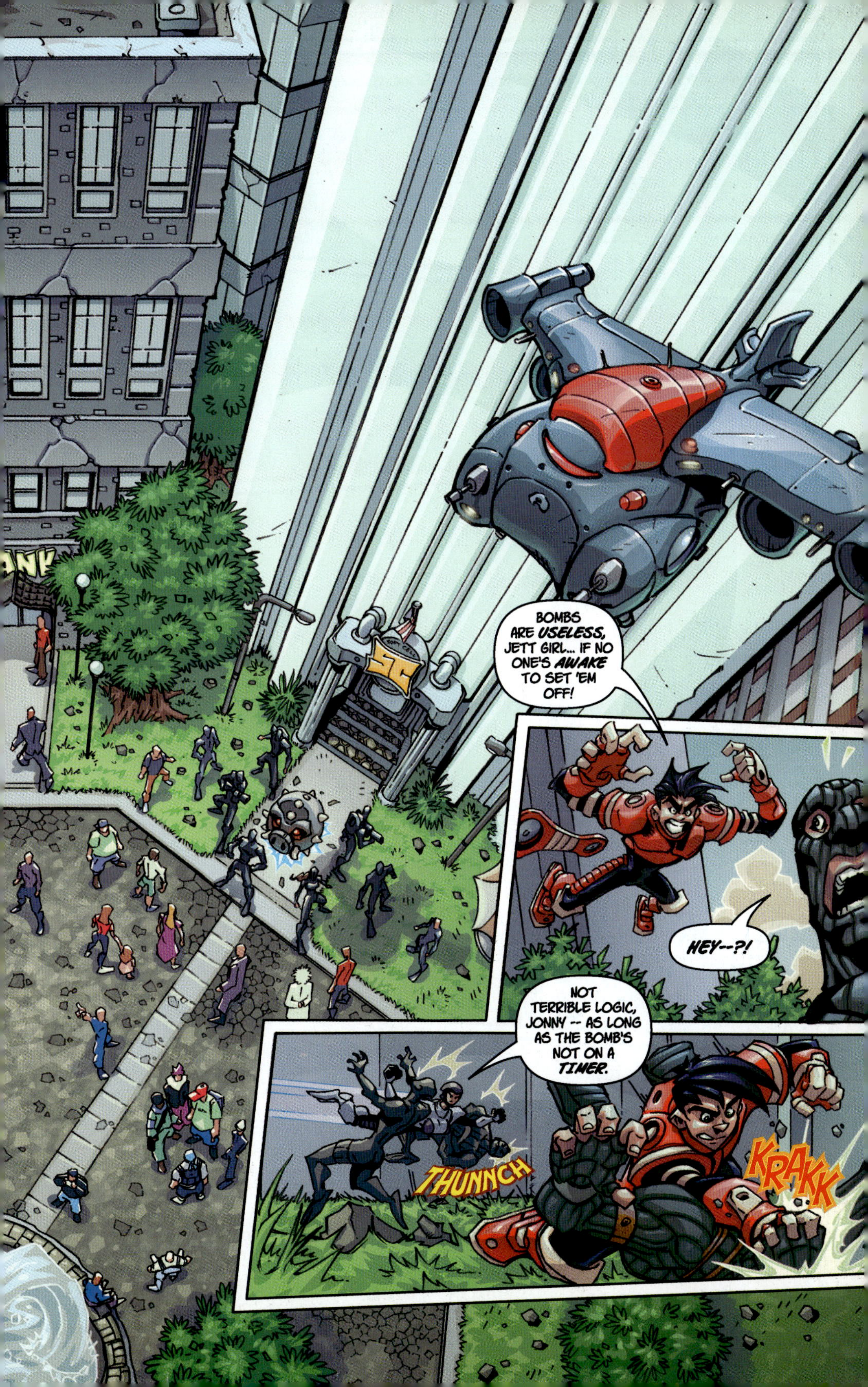
BOMBS ARE *USELESS*, JETT GIRL... IF NO ONE'S *AWAKE* TO SET 'EM OFF!
HEY--?!
NOT TERRIBLE LOGIC, JONNY -- AS LONG AS THE BOMB'S NOT ON A *TIMER*.
THUNNCH
KRAKK

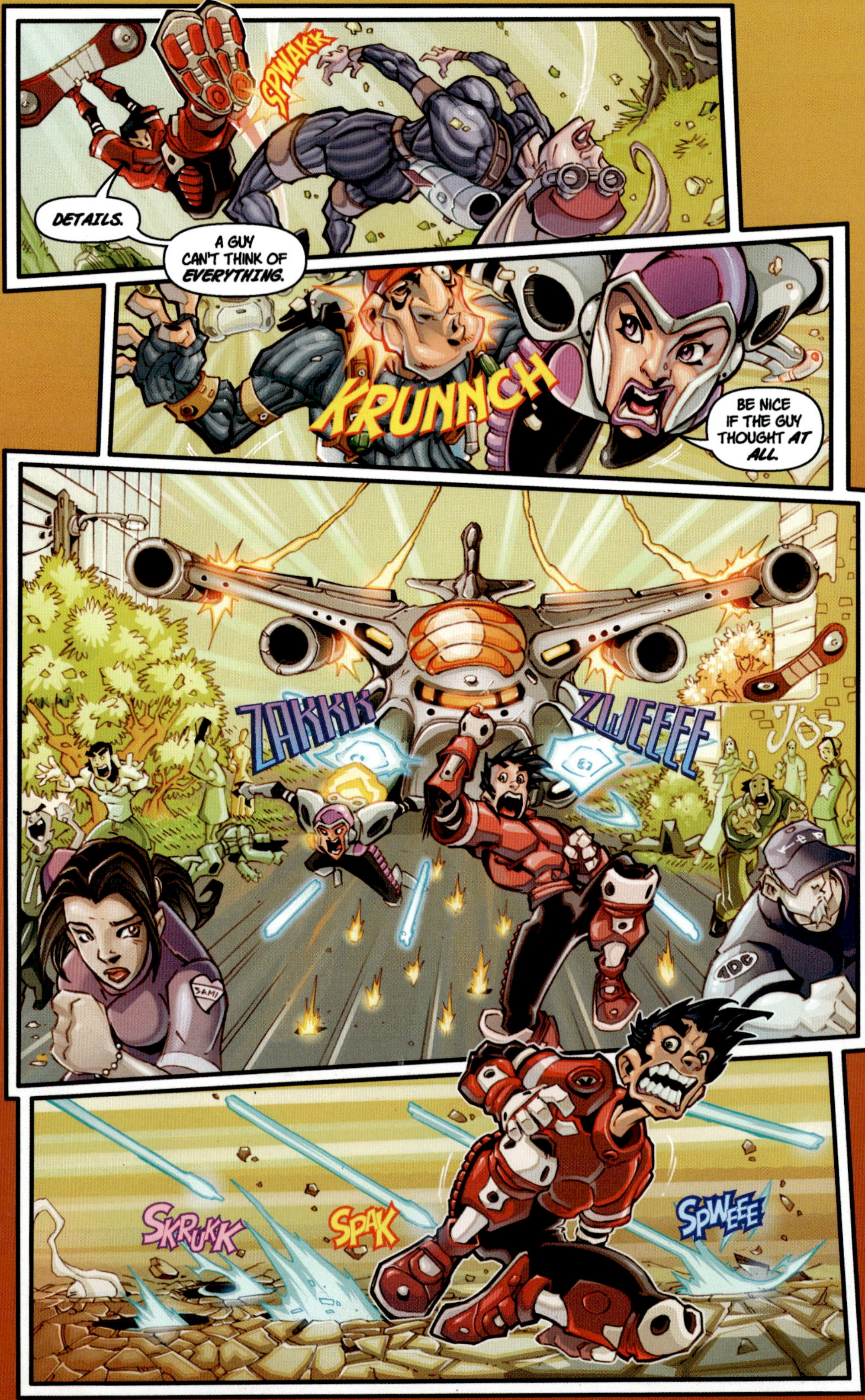
SPWAKK
DETAILS.
A GUY CAN'T THINK OF *EVERYTHING.*
KRUNNCH
BE NICE IF THE GUY THOUGHT *AT ALL.*
ZAKKK
ZWEEEE
SKRUKK
SPAK
SPWEEE

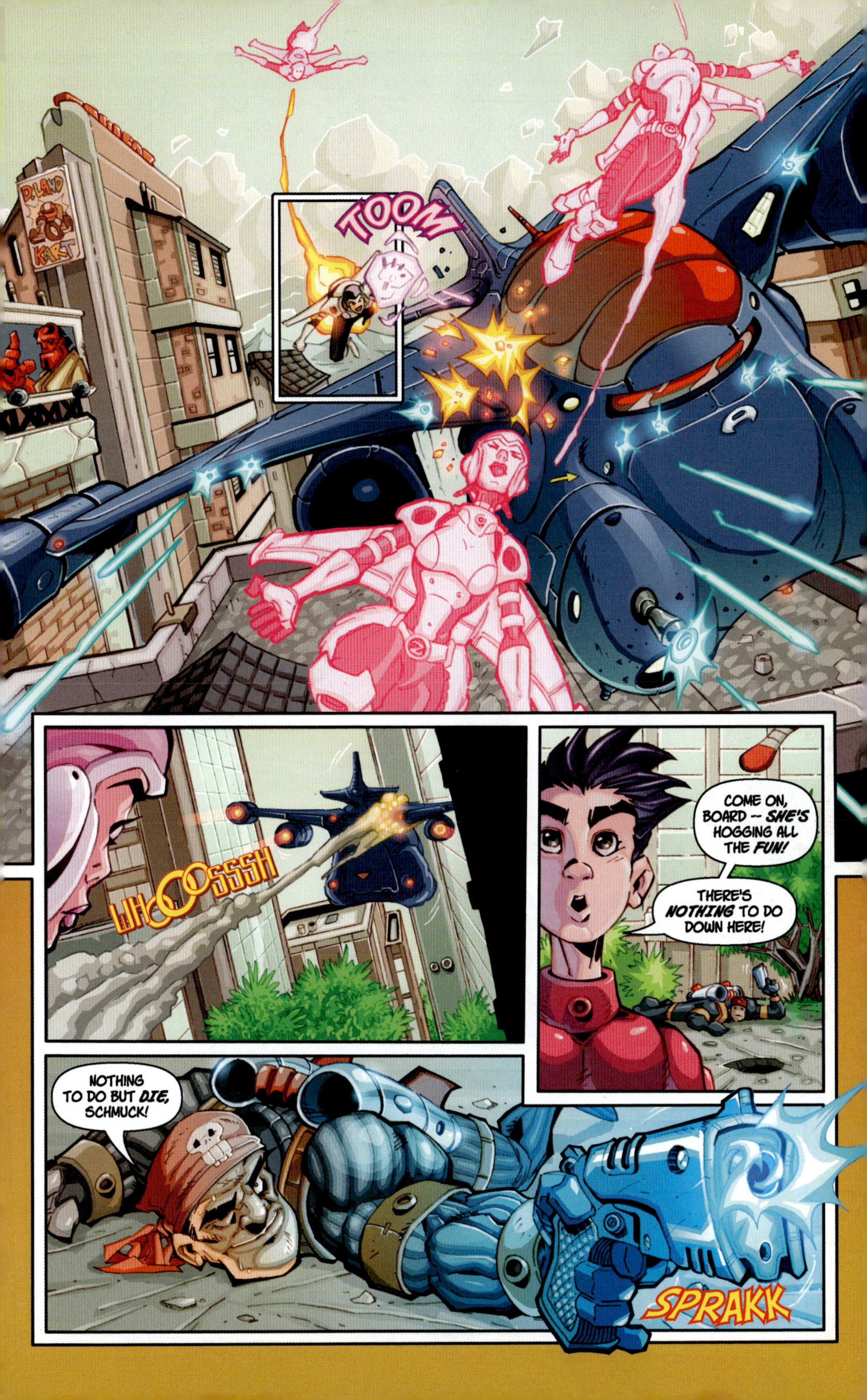
TOOM
D. LAND KART
WHOOSSSH
COME ON, BOARD -- SHE'S HOGGING ALL THE FUN!
THERE'S NOTHING TO DO DOWN HERE!
NOTHING TO DO BUT DIE, SCHMUCK!
SPRAKK

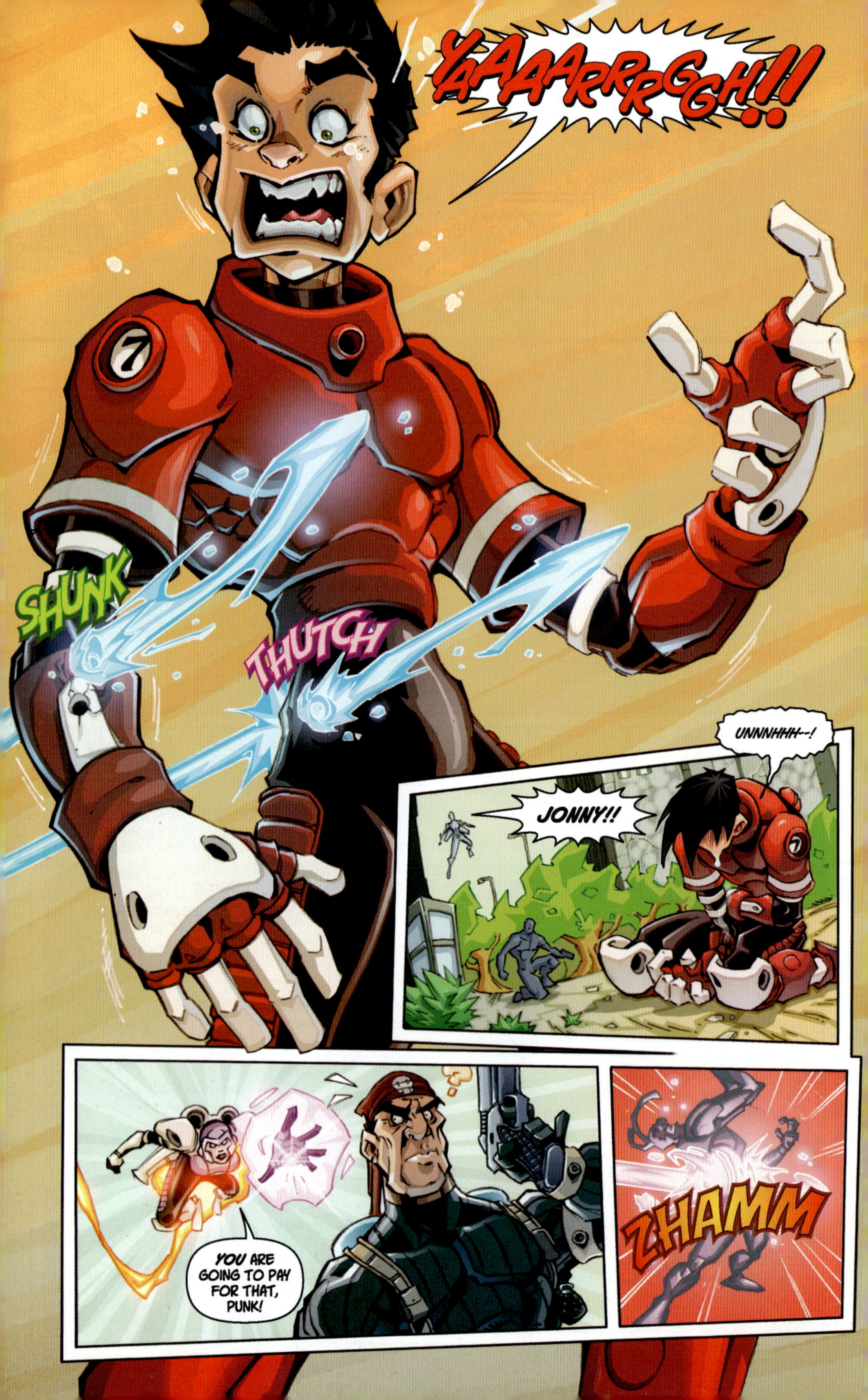
YAAAARRRGGH!!!
SHUNK
THUTCH
UNNNHHH--!
JONNY!!
YOU ARE GOING TO PAY FOR THAT, PUNK!
ZHAMM

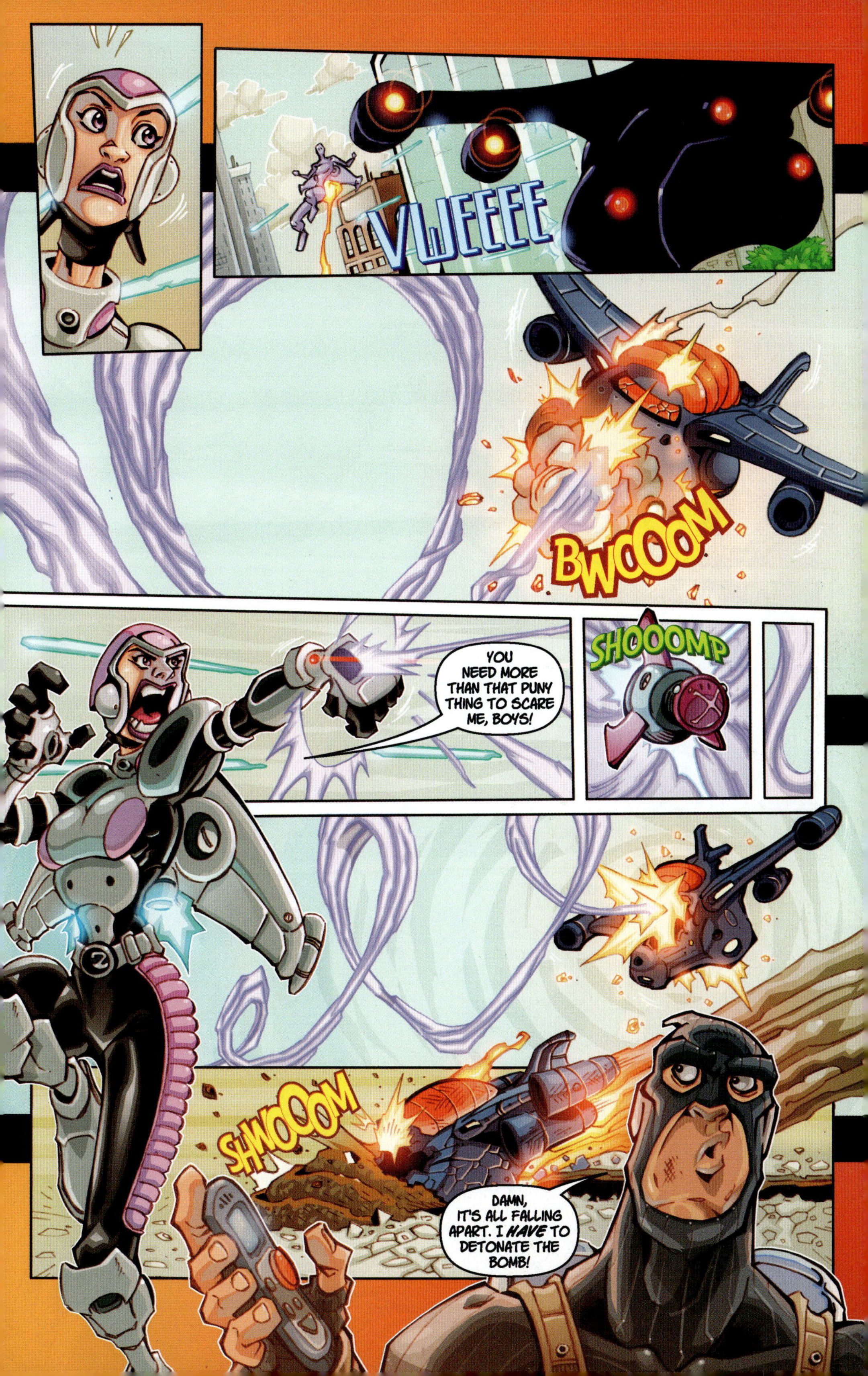
VWEEEE
BWOOOM
YOU NEED MORE THAN THAT PUNY THING TO SCARE ME, BOYS!
SHOOOMP
SHWOOOM
DAMN, IT'S ALL FALLING APART. I *HAVE* TO DETONATE THE BOMB!

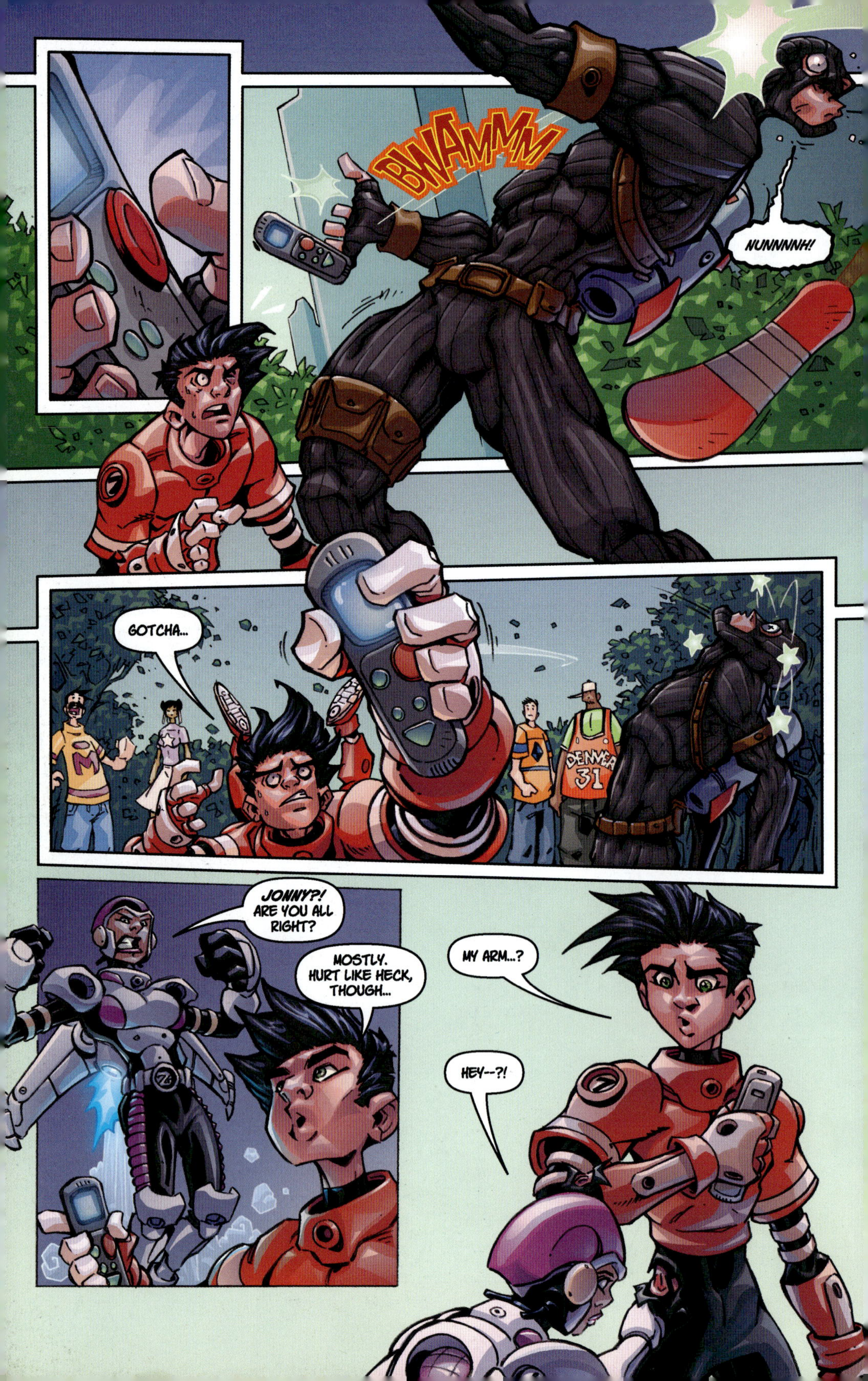
BWAMMM
NUNNNNH!
GOTCHA...
JONNY?! ARE YOU ALL RIGHT?
MOSTLY. HURT LIKE HECK, THOUGH...
MY ARM...?
HEY--?!

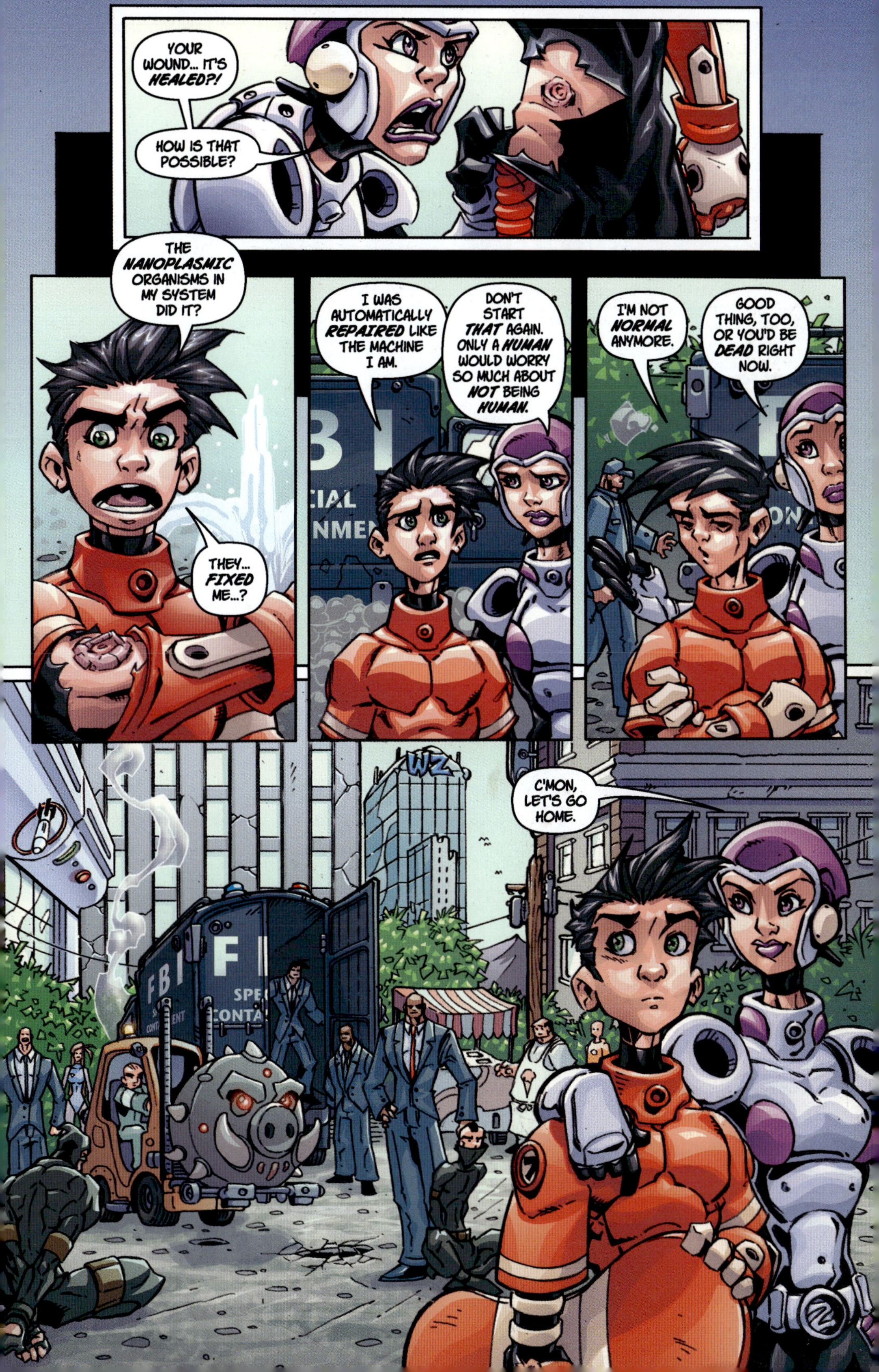
YOUR WOUND... IT'S HEALED?!
HOW IS THAT POSSIBLE?
THE NANOPLASMIC ORGANISMS IN MY SYSTEM DID IT?
THEY... FIXED ME...?
I WAS AUTOMATICALLY REPAIRED LIKE THE MACHINE I AM.
DON'T START THAT AGAIN. ONLY A HUMAN WOULD WORRY SO MUCH ABOUT NOT BEING HUMAN.
I'M NOT NORMAL ANYMORE.
GOOD THING, TOO, OR YOU'D BE DEAD RIGHT NOW.
FBI
C'MON, LET'S GO HOME.

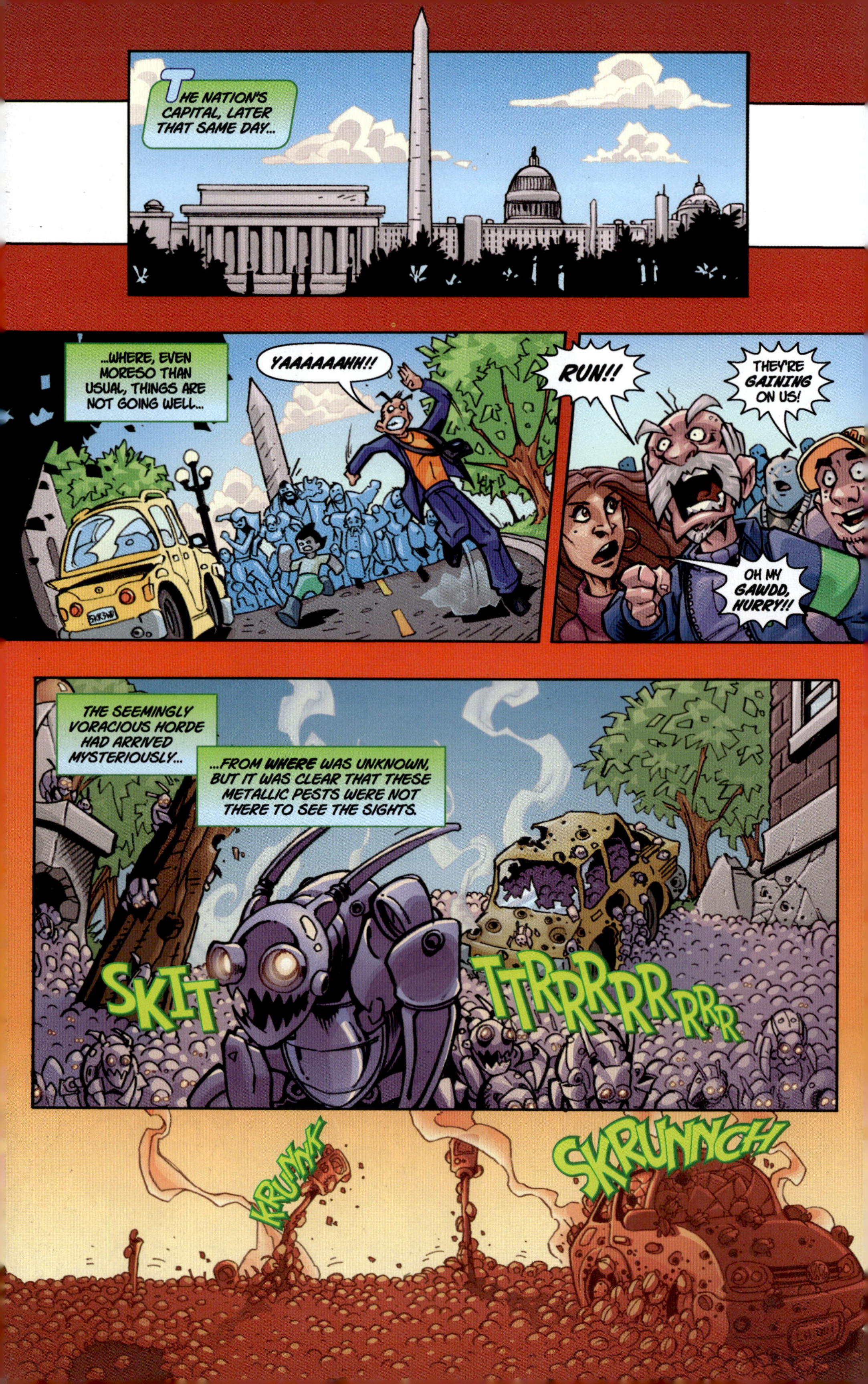
THE NATION'S CAPITAL, LATER THAT SAME DAY...
...WHERE, EVEN MORESO THAN USUAL, THINGS ARE NOT GOING WELL...
YAAAAAAHH!!
RUN!!
THEY'RE GAINING ON US!
OH MY GAWDD, HURRY!!
THE SEEMINGLY VORACIOUS HORDE HAD ARRIVED MYSTERIOUSLY...
...FROM WHERE WAS UNKNOWN, BUT IT WAS CLEAR THAT THESE METALLIC PESTS WERE NOT THERE TO SEE THE SIGHTS.
SKIT
TTRRRRRRRRR
KRUNK
SKRUNNCH!

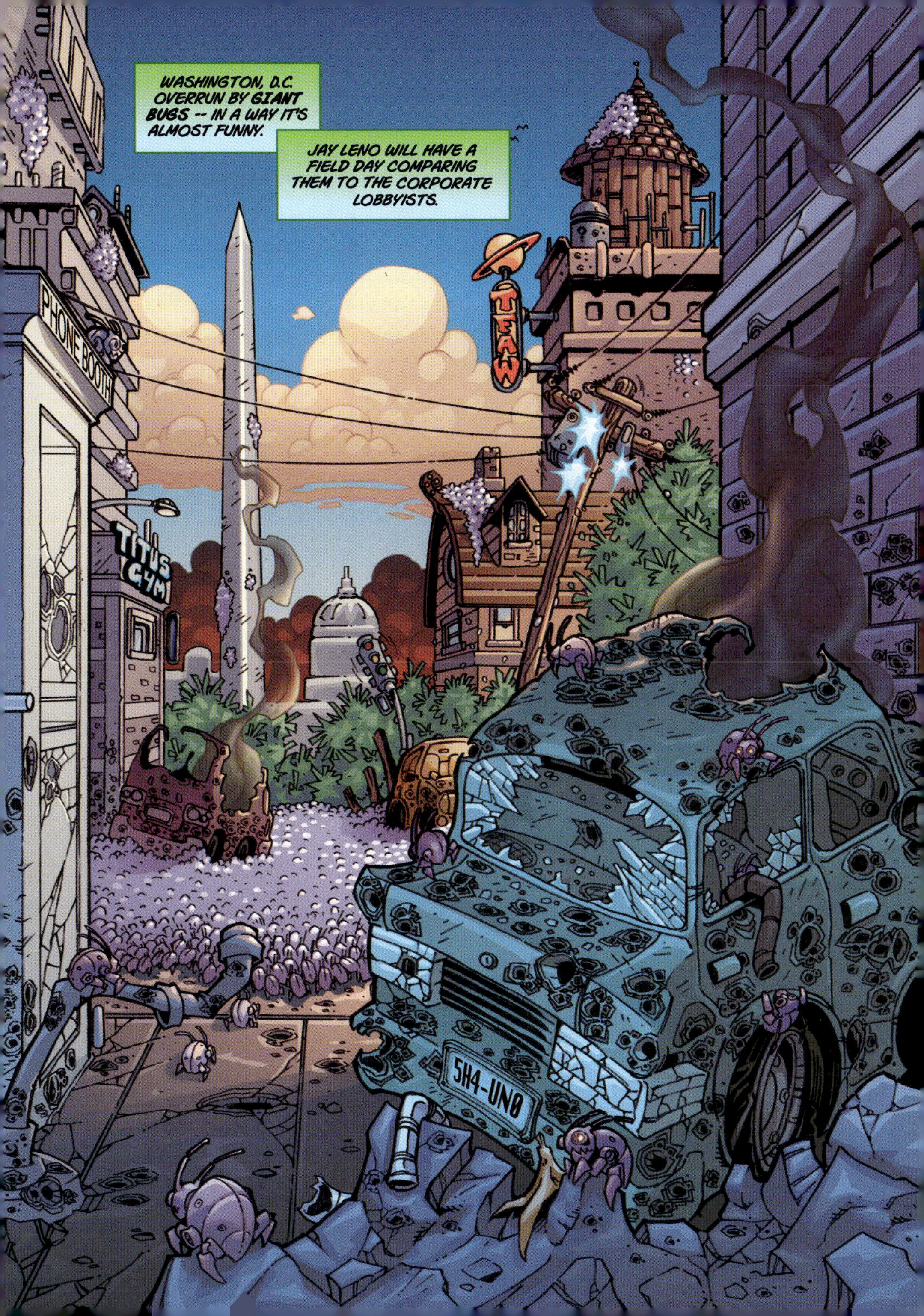
WASHINGTON, D.C. OVERRUN BY GIANT BUGS -- IN A WAY IT'S ALMOST FUNNY.
JAY LENO WILL HAVE A FIELD DAY COMPARING THEM TO THE CORPORATE LOBBYISTS.
PHONE BOOTH
TITUS GYM
5H4-UN0

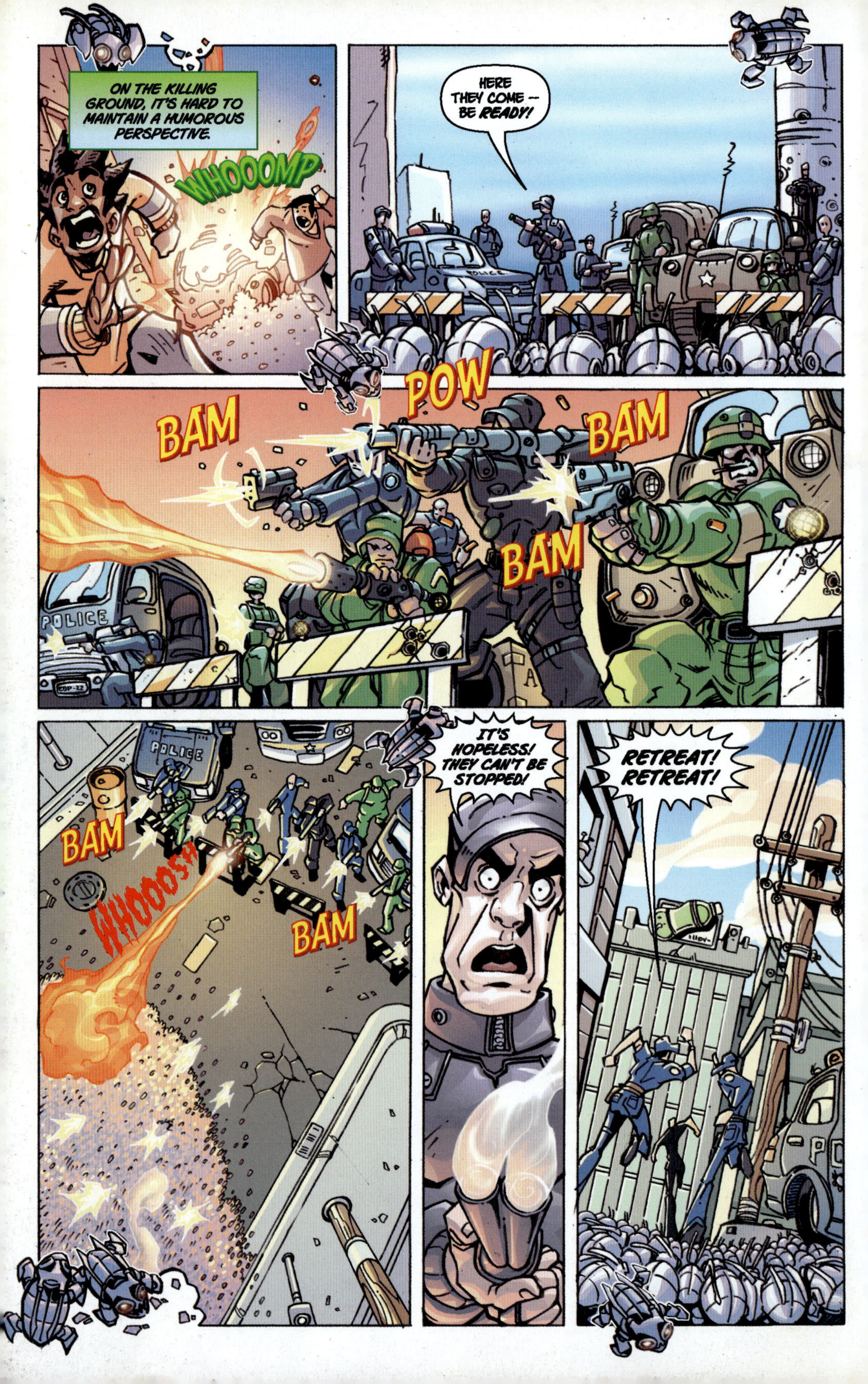
ON THE KILLING GROUND, IT'S HARD TO MAINTAIN A HUMOROUS PERSPECTIVE.
WHOOOMP
HERE THEY COME -- BE READY!
POLICE
BAM
POW
BAM
BAM
POLICE
POLICE
BAM
WHOOOSH
BAM
IT'S HOPELESS! THEY CAN'T BE STOPPED!
RETREAT! RETREAT!

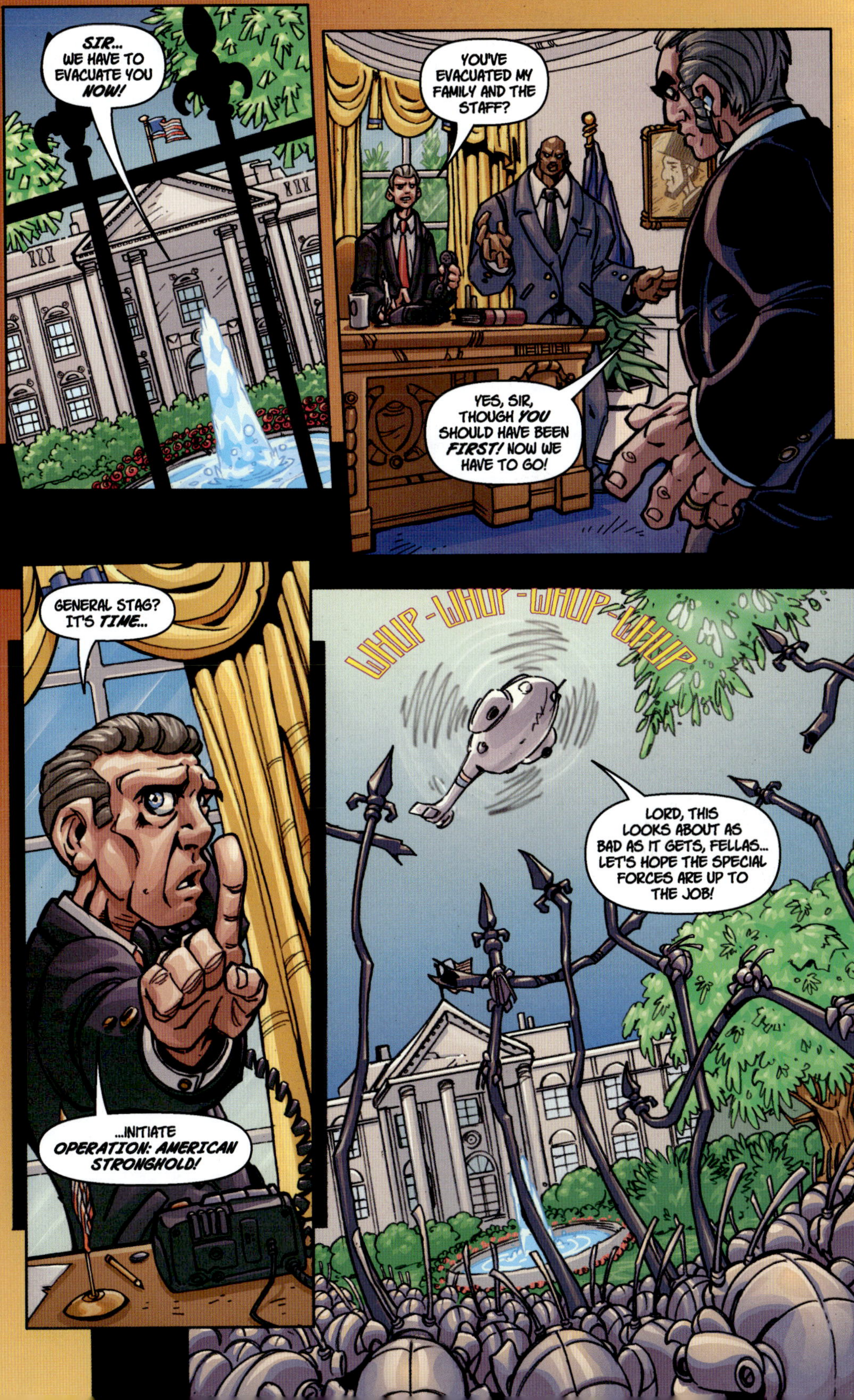
SIR... WE HAVE TO EVACUATE YOU NOW!
YOU'VE EVACUATED MY FAMILY AND THE STAFF?
YES, SIR, THOUGH YOU SHOULD HAVE BEEN FIRST! NOW WE HAVE TO GO!
GENERAL STAG? IT'S TIME...
...INITIATE OPERATION: AMERICAN STRONGHOLD!
WHUP-WHUP-WHUP-WHUP
LORD, THIS LOOKS ABOUT AS BAD AS IT GETS, FELLAS... LET'S HOPE THE SPECIAL FORCES ARE UP TO THE JOB!

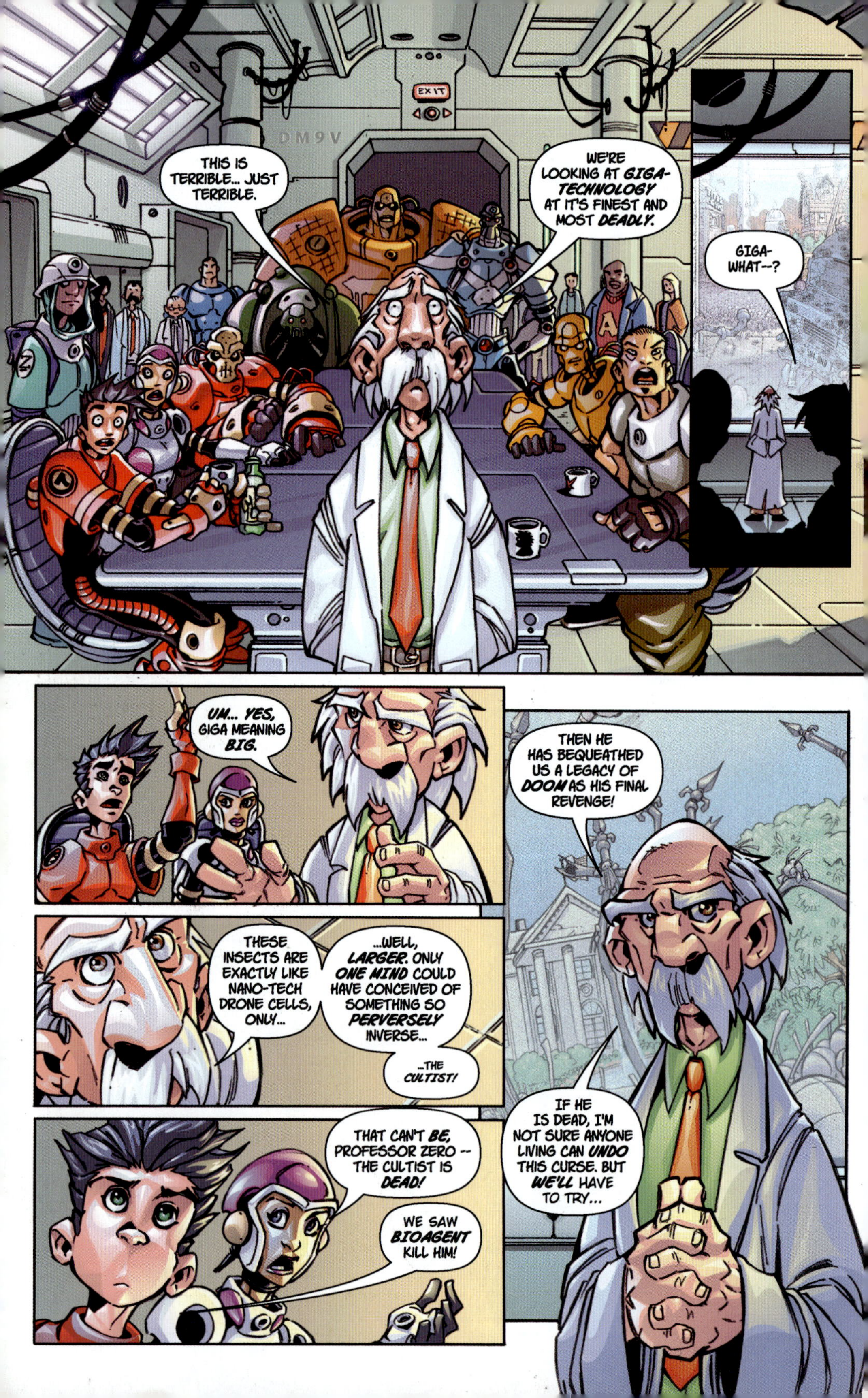

DM9V
EXIT
THIS IS TERRIBLE... JUST TERRIBLE.
WE'RE LOOKING AT GIGA-TECHNOLOGY AT IT'S FINEST AND MOST DEADLY.
GIGA-WHAT--?
UM... YES, GIGA MEANING BIG.
THESE INSECTS ARE EXACTLY LIKE NANO-TECH DRONE CELLS, ONLY...
...WELL, LARGER. ONLY ONE MIND COULD HAVE CONCEIVED OF SOMETHING SO PERVERSELY INVERSE...
...THE CULTIST!
THAT CAN'T BE, PROFESSOR ZERO -- THE CULTIST IS DEAD!
WE SAW BIOAGENT KILL HIM!
THEN HE HAS BEQUEATHED US A LEGACY OF DOOM AS HIS FINAL REVENGE!
IF HE IS DEAD, I'M NOT SURE ANYONE LIVING CAN UNDO THIS CURSE. BUT WE'LL HAVE TO TRY...

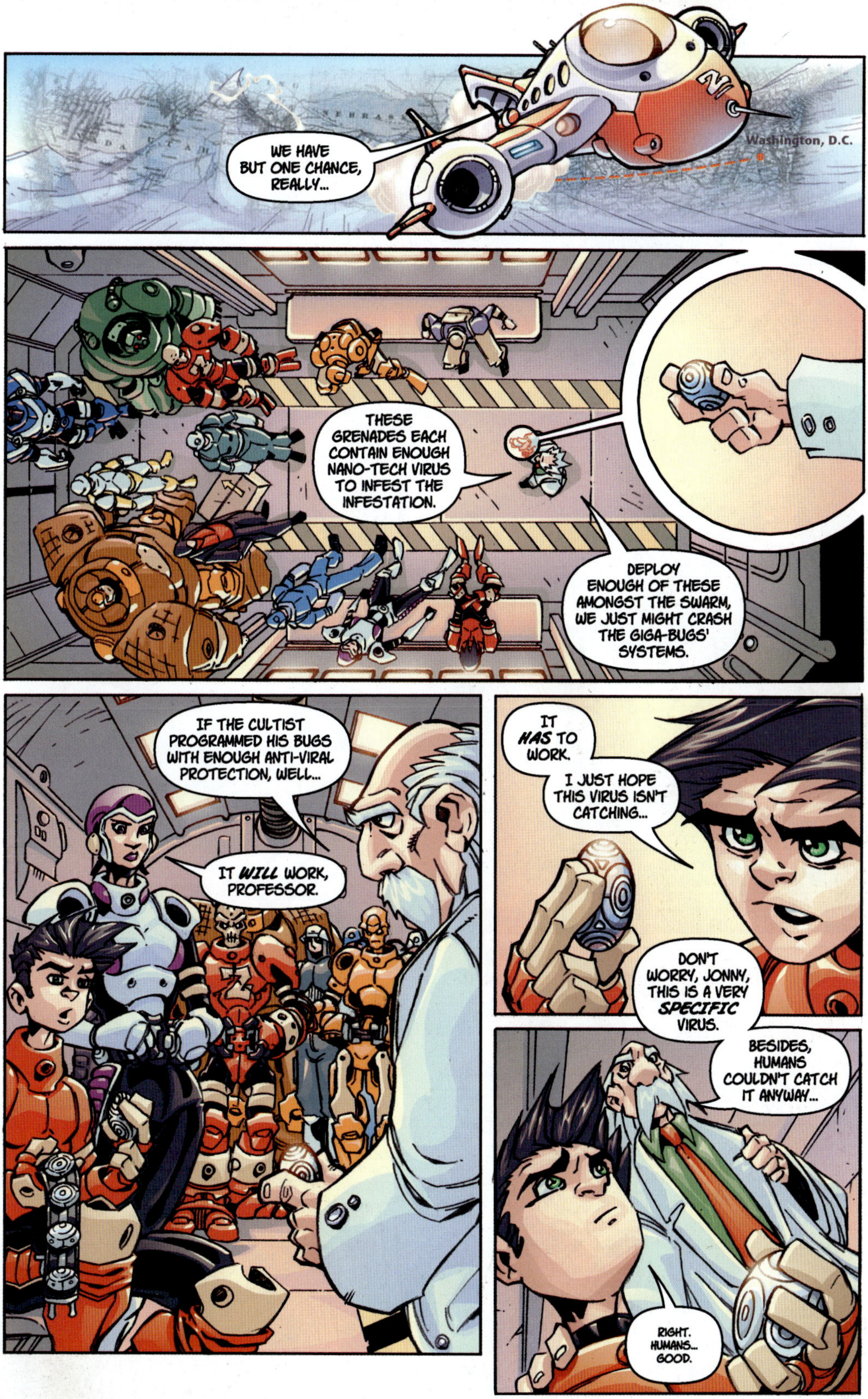
Washington, D.C.
WE HAVE BUT ONE CHANCE, REALLY...
THESE GRENADES EACH CONTAIN ENOUGH NANO-TECH VIRUS TO INFEST THE INFESTATION.
DEPLOY ENOUGH OF THESE AMONGST THE SWARM, WE JUST MIGHT CRASH THE GIGA-BUGS' SYSTEMS.
IF THE CULTIST PROGRAMMED HIS BUGS WITH ENOUGH ANTI-VIRAL PROTECTION, WELL...
IT WILL WORK, PROFESSOR.
IT HAS TO WORK.
I JUST HOPE THIS VIRUS ISN'T CATCHING...
DON'T WORRY, JONNY, THIS IS A VERY SPECIFIC VIRUS.
BESIDES, HUMANS COULDN'T CATCH IT ANYWAY...
RIGHT. HUMANS... GOOD.

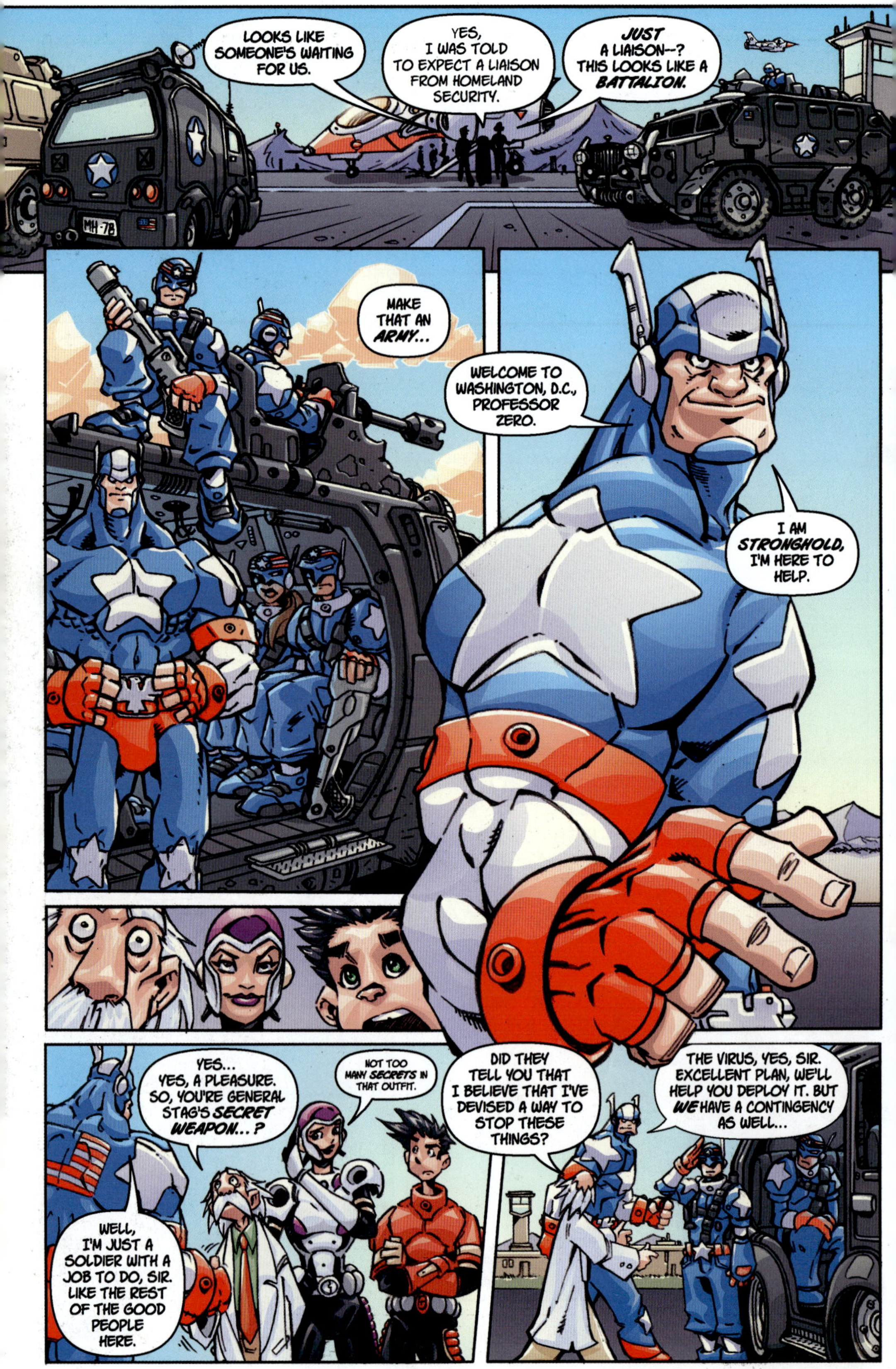
LOOKS LIKE SOMEONE'S WAITING FOR US.
YES, I WAS TOLD TO EXPECT A LIAISON FROM HOMELAND SECURITY.
JUST A LIAISON--? THIS LOOKS LIKE A BATTALION.
MH-78
MAKE THAT AN ARMY...
WELCOME TO WASHINGTON, D.C., PROFESSOR ZERO.
I AM STRONGHOLD, I'M HERE TO HELP.
YES... YES, A PLEASURE. SO, YOU'RE GENERAL STAG'S SECRET WEAPON...?
NOT TOO MANY SECRETS IN THAT OUTFIT.
WELL, I'M JUST A SOLDIER WITH A JOB TO DO, SIR. LIKE THE REST OF THE GOOD PEOPLE HERE.
DID THEY TELL YOU THAT I BELIEVE THAT I'VE DEVISED A WAY TO STOP THESE THINGS?
THE VIRUS, YES, SIR. EXCELLENT PLAN, WE'LL HELP YOU DEPLOY IT. BUT WE HAVE A CONTINGENCY AS WELL...

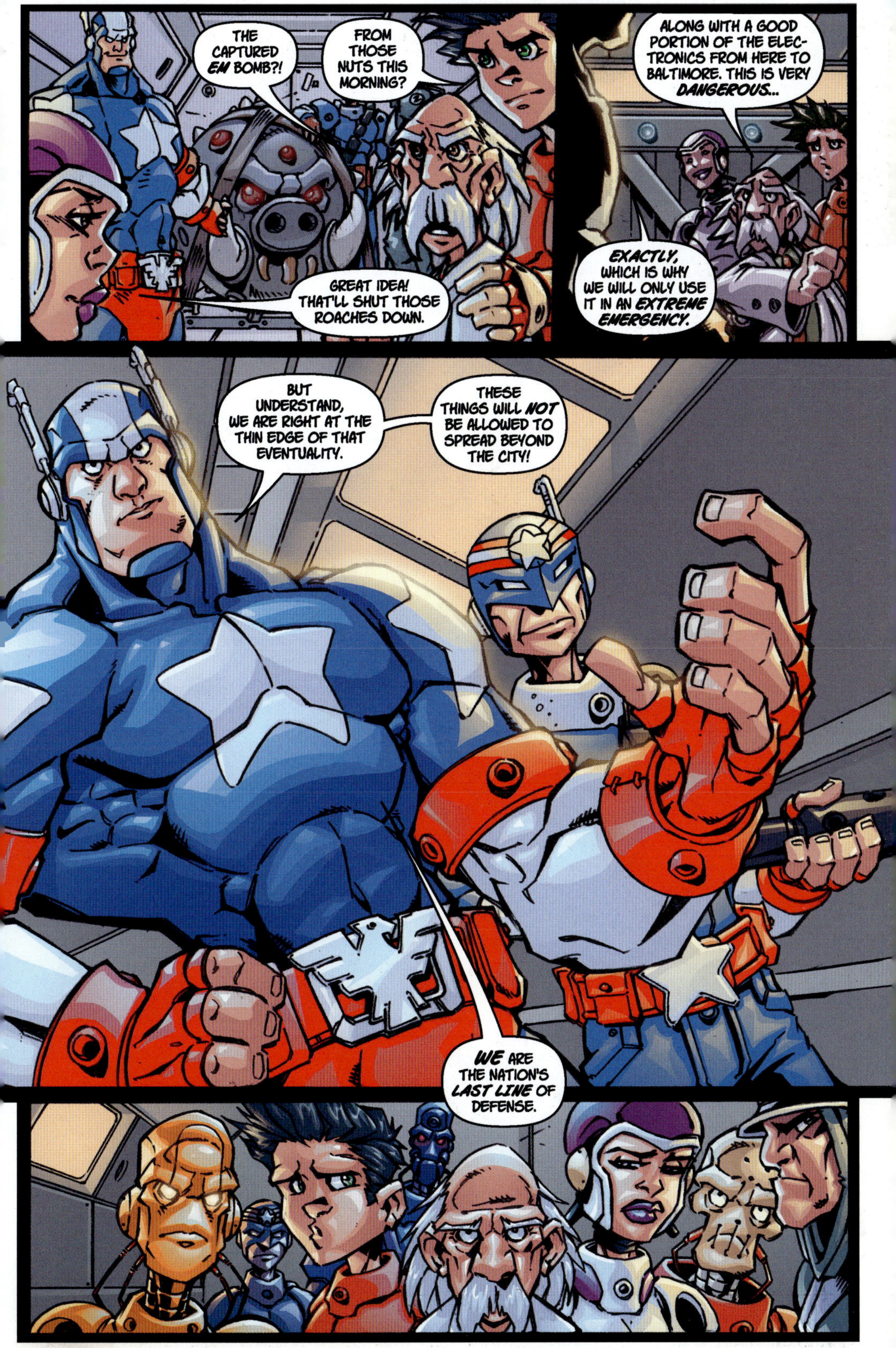
THE CAPTURED EM BOMB?!
FROM THOSE NUTS THIS MORNING?
GREAT IDEA! THAT'LL SHUT THOSE ROACHES DOWN.
ALONG WITH A GOOD PORTION OF THE ELECTRONICS FROM HERE TO BALTIMORE. THIS IS VERY DANGEROUS...
EXACTLY, WHICH IS WHY WE WILL ONLY USE IT IN AN EXTREME EMERGENCY.
BUT UNDERSTAND, WE ARE RIGHT AT THE THIN EDGE OF THAT EVENTUALITY.
THESE THINGS WILL NOT BE ALLOWED TO SPREAD BEYOND THE CITY!
WE ARE THE NATION'S LAST LINE OF DEFENSE.

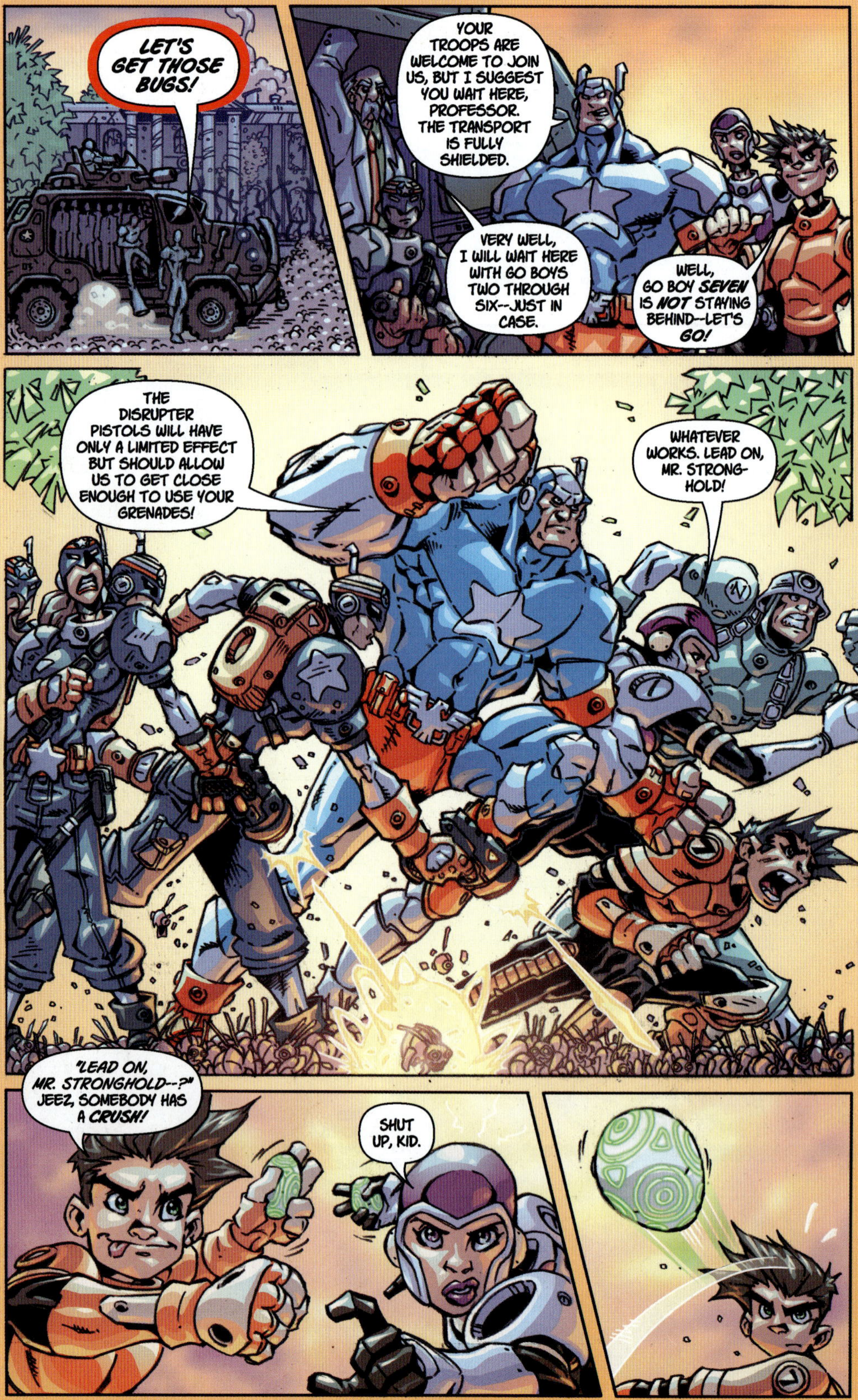

LET'S GET THOSE BUGS!
YOUR TROOPS ARE WELCOME TO JOIN US, BUT I SUGGEST YOU WAIT HERE, PROFESSOR. THE TRANSPORT IS FULLY SHIELDED.
VERY WELL, I WILL WAIT HERE WITH GO BOYS TWO THROUGH SIX--JUST IN CASE.
WELL, GO BOY *SEVEN* IS *NOT* STAYING BEHIND--LET'S *GO!*
THE DISRUPTER PISTOLS WILL HAVE ONLY A LIMITED EFFECT BUT SHOULD ALLOW US TO GET CLOSE ENOUGH TO USE YOUR GRENADES!
WHATEVER WORKS. LEAD ON, MR. STRONGHOLD!
"LEAD ON, MR. STRONGHOLD--?" JEEZ, SOMEBODY HAS A *CRUSH!*
SHUT UP, KID.

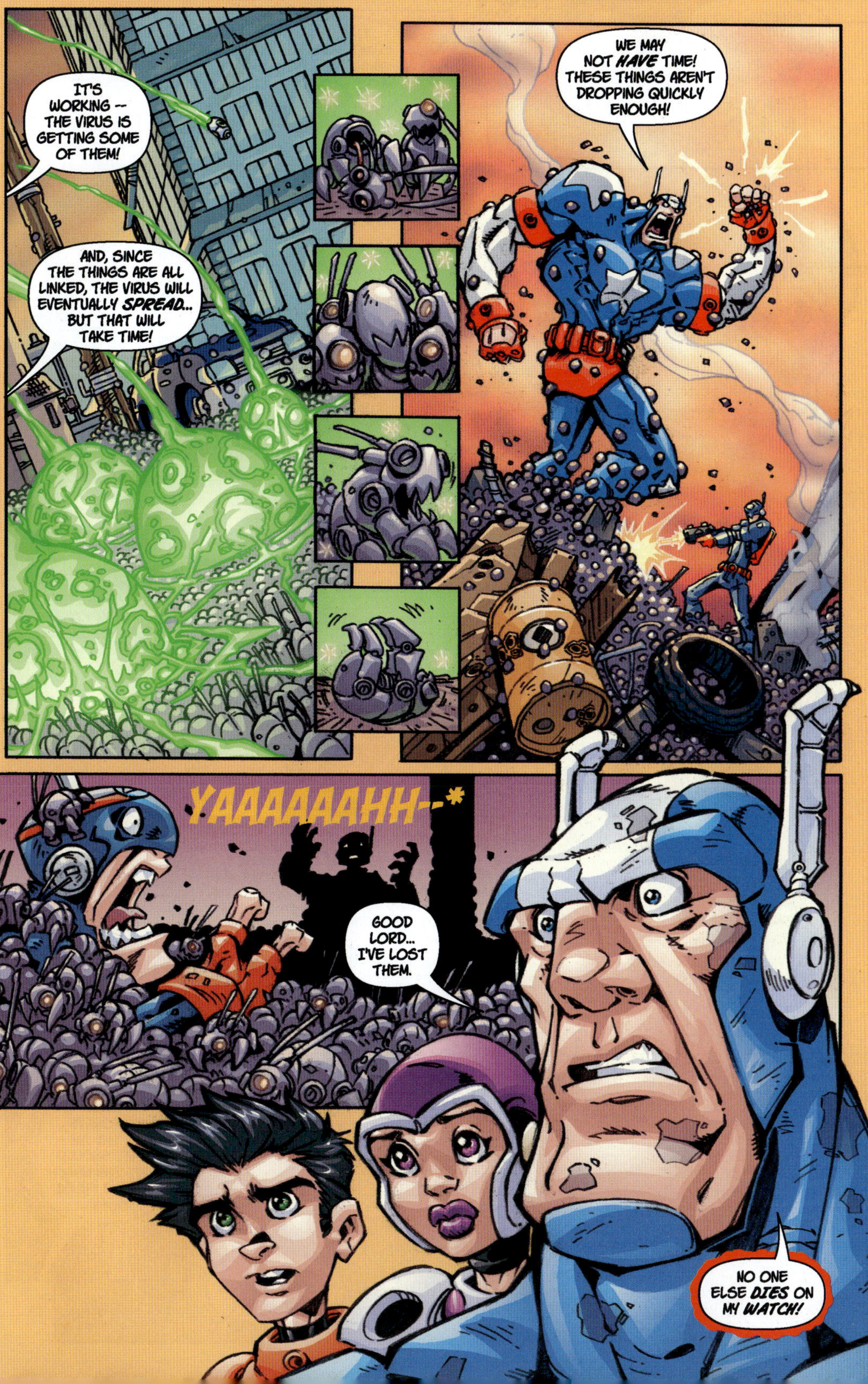
IT'S WORKING -- THE VIRUS IS GETTING SOME OF THEM!
AND, SINCE THE THINGS ARE ALL LINKED, THE VIRUS WILL EVENTUALLY SPREAD... BUT THAT WILL TAKE TIME!
WE MAY NOT HAVE TIME! THESE THINGS AREN'T DROPPING QUICKLY ENOUGH!
YAAAAAAHH--*
GOOD LORD... I'VE LOST THEM.
NO ONE ELSE DIES ON MY WATCH!

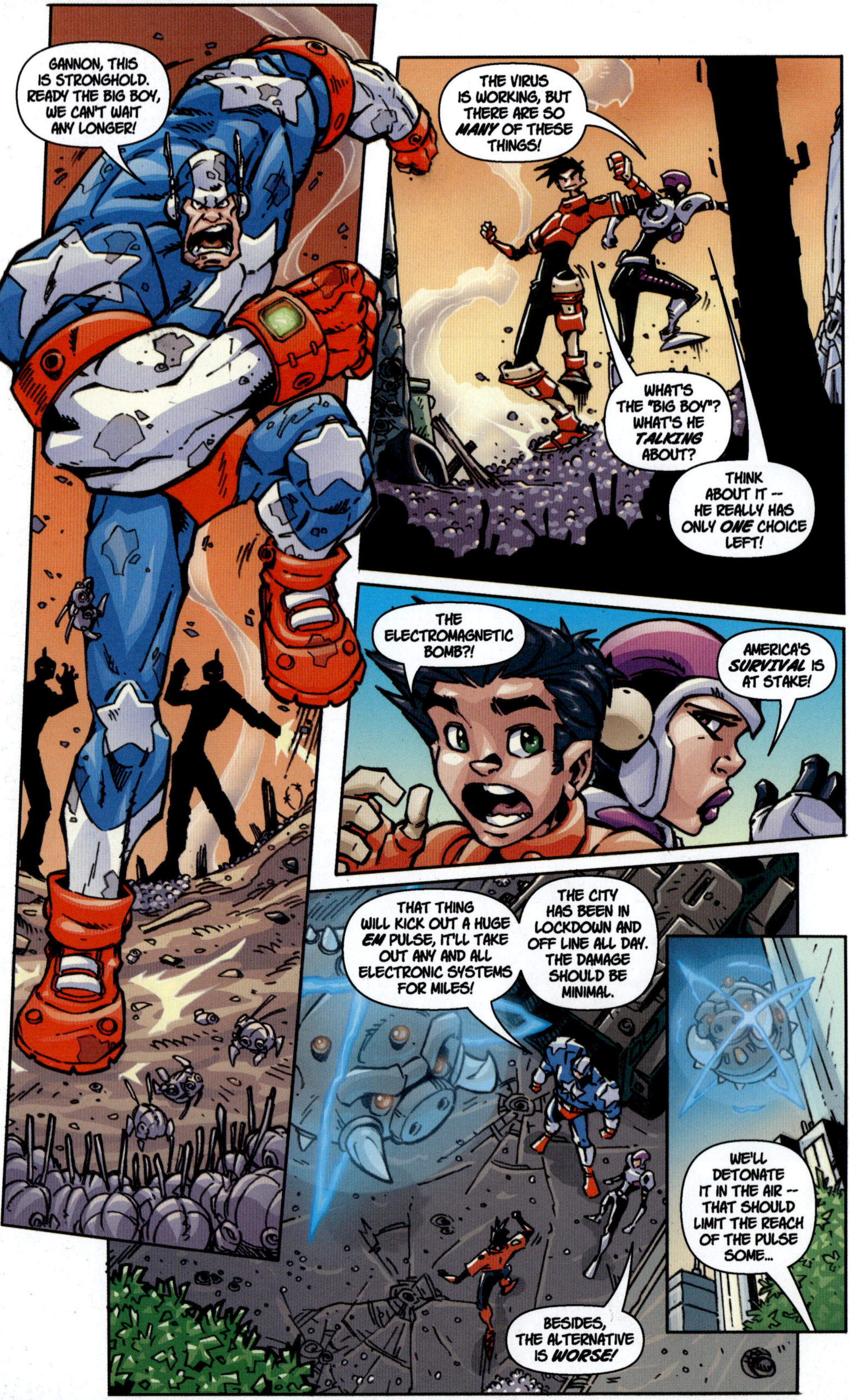
GANNON, THIS IS STRONGHOLD. READY THE BIG BOY, WE CAN'T WAIT ANY LONGER!
THE VIRUS IS WORKING, BUT THERE ARE SO MANY OF THESE THINGS!
WHAT'S THE "BIG BOY"? WHAT'S HE TALKING ABOUT?
THINK ABOUT IT -- HE REALLY HAS ONLY ONE CHOICE LEFT!
THE ELECTROMAGNETIC BOMB?!
AMERICA'S SURVIVAL IS AT STAKE!
THAT THING WILL KICK OUT A HUGE EM PULSE, IT'LL TAKE OUT ANY AND ALL ELECTRONIC SYSTEMS FOR MILES!
THE CITY HAS BEEN IN LOCKDOWN AND OFF LINE ALL DAY. THE DAMAGE SHOULD BE MINIMAL.
WE'LL DETONATE IT IN THE AIR -- THAT SHOULD LIMIT THE REACH OF THE PULSE SOME...
BESIDES, THE ALTERNATIVE IS WORSE!

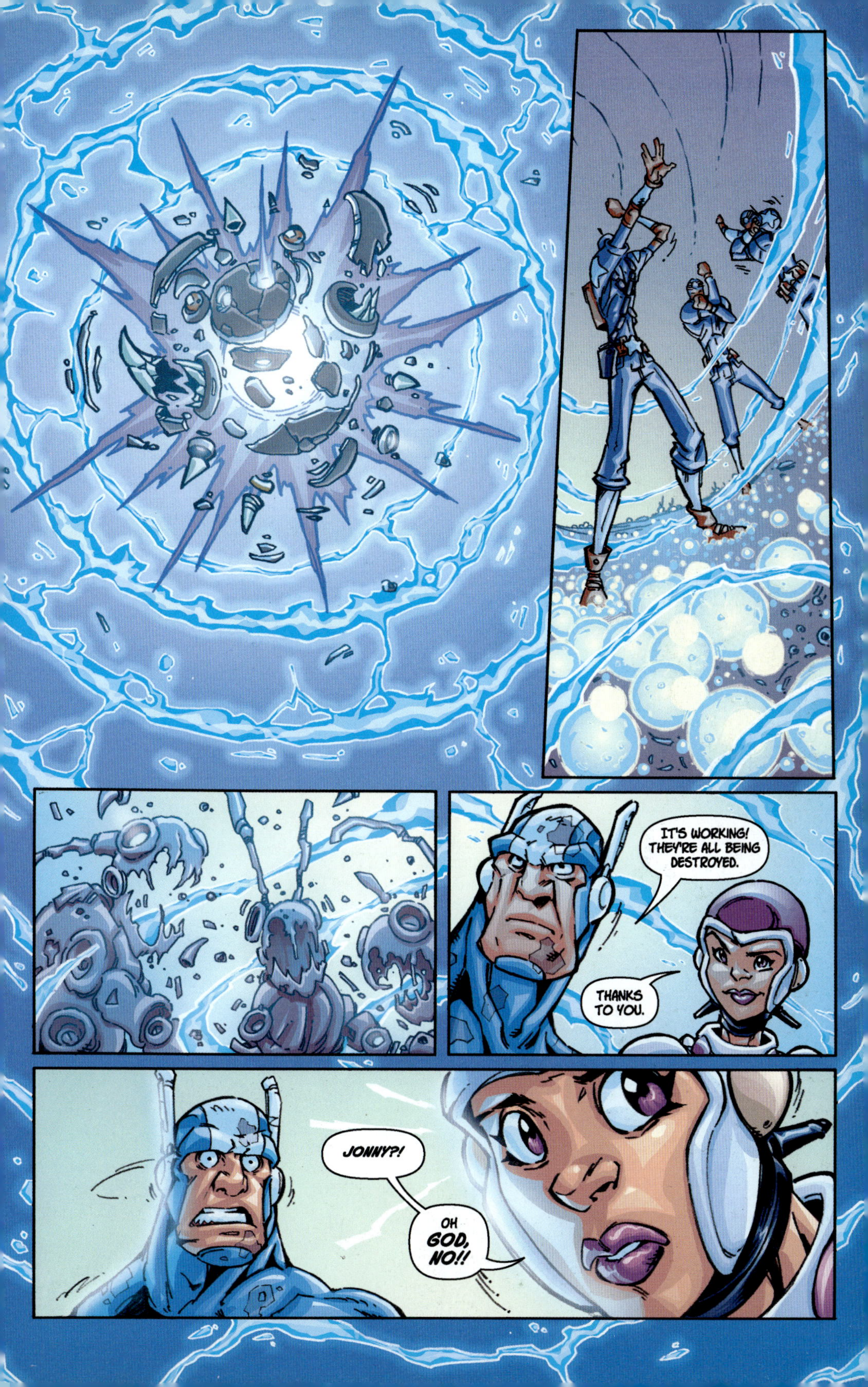
IT'S WORKING! THEY'RE ALL BEING DESTROYED.
THANKS TO YOU.
JONNY?!
OH GOD, NO!!

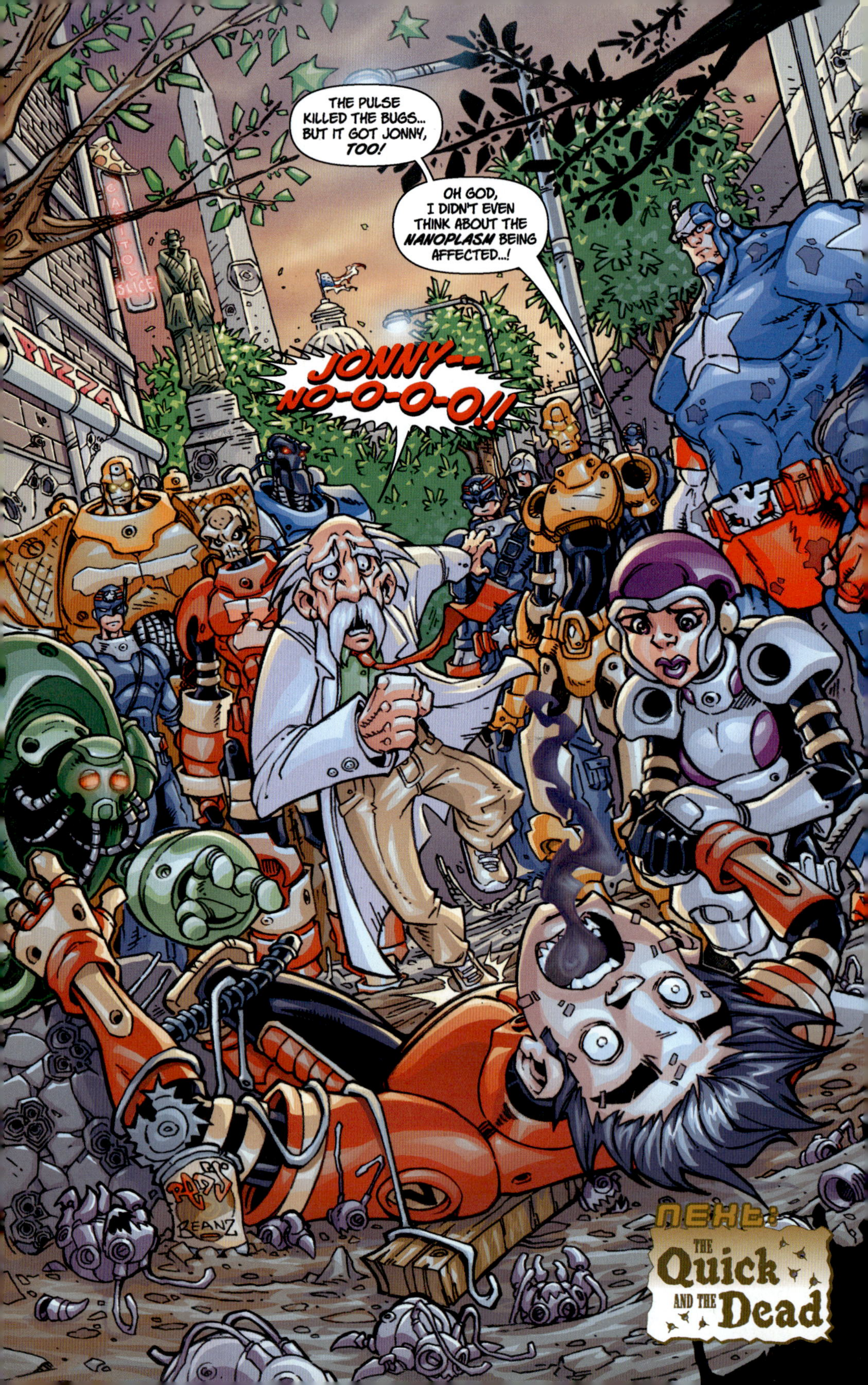
THE PULSE KILLED THE BUGS... BUT IT GOT JONNY, *TOO!*
OH GOD, I DIDN'T EVEN THINK ABOUT THE *NANOPLASM* BEING AFFECTED...!
JONNY-- NO-O-O-O!!
PIZZA
CAPITOL SLICE
NEXT: THE Quick AND THE Dead

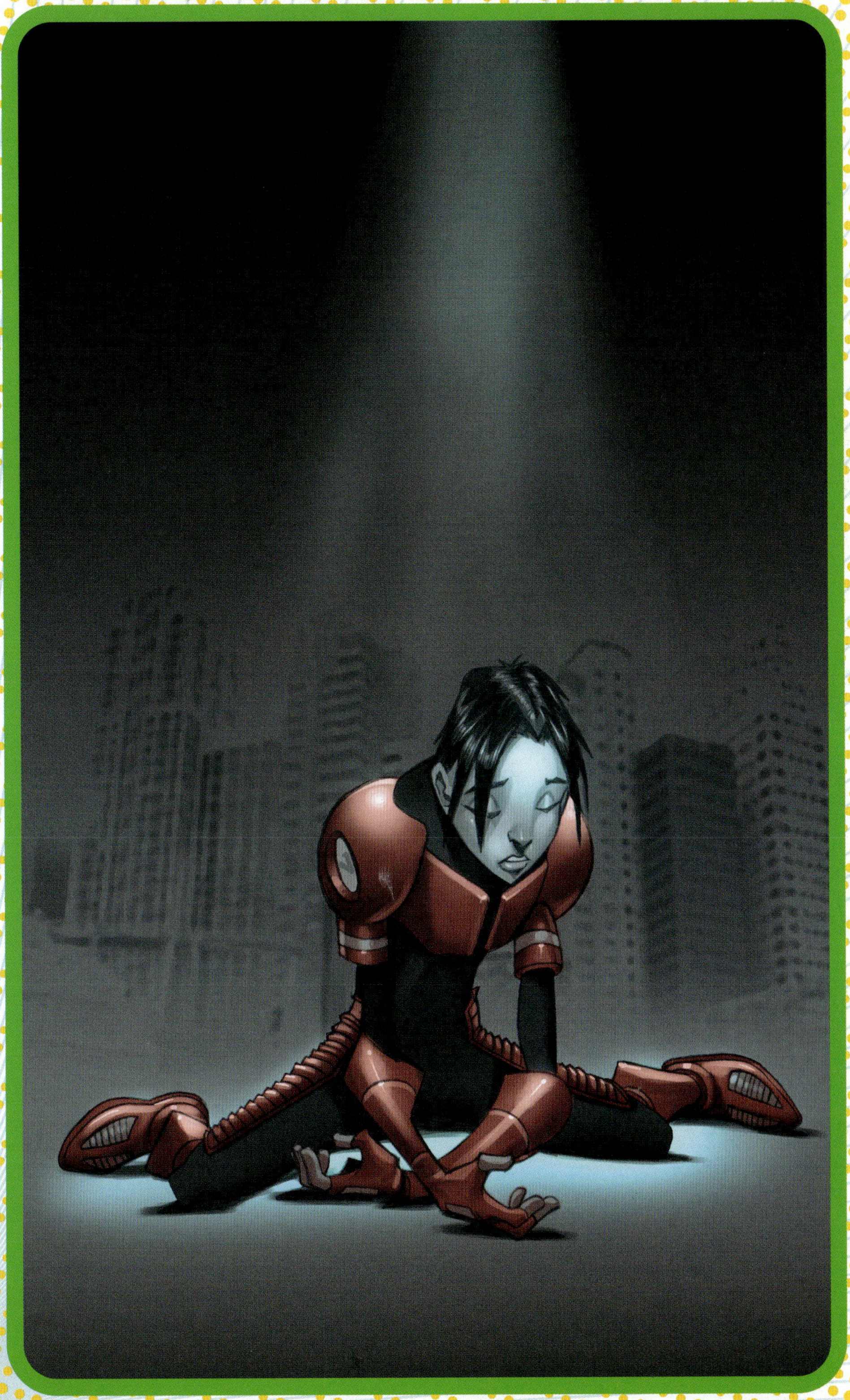

"THE QUICK AND THE DEAD"

SCRIPT BRIAN AUGUSTYN

PENCILS TODD DEMONG

INKS KRIS JUSTICE

COLORS DAN JACKSON

LETTERS MICHAEL DAVID THOMAS

COVER FRANCISCO RUIZ VELASCO

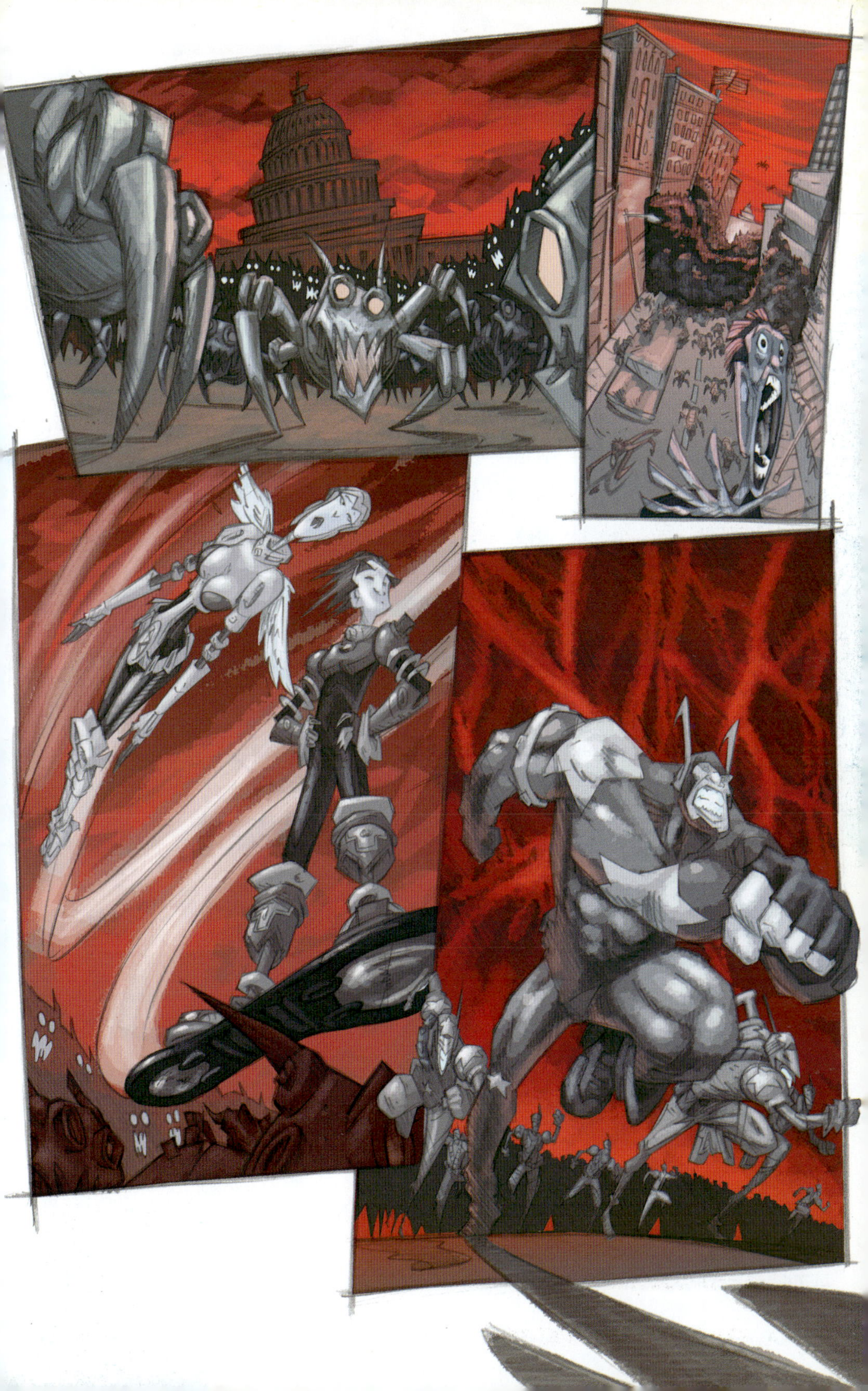

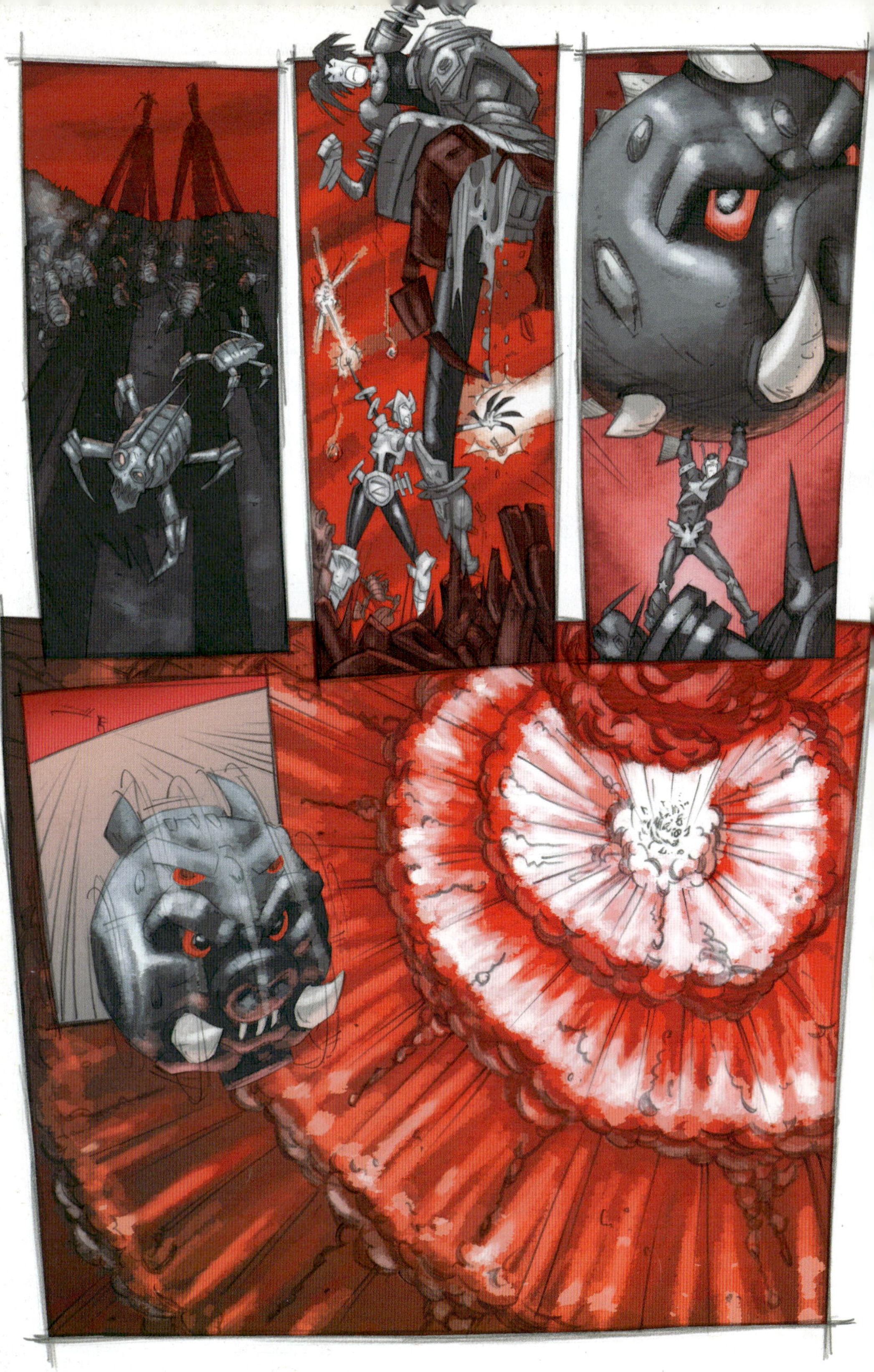

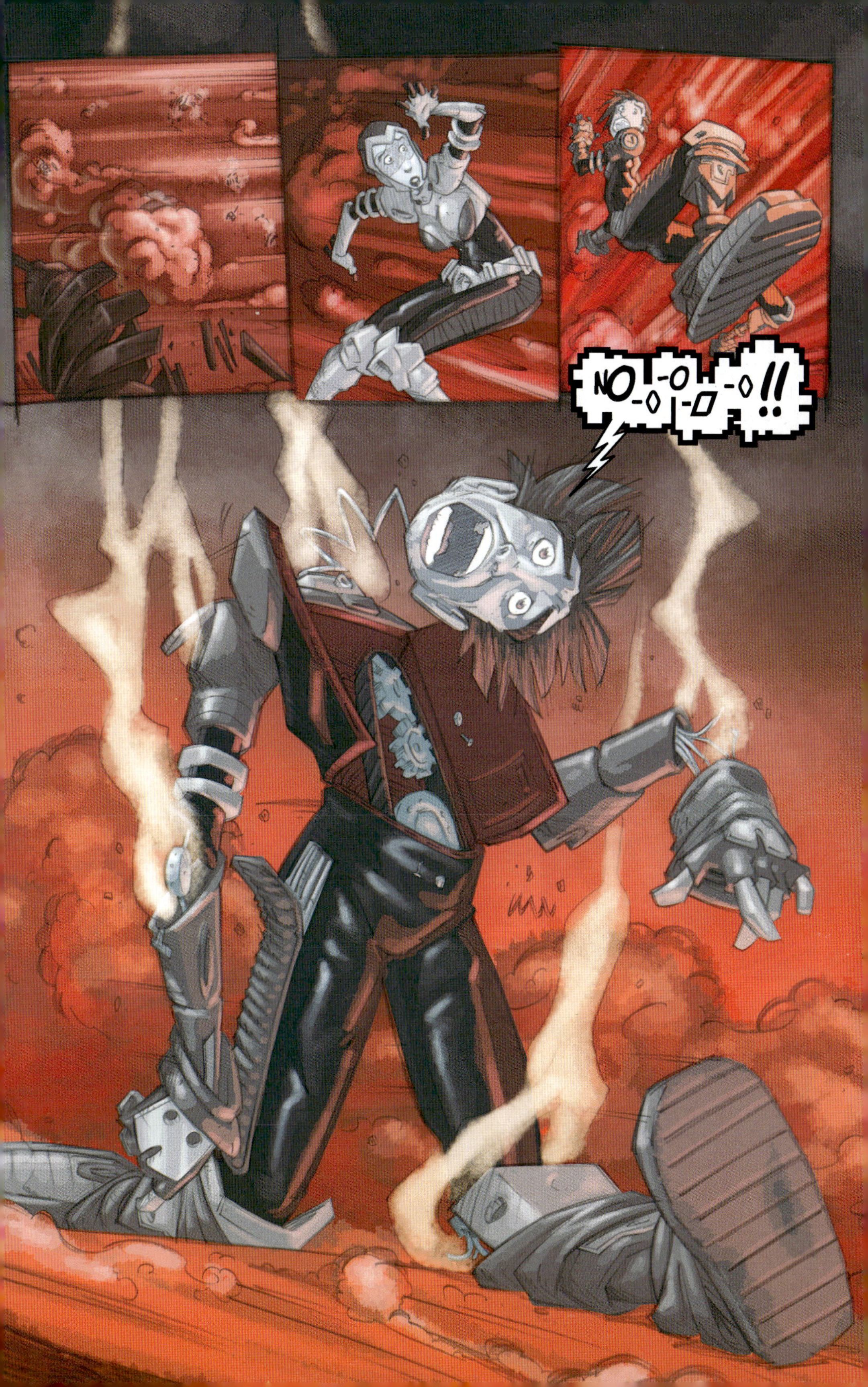
NO-O-O-O-O!!

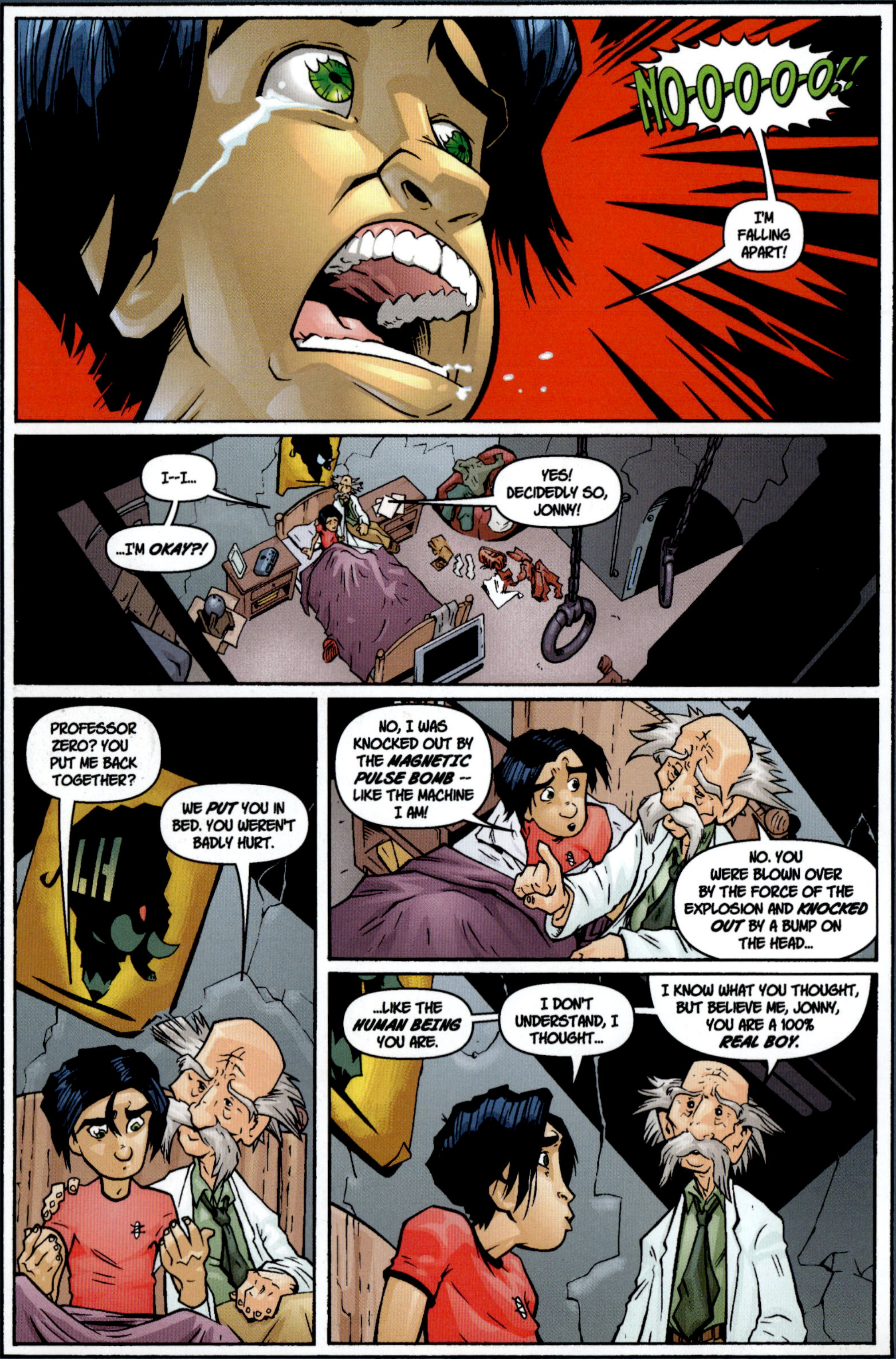
NO-O-O-O-O!!
I'M FALLING APART!
I--I...
...I'M OKAY?!
YES! DECIDEDLY SO, JONNY!
PROFESSOR ZERO? YOU PUT ME BACK TOGETHER?
WE PUT YOU IN BED. YOU WEREN'T BADLY HURT.
NO, I WAS KNOCKED OUT BY THE MAGNETIC PULSE BOMB -- LIKE THE MACHINE I AM!
NO. YOU WERE BLOWN OVER BY THE FORCE OF THE EXPLOSION AND KNOCKED OUT BY A BUMP ON THE HEAD...
...LIKE THE HUMAN BEING YOU ARE.
I DON'T UNDERSTAND, I THOUGHT...
I KNOW WHAT YOU THOUGHT, BUT BELIEVE ME, JONNY, YOU ARE A 100% REAL BOY.

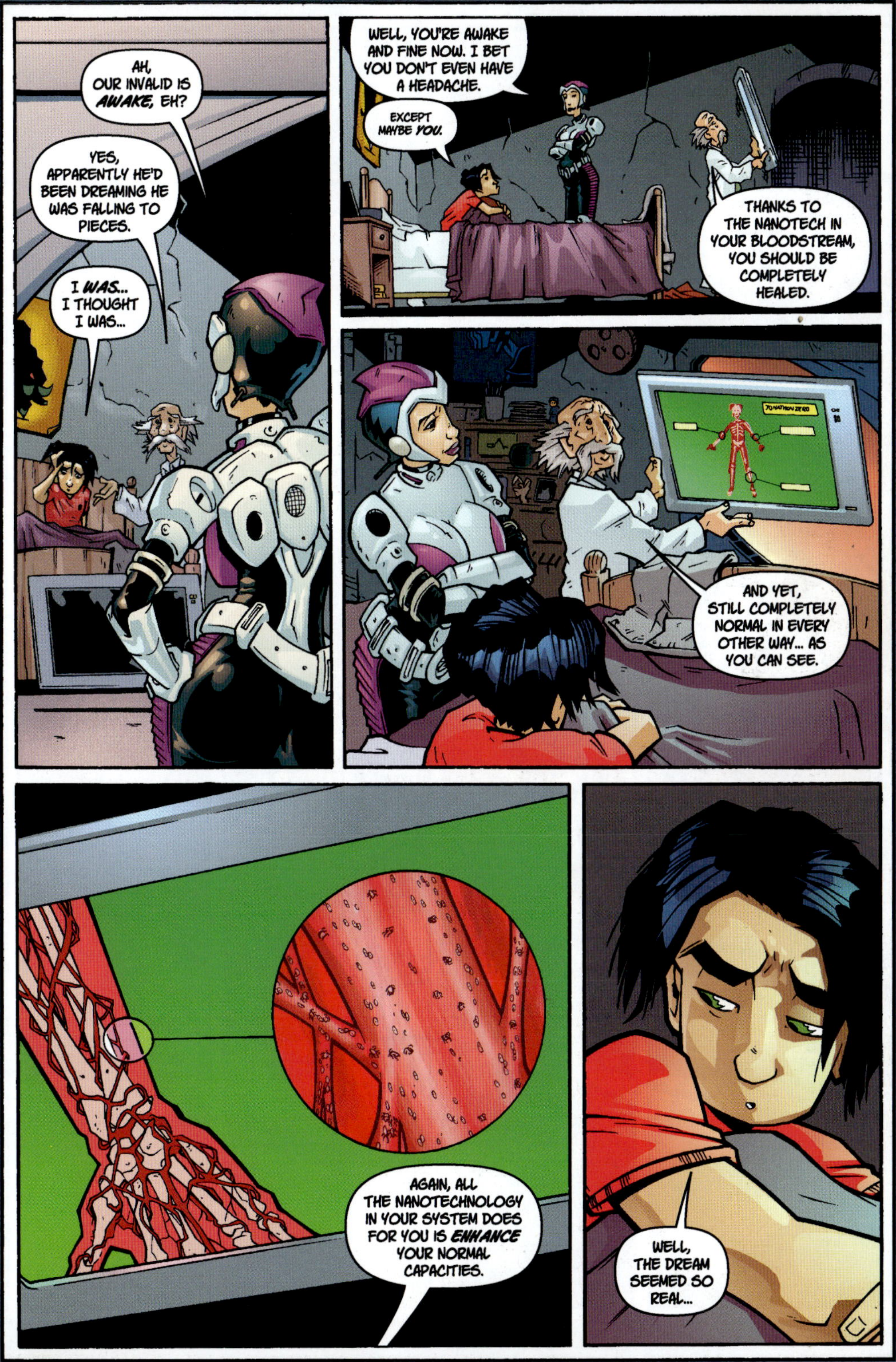
AH, OUR INVALID IS AWAKE, EH?
YES, APPARENTLY HE'D BEEN DREAMING HE WAS FALLING TO PIECES.
I WAS... I THOUGHT I WAS...
WELL, YOU'RE AWAKE AND FINE NOW. I BET YOU DON'T EVEN HAVE A HEADACHE.
EXCEPT MAYBE YOU.
THANKS TO THE NANOTECH IN YOUR BLOODSTREAM, YOU SHOULD BE COMPLETELY HEALED.
AND YET, STILL COMPLETELY NORMAL IN EVERY OTHER WAY... AS YOU CAN SEE.
AGAIN, ALL THE NANOTECHNOLOGY IN YOUR SYSTEM DOES FOR YOU IS ENHANCE YOUR NORMAL CAPACITIES.
WELL, THE DREAM SEEMED SO REAL...

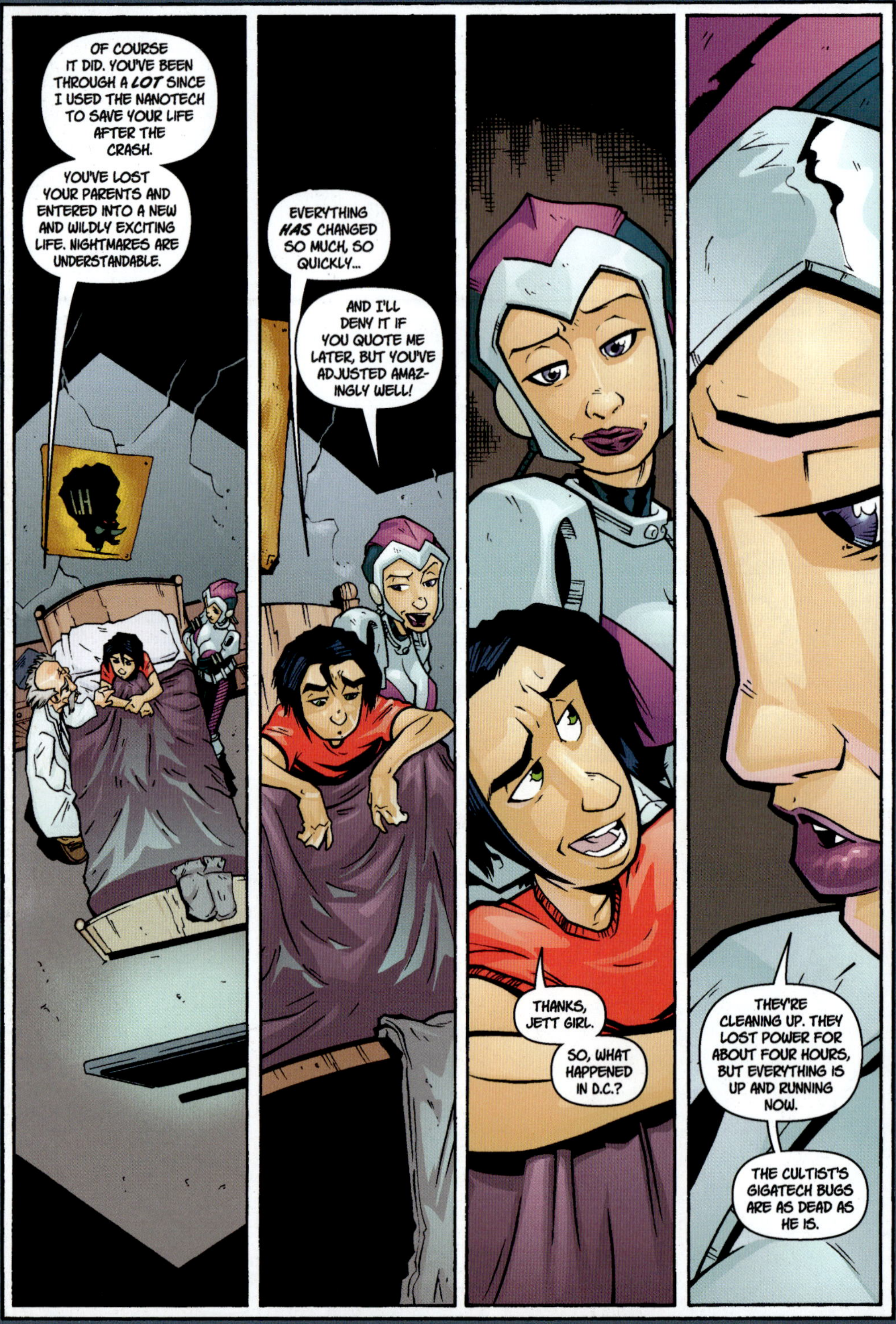
OF COURSE IT DID. YOU'VE BEEN THROUGH A *LOT* SINCE I USED THE NANOTECH TO SAVE YOUR LIFE AFTER THE CRASH.
YOU'VE LOST YOUR PARENTS AND ENTERED INTO A NEW AND WILDLY EXCITING LIFE. NIGHTMARES ARE UNDERSTANDABLE.
EVERYTHING *HAS* CHANGED SO MUCH, SO QUICKLY...
AND I'LL DENY IT IF YOU QUOTE ME LATER, BUT YOU'VE ADJUSTED AMAZINGLY WELL!
THANKS, JETT GIRL.
SO, WHAT HAPPENED IN D.C.?
THEY'RE CLEANING UP. THEY LOST POWER FOR ABOUT FOUR HOURS, BUT EVERYTHING IS UP AND RUNNING NOW.
THE CULTIST'S GIGATECH BUGS ARE AS DEAD AS HE IS.

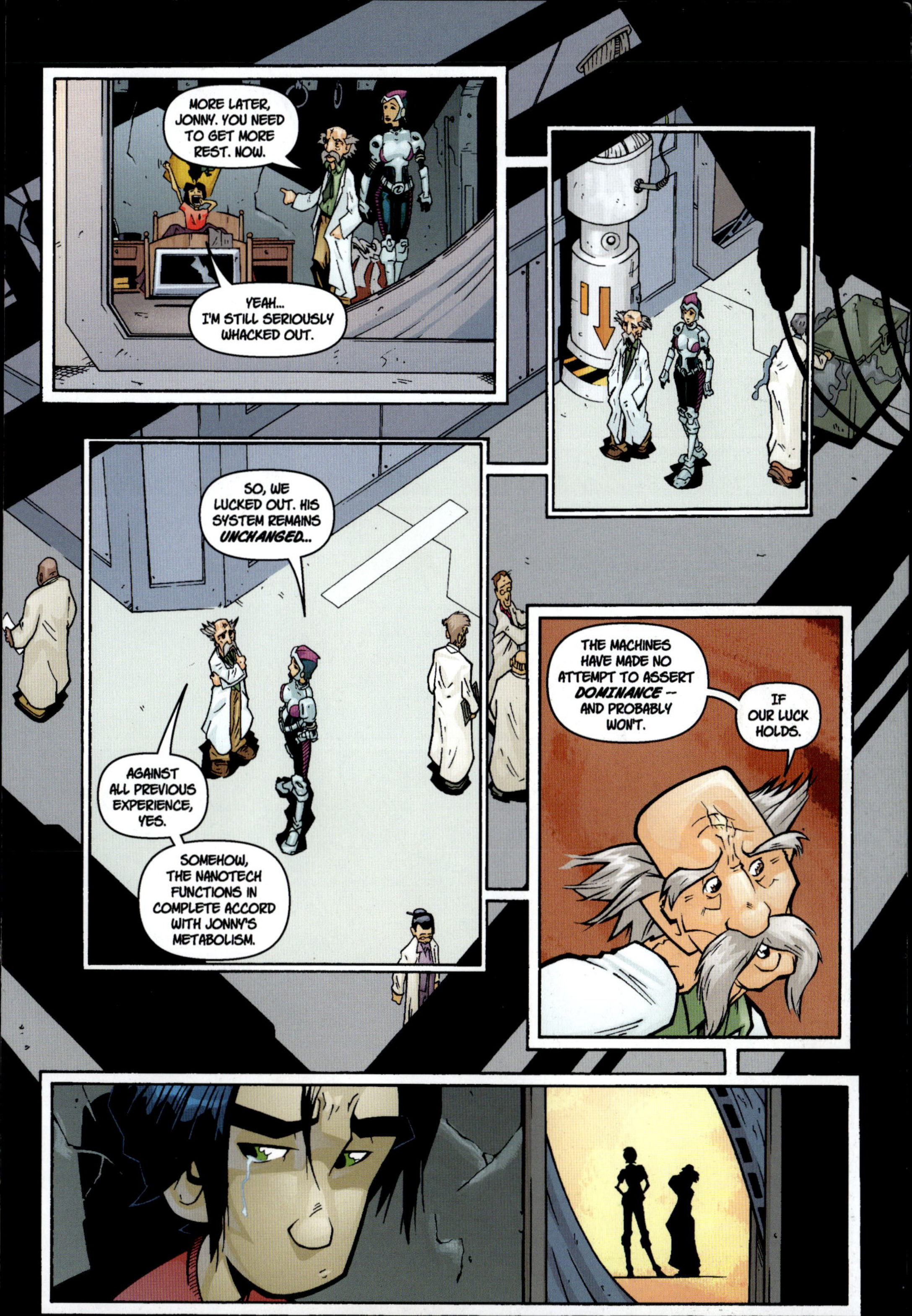
MORE LATER, JONNY. YOU NEED TO GET MORE REST. NOW.
YEAH... I'M STILL SERIOUSLY WHACKED OUT.
SO, WE LUCKED OUT. HIS SYSTEM REMAINS *UNCHANGED*...
AGAINST ALL PREVIOUS EXPERIENCE, YES.
SOMEHOW, THE NANOTECH FUNCTIONS IN COMPLETE ACCORD WITH JONNY'S METABOLISM.
THE MACHINES HAVE MADE NO ATTEMPT TO ASSERT *DOMINANCE* -- AND PROBABLY WON'T.
IF OUR LUCK HOLDS.

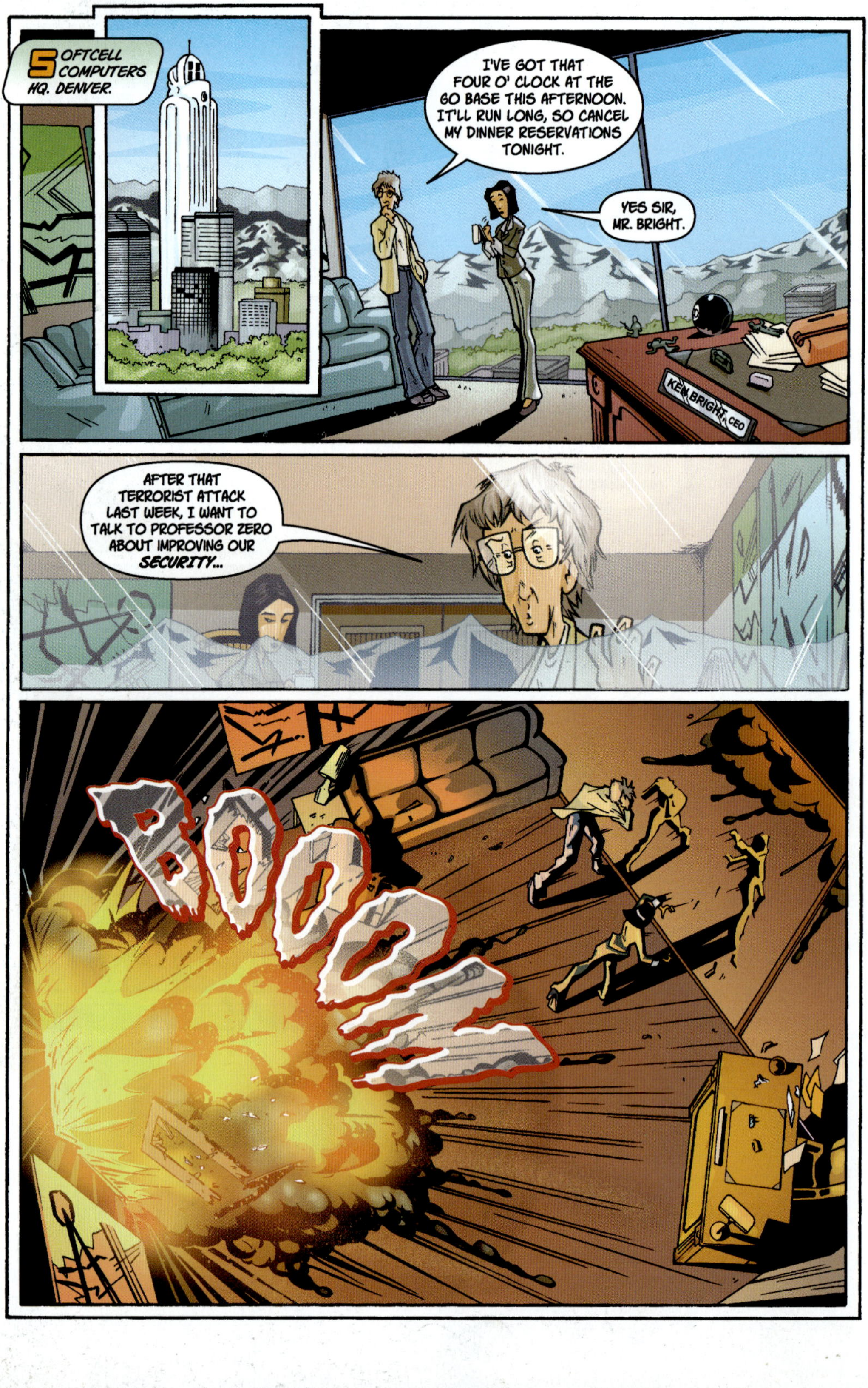
SOFTCELL COMPUTERS HQ. DENVER.
I'VE GOT THAT FOUR O' CLOCK AT THE GO BASE THIS AFTERNOON. IT'LL RUN LONG, SO CANCEL MY DINNER RESERVATIONS TONIGHT.
YES SIR, MR. BRIGHT.
KEN BRIGHT, CEO
AFTER THAT TERRORIST ATTACK LAST WEEK, I WANT TO TALK TO PROFESSOR ZERO ABOUT IMPROVING OUR *SECURITY...*
BOOOM

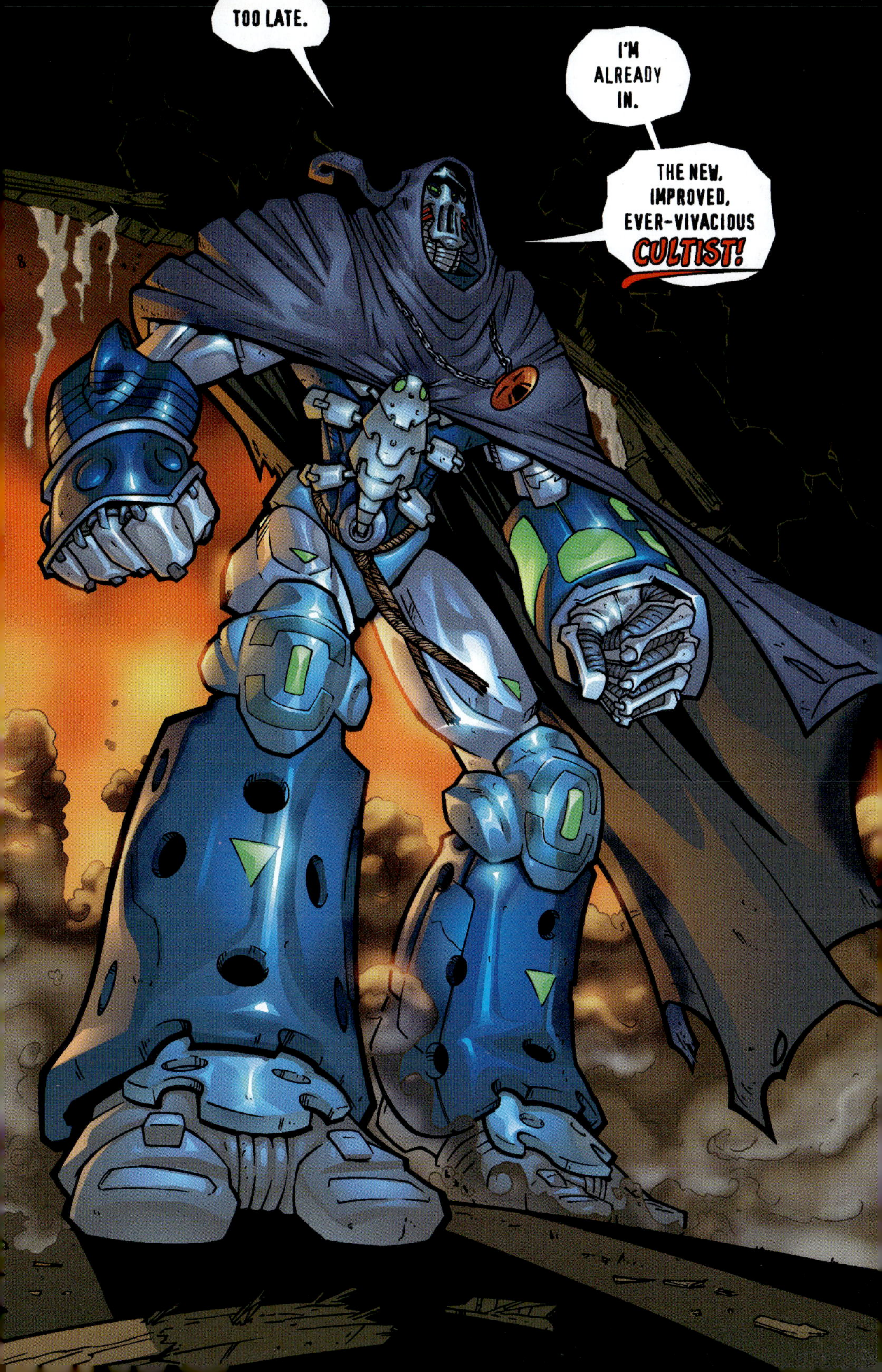
TOO LATE.
I'M ALREADY IN.
THE NEW, IMPROVED, EVER-VIVACIOUS CULTIST!

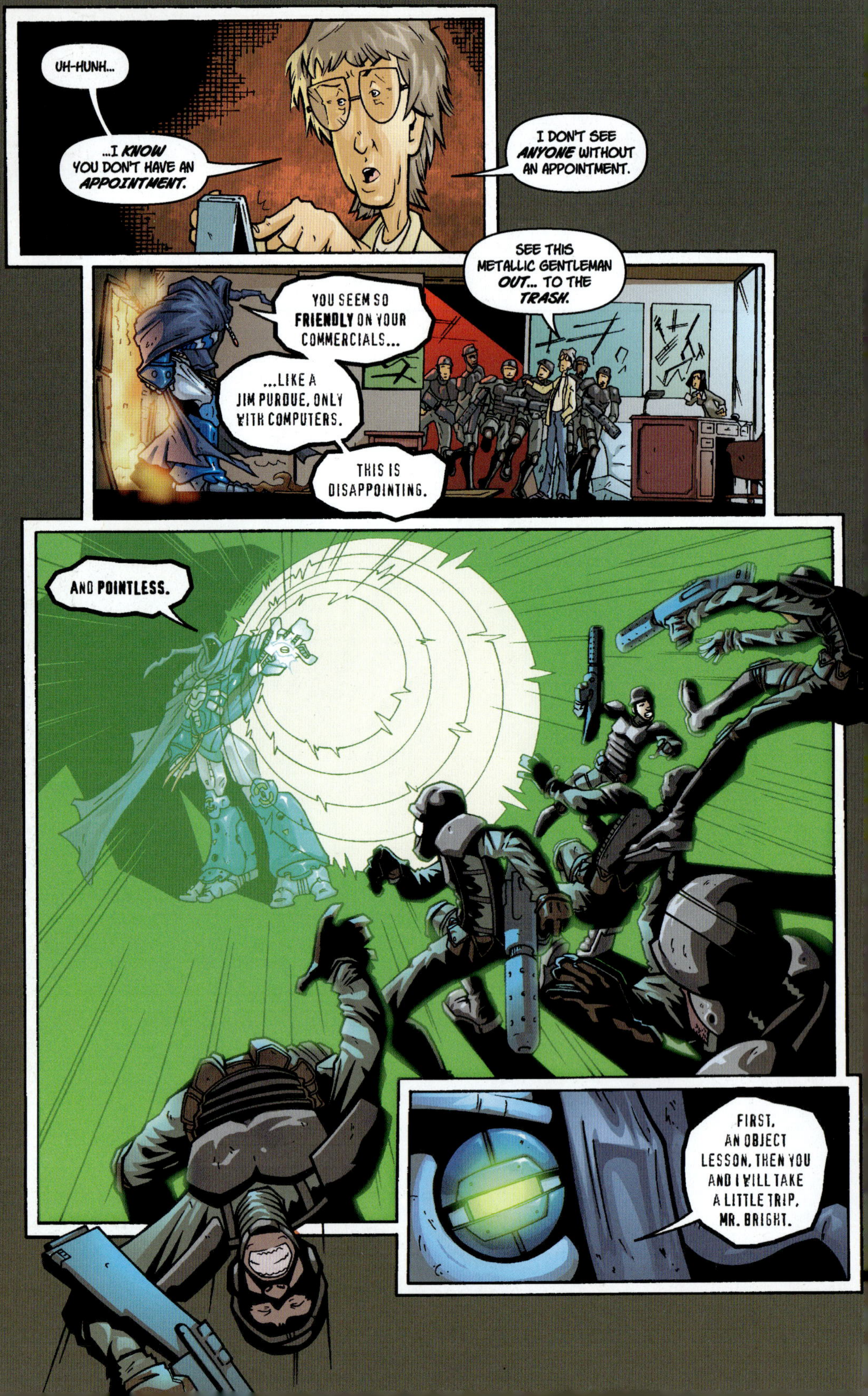

UH-HUNH...
...I KNOW YOU DON'T HAVE AN APPOINTMENT.
I DON'T SEE ANYONE WITHOUT AN APPOINTMENT.
SEE THIS METALLIC GENTLEMAN OUT... TO THE TRASH.
YOU SEEM SO FRIENDLY ON YOUR COMMERCIALS...
...LIKE A JIM PURDUE, ONLY WITH COMPUTERS.
THIS IS DISAPPOINTING.
AND POINTLESS.
FIRST, AN OBJECT LESSON, THEN YOU AND I WILL TAKE A LITTLE TRIP, MR. BRIGHT.

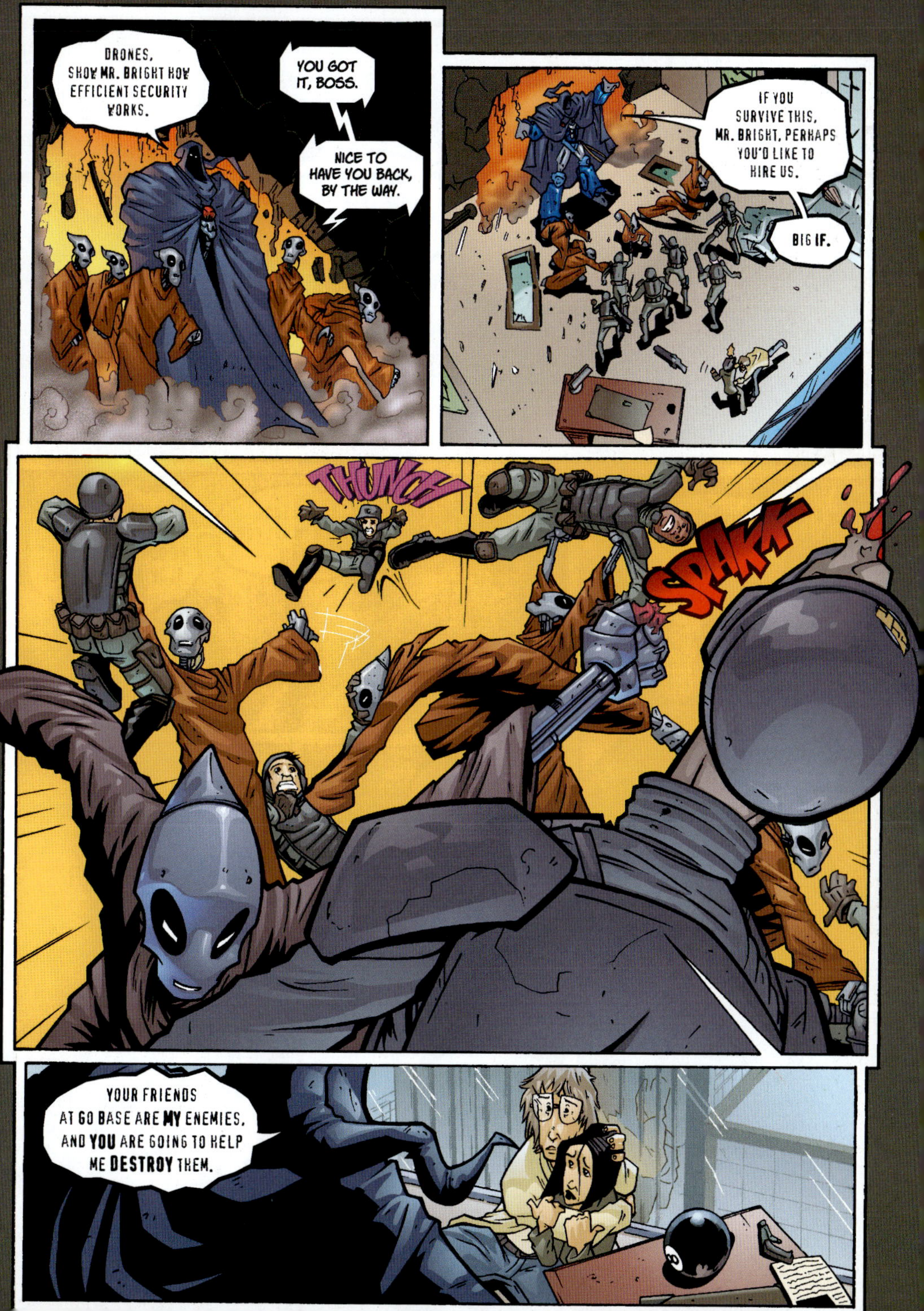
DRONES, SHOW MR. BRIGHT HOW EFFICIENT SECURITY WORKS.
YOU GOT IT, BOSS.
NICE TO HAVE YOU BACK, BY THE WAY.
IF YOU SURVIVE THIS, MR. BRIGHT, PERHAPS YOU'D LIKE TO HIRE US.
BIG IF.
THUNCH
SPAKT
YOUR FRIENDS AT GO BASE ARE MY ENEMIES, AND YOU ARE GOING TO HELP ME DESTROY THEM.

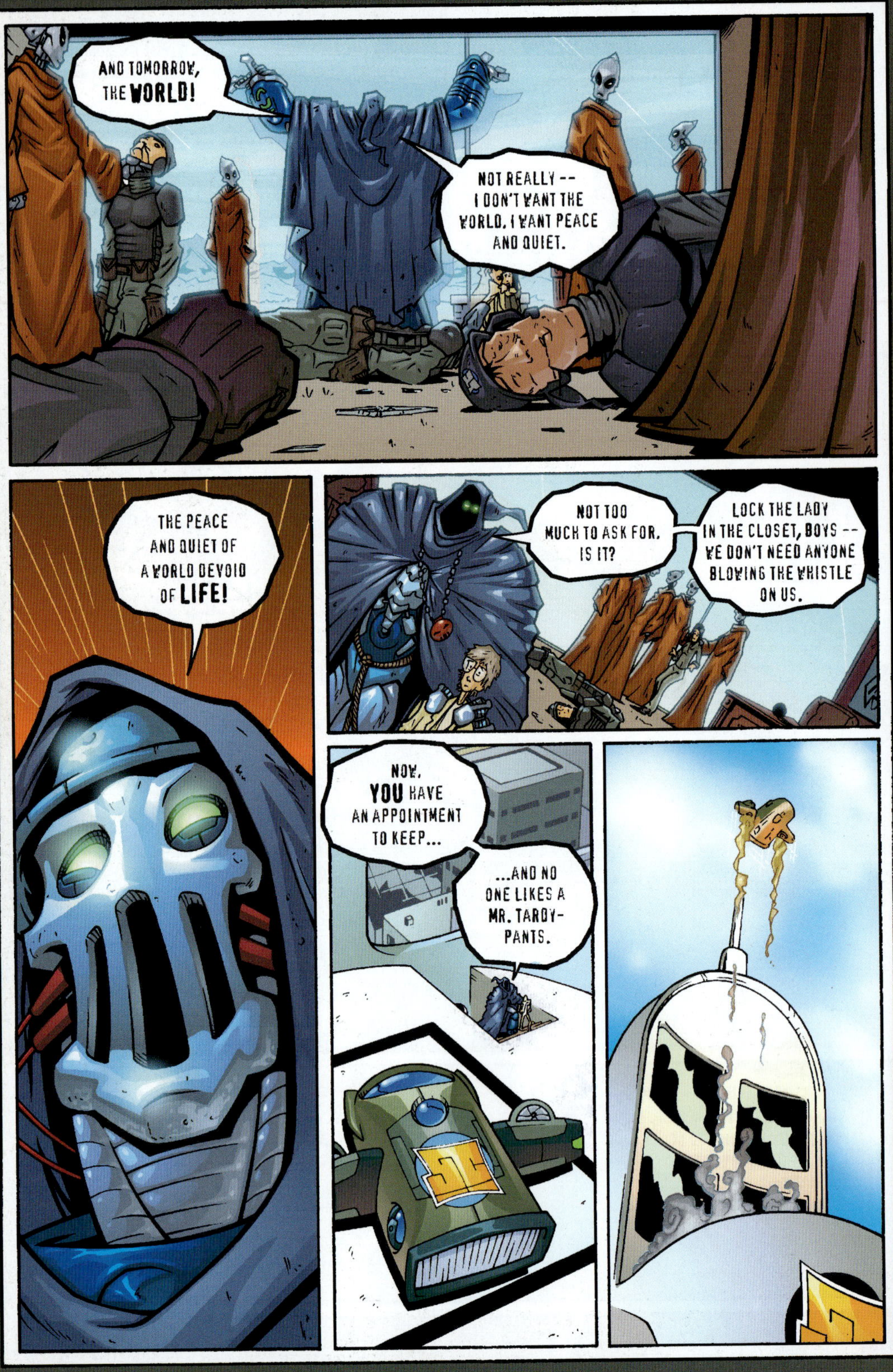
AND TOMORROW, THE WORLD!
NOT REALLY -- I DON'T WANT THE WORLD. I WANT PEACE AND QUIET.
THE PEACE AND QUIET OF A WORLD DEVOID OF LIFE!
NOT TOO MUCH TO ASK FOR. IS IT?
LOCK THE LADY IN THE CLOSET, BOYS -- WE DON'T NEED ANYONE BLOWING THE WHISTLE ON US.
NOW, YOU HAVE AN APPOINTMENT TO KEEP...
...AND NO ONE LIKES A MR. TARDY-PANTS.

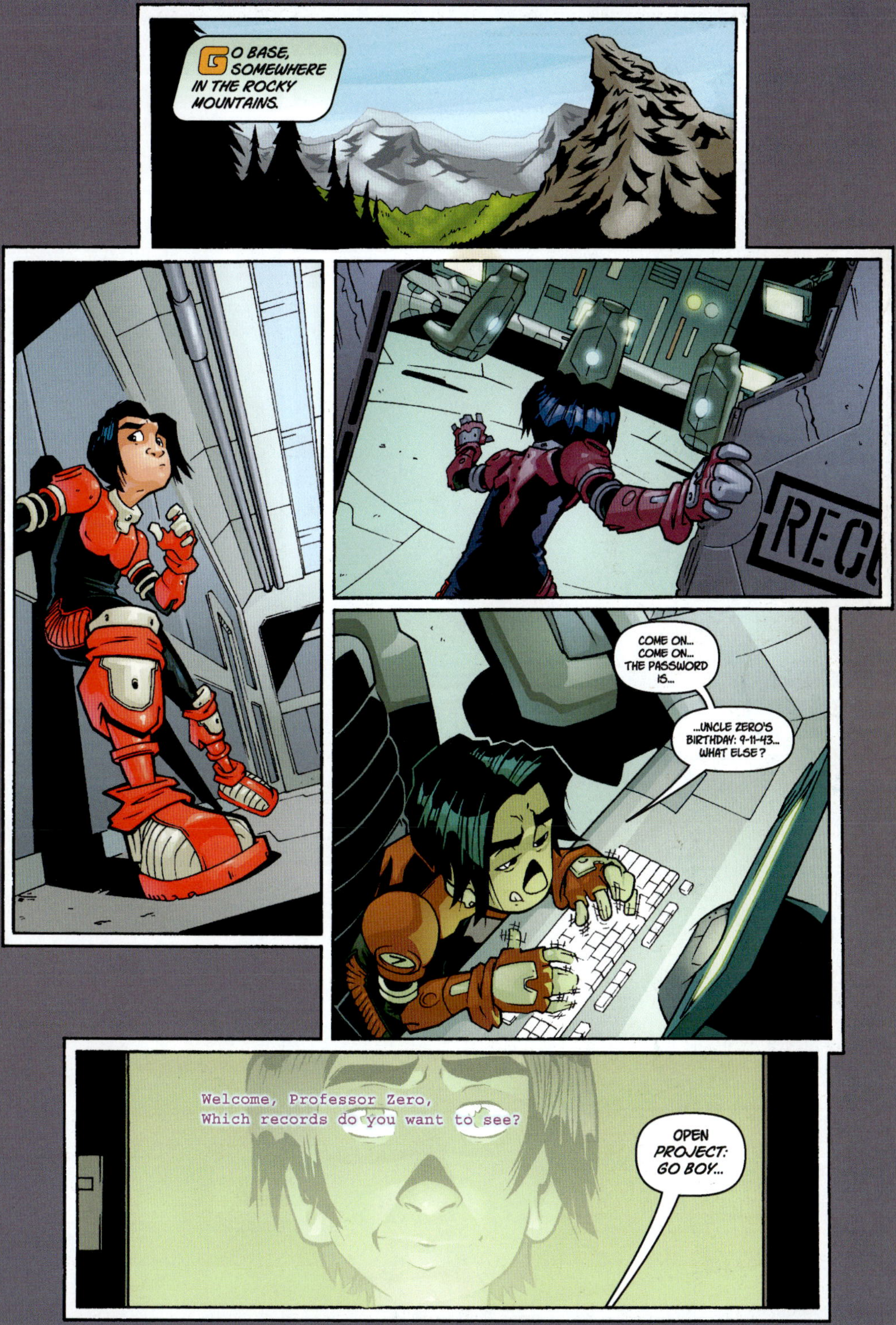
GO BASE, SOMEWHERE IN THE ROCKY MOUNTAINS.
REC
COME ON... COME ON... THE PASSWORD IS...
...UNCLE ZERO'S BIRTHDAY: 9-11-43... WHAT ELSE?
Welcome, Professor Zero,
Which records do you want to see?
OPEN PROJECT: GO BOY...

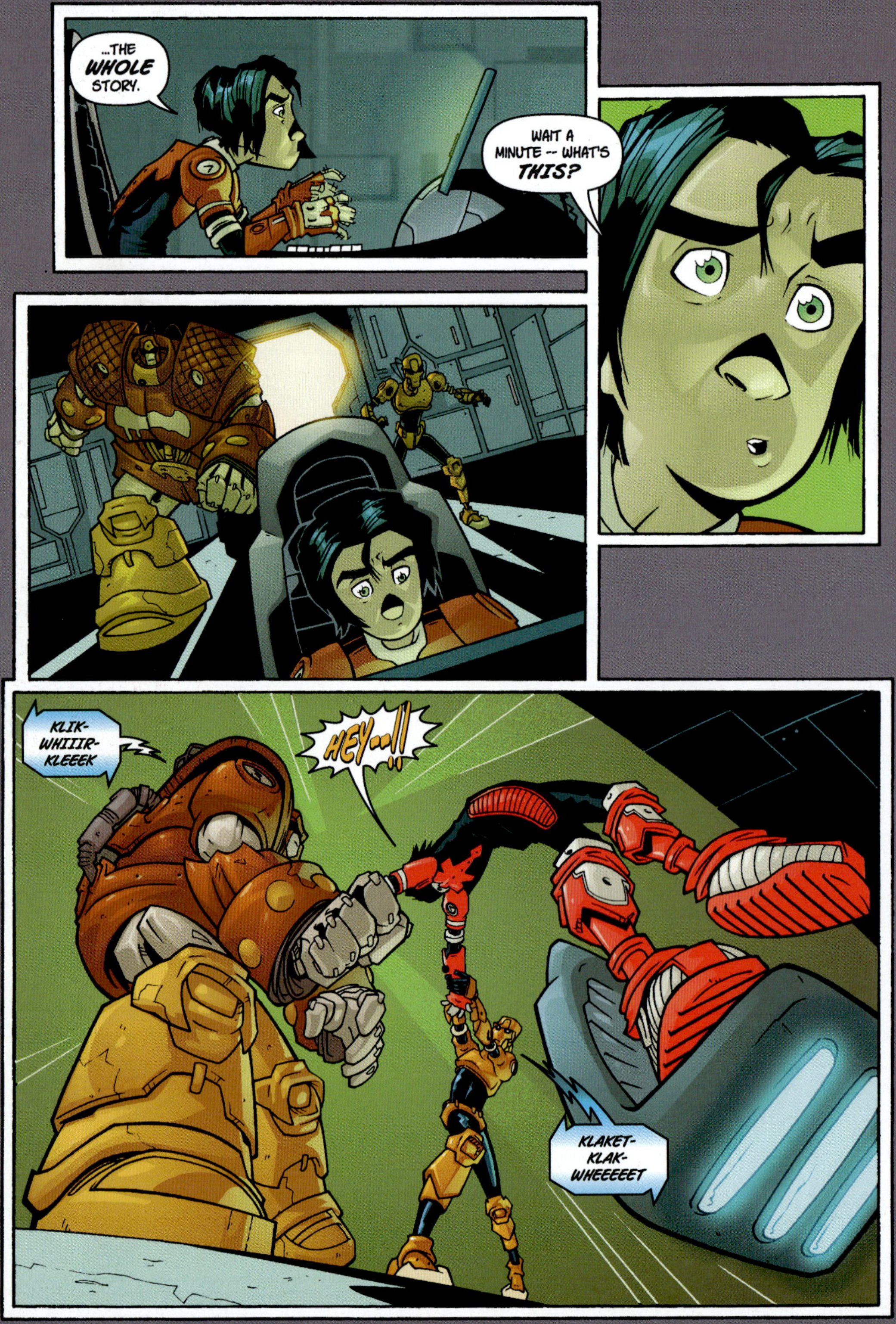
...THE WHOLE STORY.
WAIT A MINUTE -- WHAT'S THIS?
KLIK-WHIIIR-KLEEEK
HEY--!!
KLAKET-KLAK-WHEEEEET

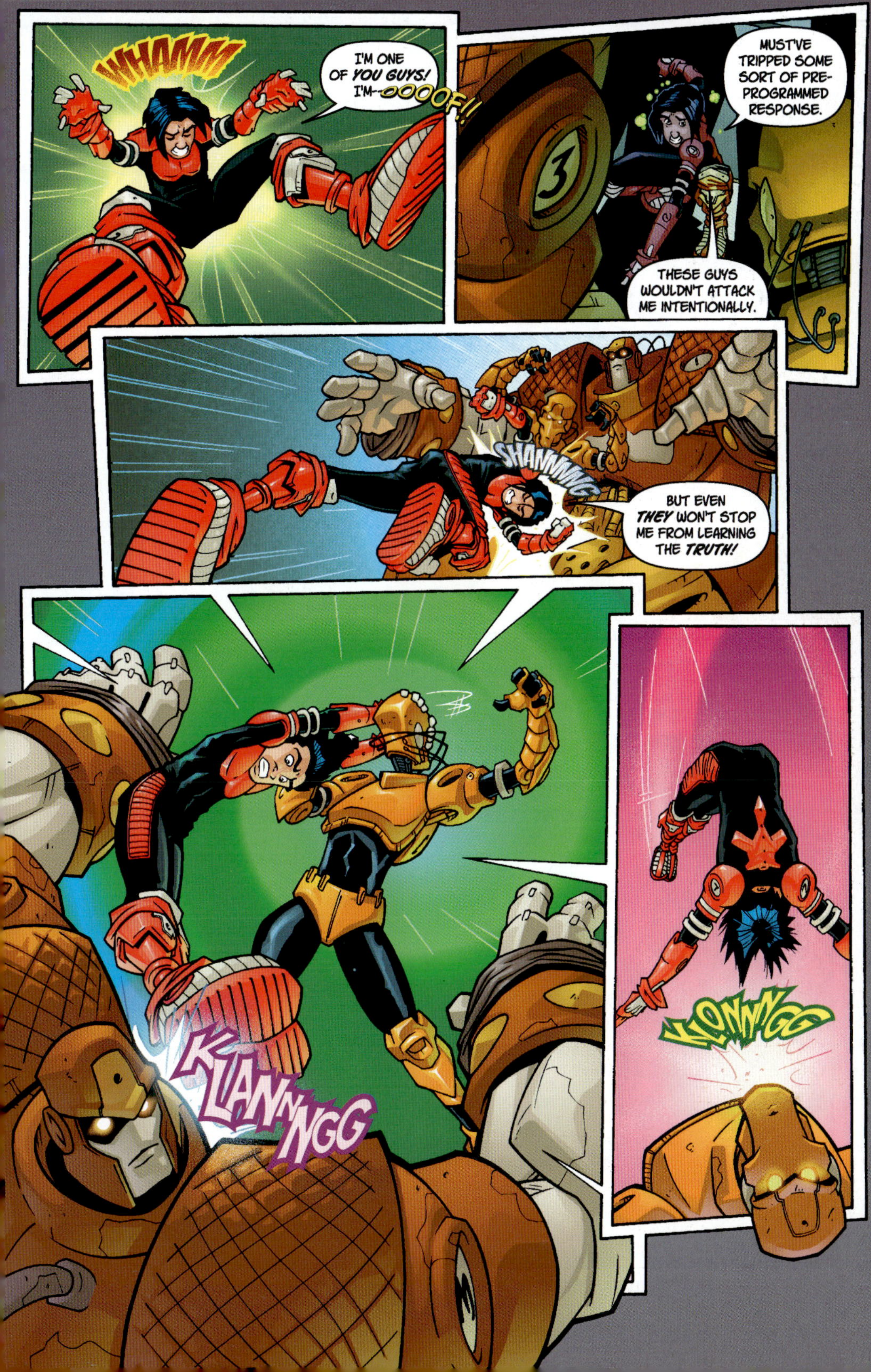
WHAMM
I'M ONE OF YOU GUYS! I'M--OOOOF!!
MUST'VE TRIPPED SOME SORT OF PRE-PROGRAMMED RESPONSE.
THESE GUYS WOULDN'T ATTACK ME INTENTIONALLY.
SHANNNNG
BUT EVEN THEY WON'T STOP ME FROM LEARNING THE TRUTH!
KLANNNGG
KLONNNGG

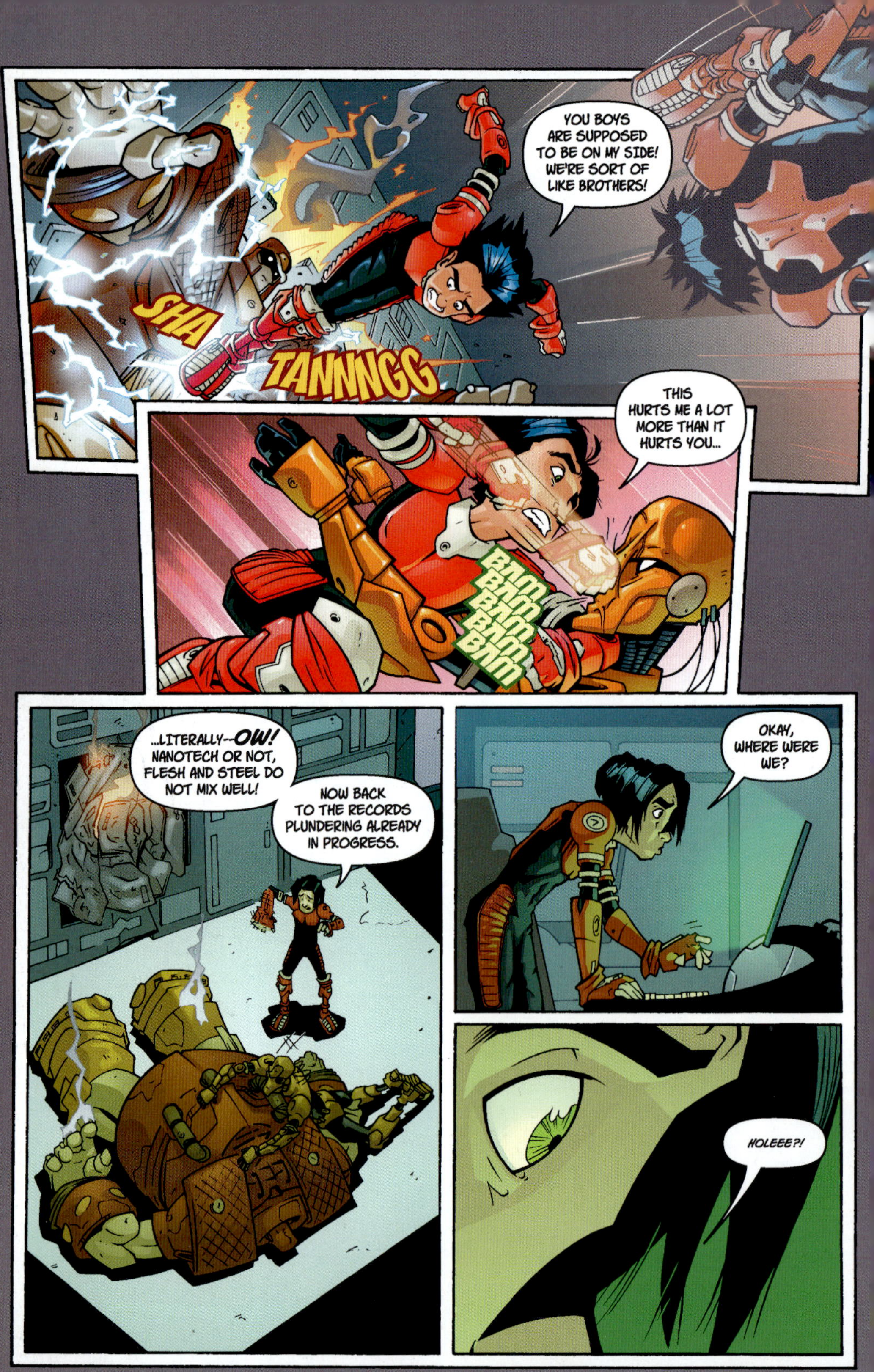
YOU BOYS ARE SUPPOSED TO BE ON MY SIDE! WE'RE SORT OF LIKE BROTHERS!
SHA
TANNNGG
THIS HURTS ME A LOT MORE THAN IT HURTS YOU...
BAM BAM BAM BAM BAM
...LITERALLY--OW! NANOTECH OR NOT, FLESH AND STEEL DO NOT MIX WELL!
NOW BACK TO THE RECORDS PLUNDERING ALREADY IN PROGRESS.
OKAY, WHERE WERE WE?
HOLEEE?!

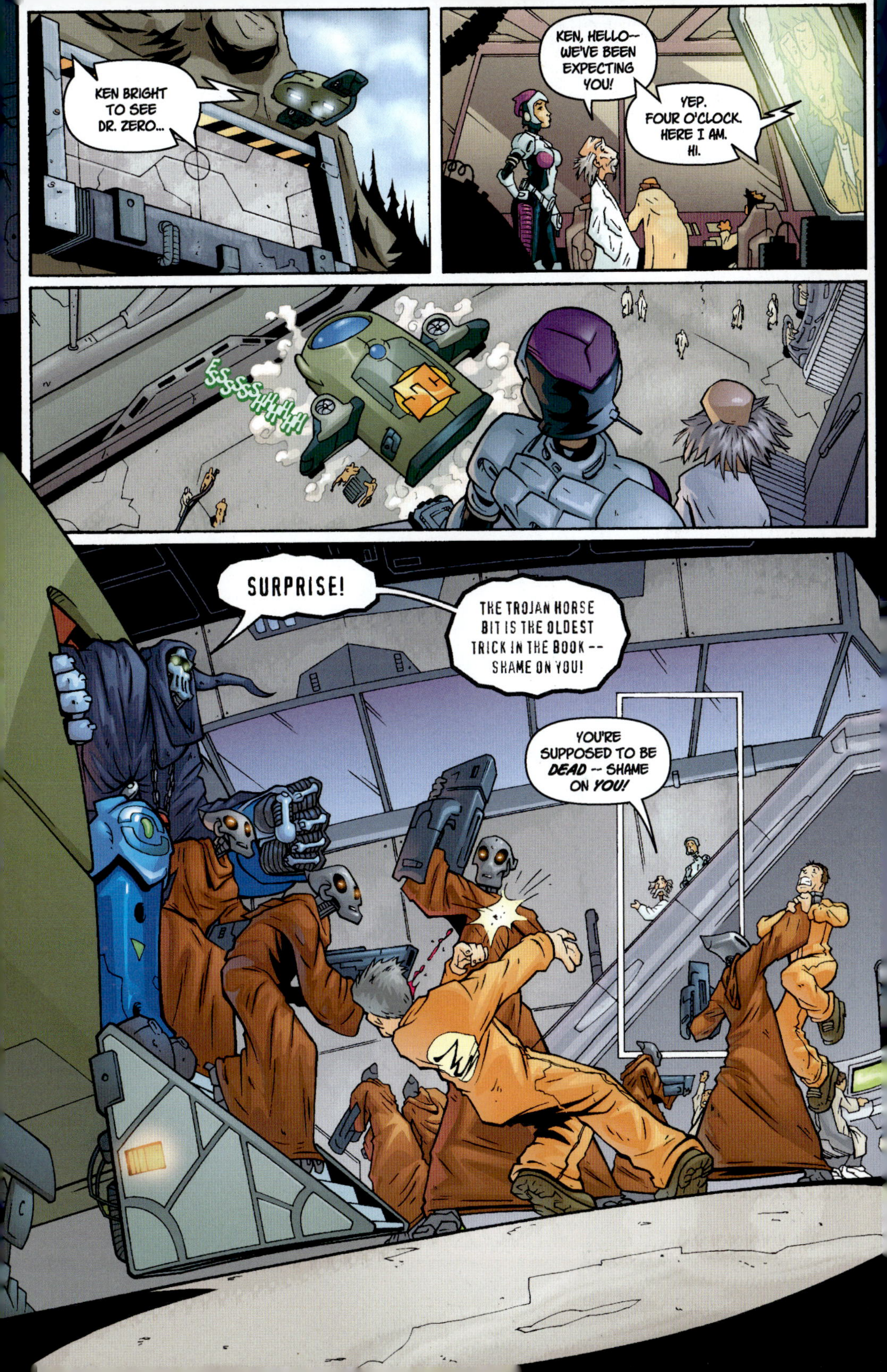
KEN BRIGHT TO SEE DR. ZERO...
KEN, HELLO-- WE'VE BEEN EXPECTING YOU!
YEP. FOUR O'CLOCK. HERE I AM. HI.
SSSSHHHHH
SURPRISE!
THE TROJAN HORSE BIT IS THE OLDEST TRICK IN THE BOOK -- SHAME ON YOU!
YOU'RE SUPPOSED TO BE *DEAD* -- SHAME ON *YOU!*

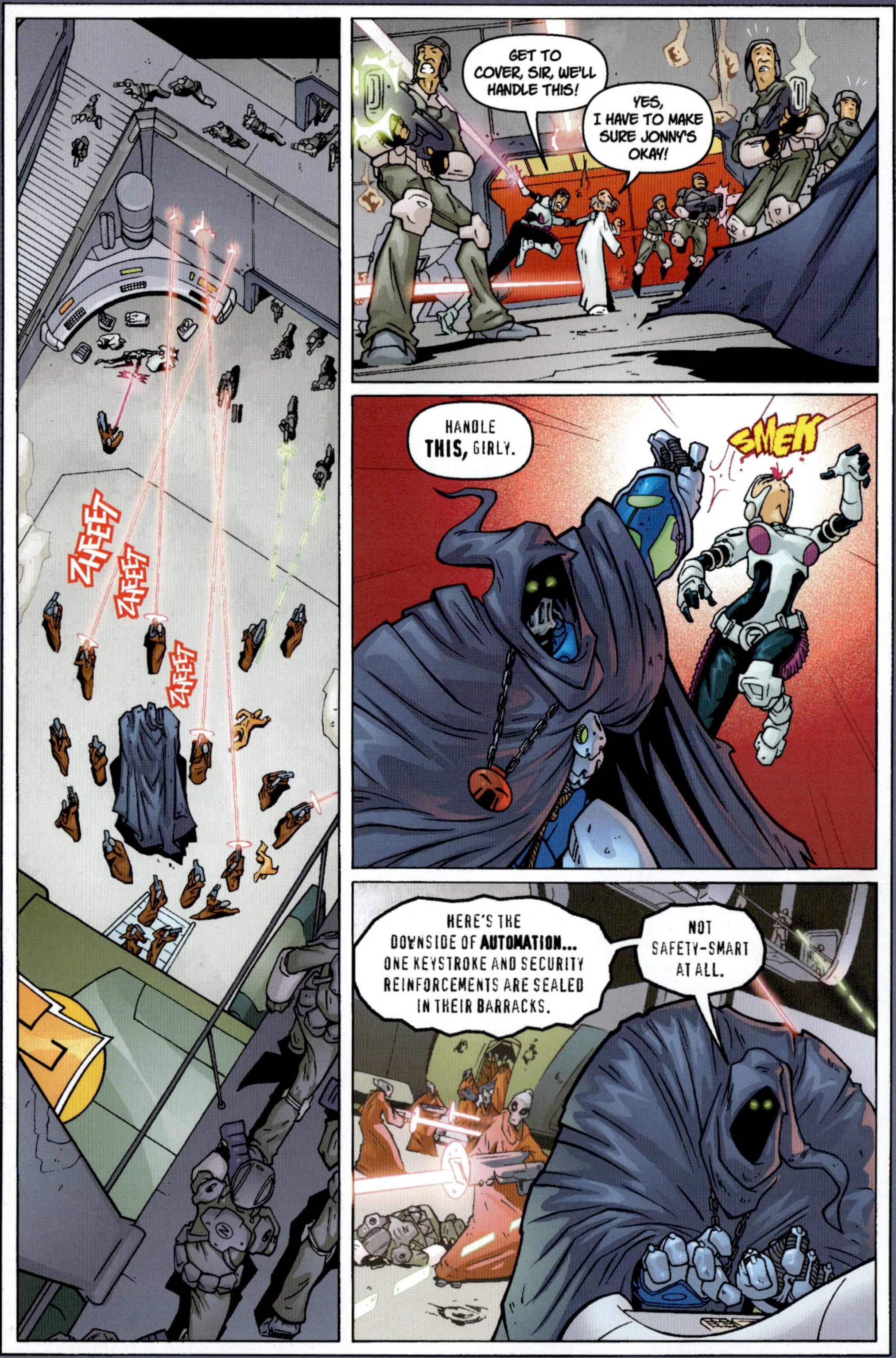
ZHEET
ZHEET
ZHEET
GET TO COVER, SIR, WE'LL HANDLE THIS!
YES, I HAVE TO MAKE SURE JONNY'S OKAY!
HANDLE THIS, GIRLY.
SMEK
HERE'S THE DOWNSIDE OF AUTOMATION... ONE KEYSTROKE AND SECURITY REINFORCEMENTS ARE SEALED IN THEIR BARRACKS.
NOT SAFETY-SMART AT ALL.

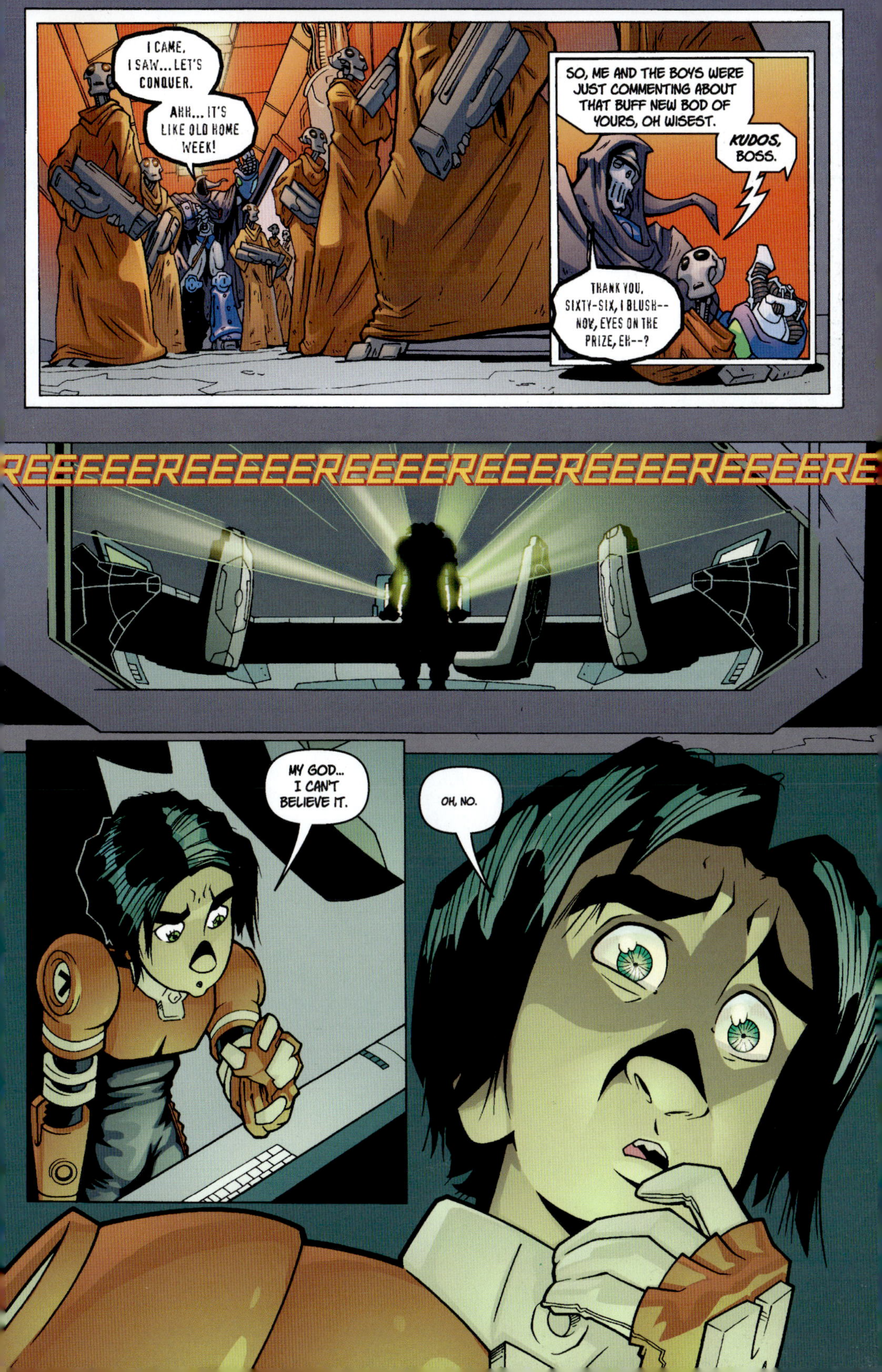
I CAME. I SAW... LET'S CONQUER.
AHH... IT'S LIKE OLD HOME WEEK!
SO, ME AND THE BOYS WERE JUST COMMENTING ABOUT THAT BUFF NEW BOD OF YOURS, OH WISEST.
KUDOS, BOSS.
THANK YOU, SIXTY-SIX, I BLUSH-- NOW, EYES ON THE PRIZE, EH--?
REEEEEREEEEEEREEEEEREEEEREEEEEREEEEERE
MY GOD... I CAN'T BELIEVE IT.
OH, NO.

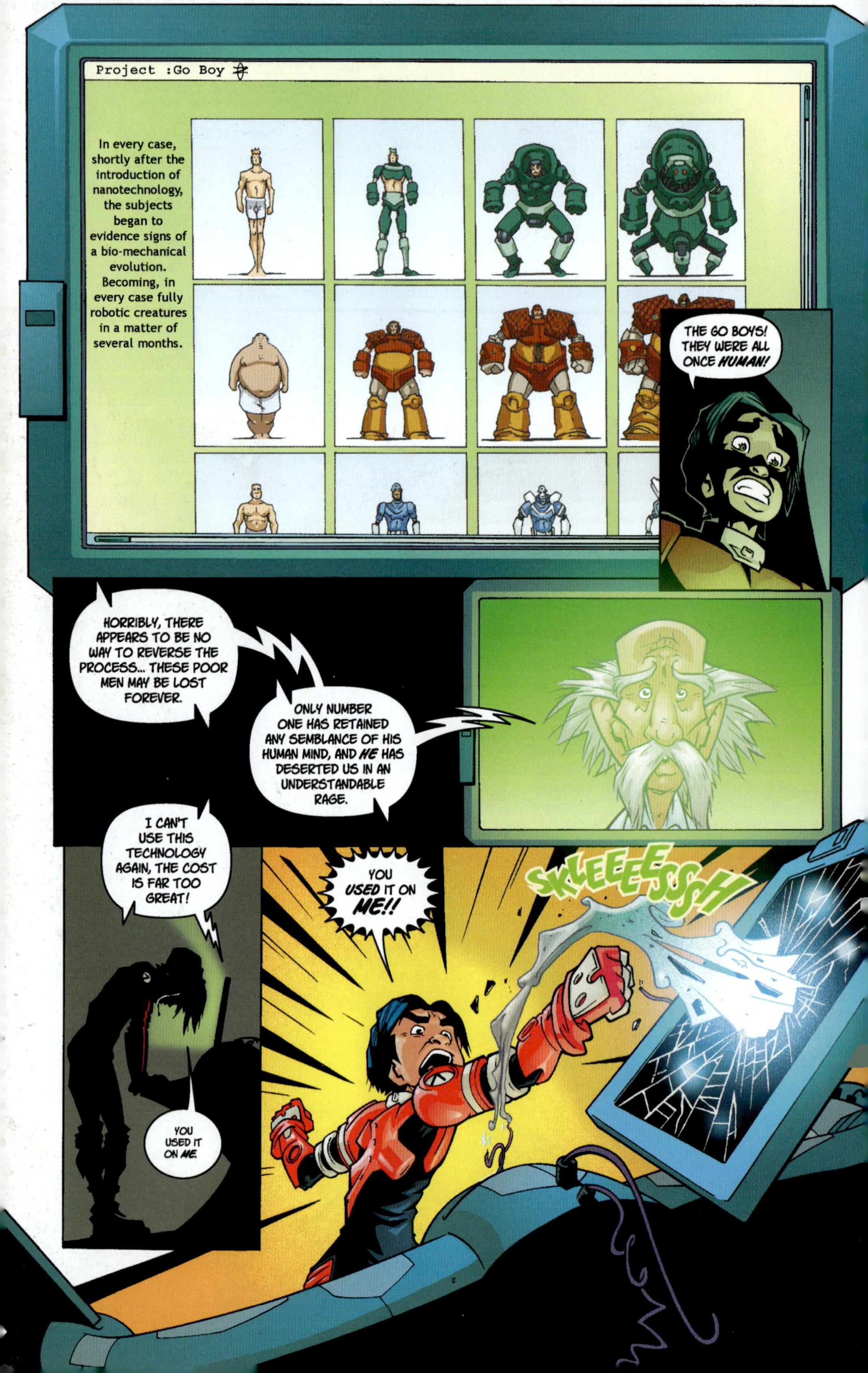
Project :Go Boy
In every case, shortly after the introduction of nanotechnology, the subjects began to evidence signs of a bio-mechanical evolution. Becoming, in every case fully robotic creatures in a matter of several months.
THE GO BOYS! THEY WERE ALL ONCE HUMAN!
HORRIBLY, THERE APPEARS TO BE NO WAY TO REVERSE THE PROCESS... THESE POOR MEN MAY BE LOST FOREVER.
ONLY NUMBER ONE HAS RETAINED ANY SEMBLANCE OF HIS HUMAN MIND, AND HE HAS DESERTED US IN AN UNDERSTANDABLE RAGE.
I CAN'T USE THIS TECHNOLOGY AGAIN, THE COST IS FAR TOO GREAT!
YOU USED IT ON ME.
YOU USED IT ON ME!!
SKLEEEESSSH

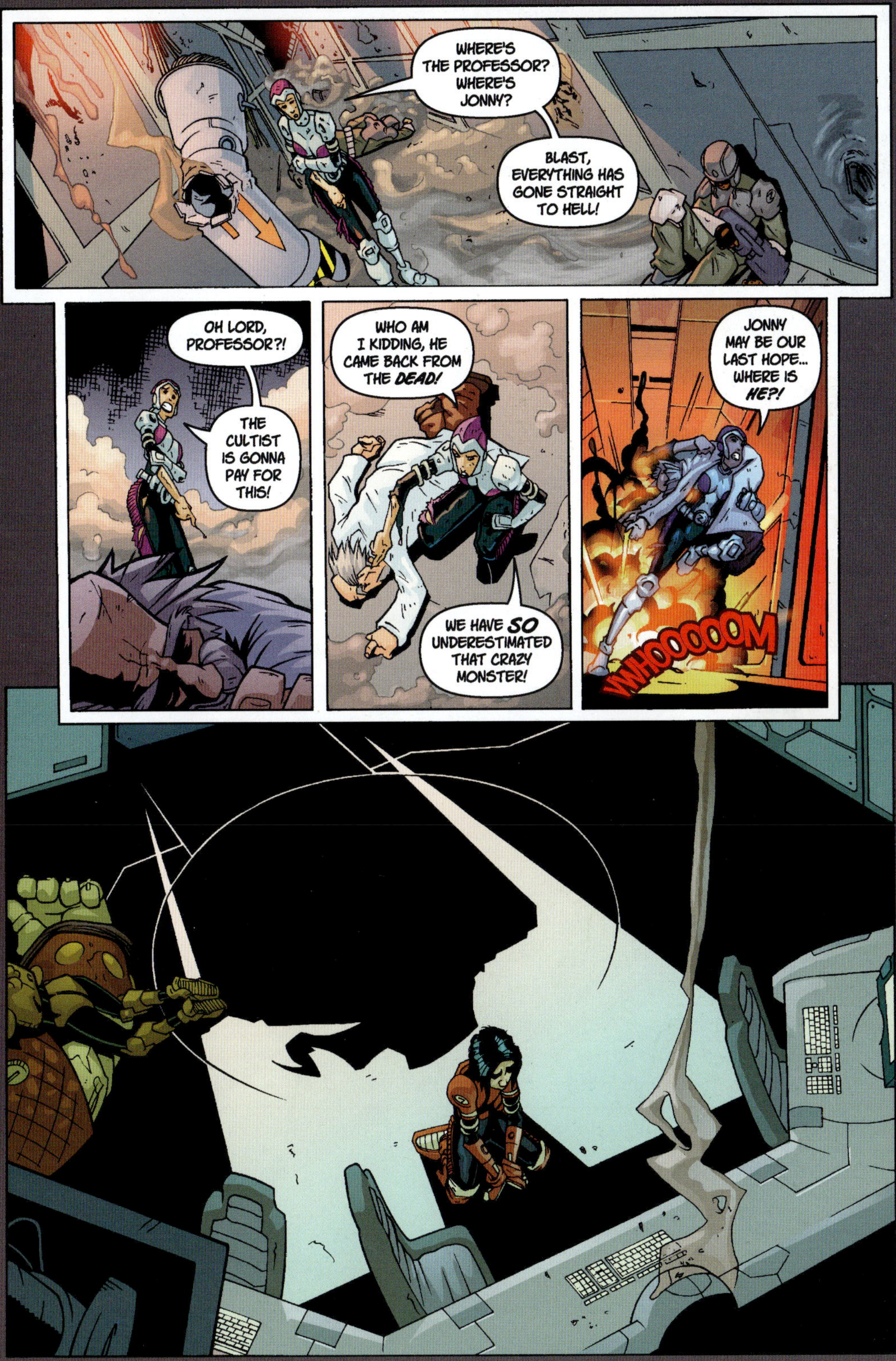
WHERE'S THE PROFESSOR? WHERE'S JONNY?
BLAST, EVERYTHING HAS GONE STRAIGHT TO HELL!
OH LORD, PROFESSOR?!
THE CULTIST IS GONNA PAY FOR THIS!
WHO AM I KIDDING, HE CAME BACK FROM THE DEAD!
WE HAVE SO UNDERESTIMATED THAT CRAZY MONSTER!
JONNY MAY BE OUR LAST HOPE... WHERE IS HE?!
VWHOOOOOM

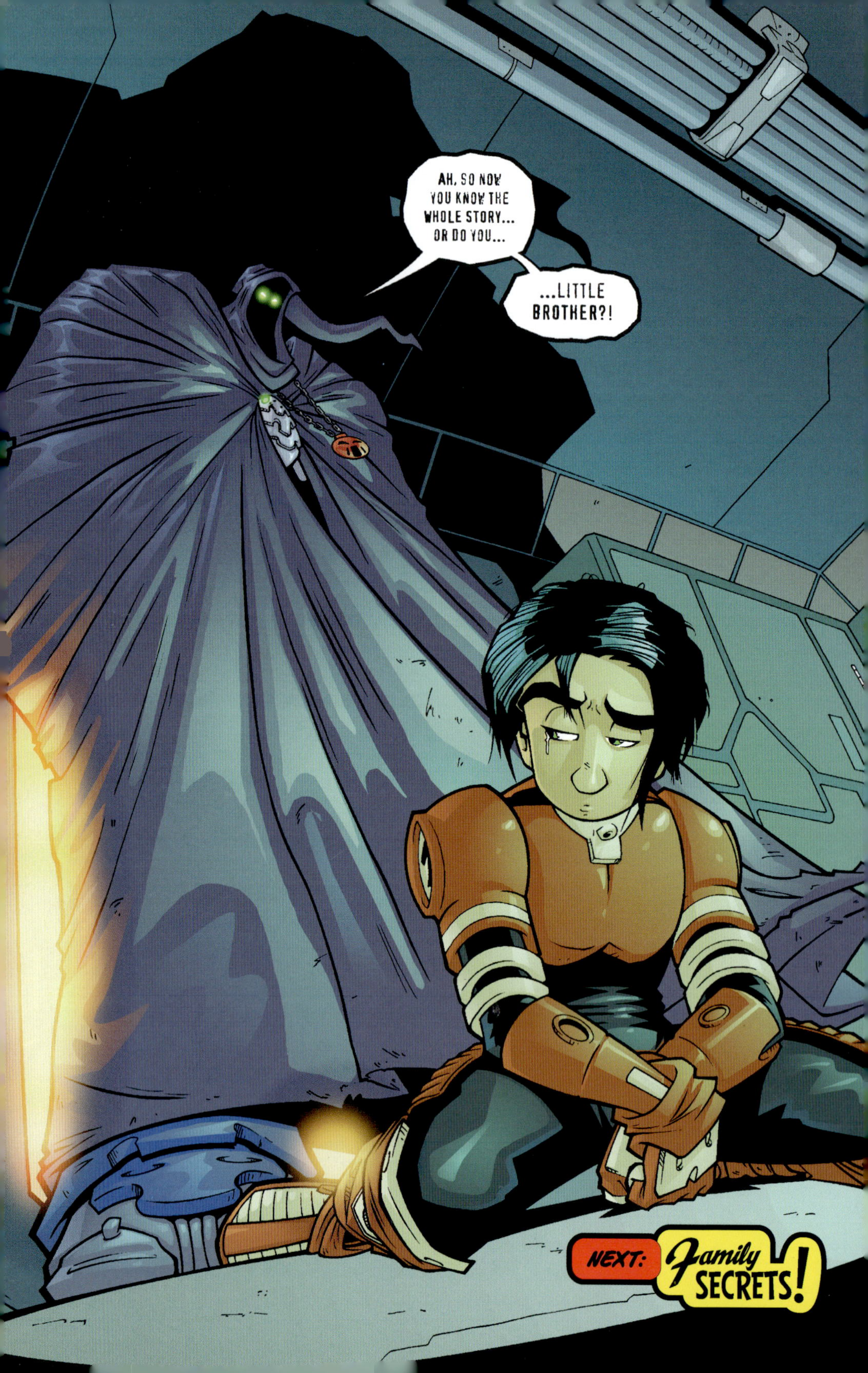
AH, SO NOW YOU KNOW THE WHOLE STORY... OR DO YOU...
...LITTLE BROTHER?!
NEXT: Family SECRETS!

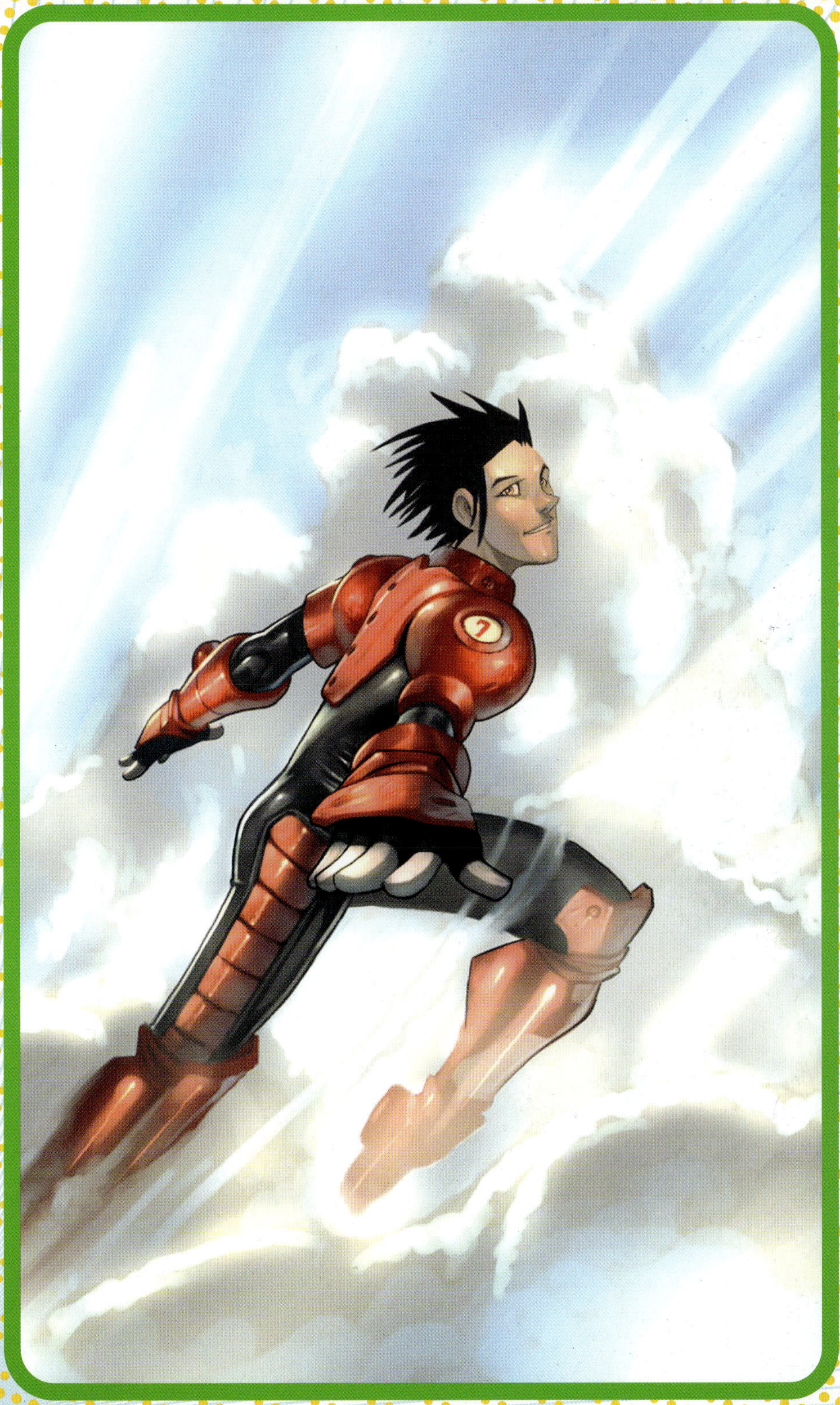

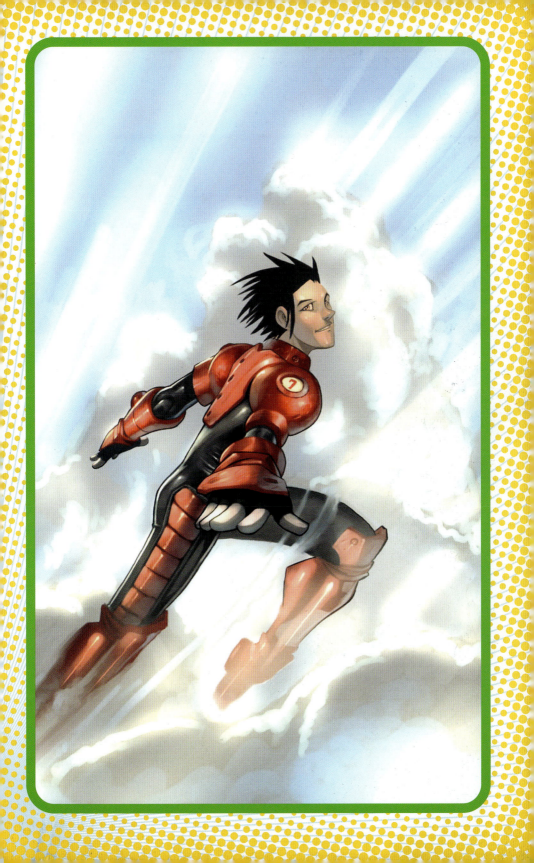

"FAMILY SECRETS"

SCRIPT	BRIAN AUGUSTYN
PENCILS	JON SOMMARIVA
INKS	VINCE RUSSELL
COLORS	DAVE NESTELLE
LETTERS	MICHAEL DAVID THOMAS

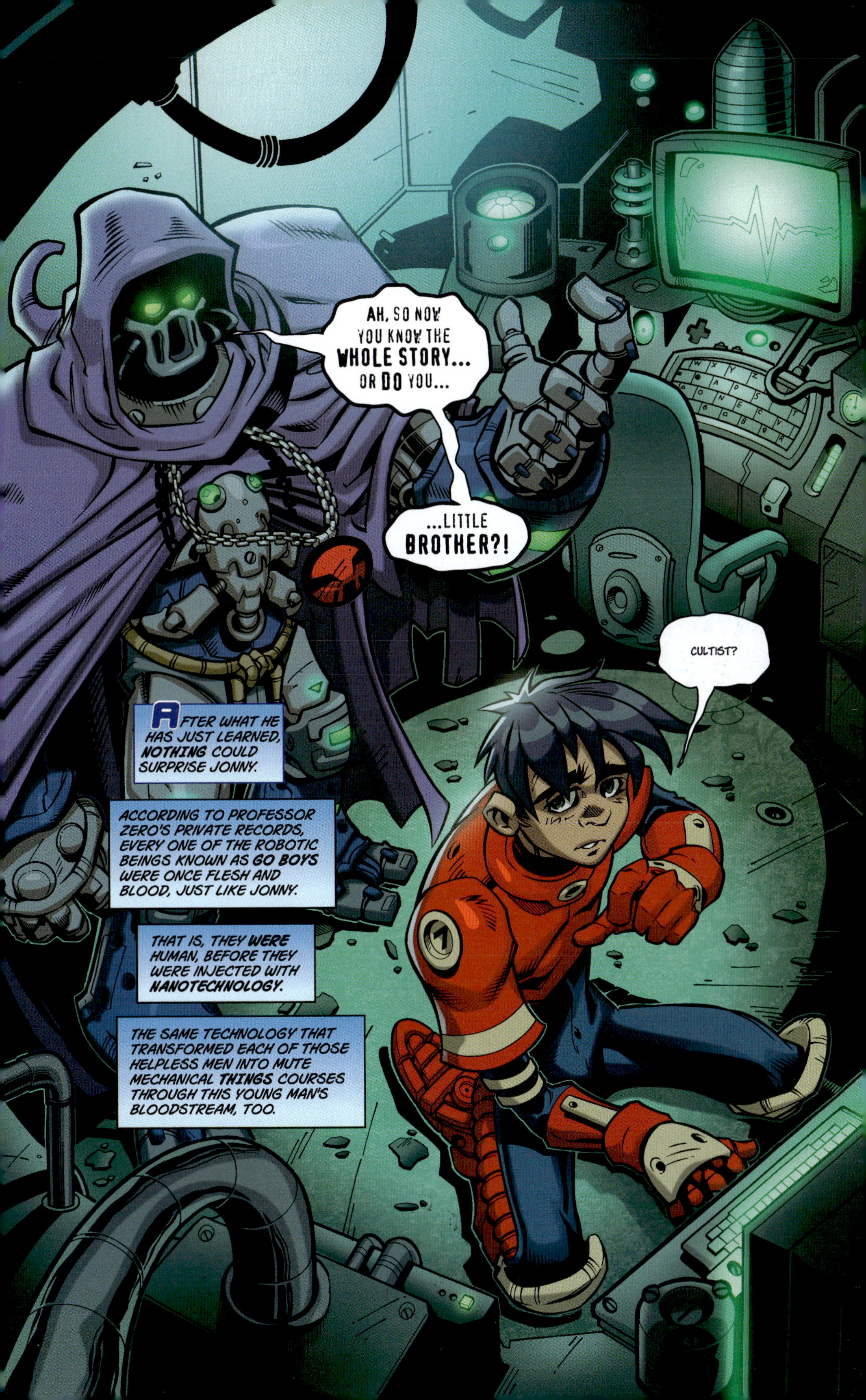
AH, SO NOW YOU KNOW THE WHOLE STORY... OR DO YOU...
...LITTLE BROTHER?!
CULTIST?
AFTER WHAT HE HAS JUST LEARNED, NOTHING COULD SURPRISE JONNY.
ACCORDING TO PROFESSOR ZERO'S PRIVATE RECORDS, EVERY ONE OF THE ROBOTIC BEINGS KNOWN AS GO BOYS WERE ONCE FLESH AND BLOOD, JUST LIKE JONNY.
THAT IS, THEY WERE HUMAN, BEFORE THEY WERE INJECTED WITH NANOTECHNOLOGY.
THE SAME TECHNOLOGY THAT TRANSFORMED EACH OF THOSE HELPLESS MEN INTO MUTE MECHANICAL THINGS COURSES THROUGH THIS YOUNG MAN'S BLOODSTREAM, TOO.

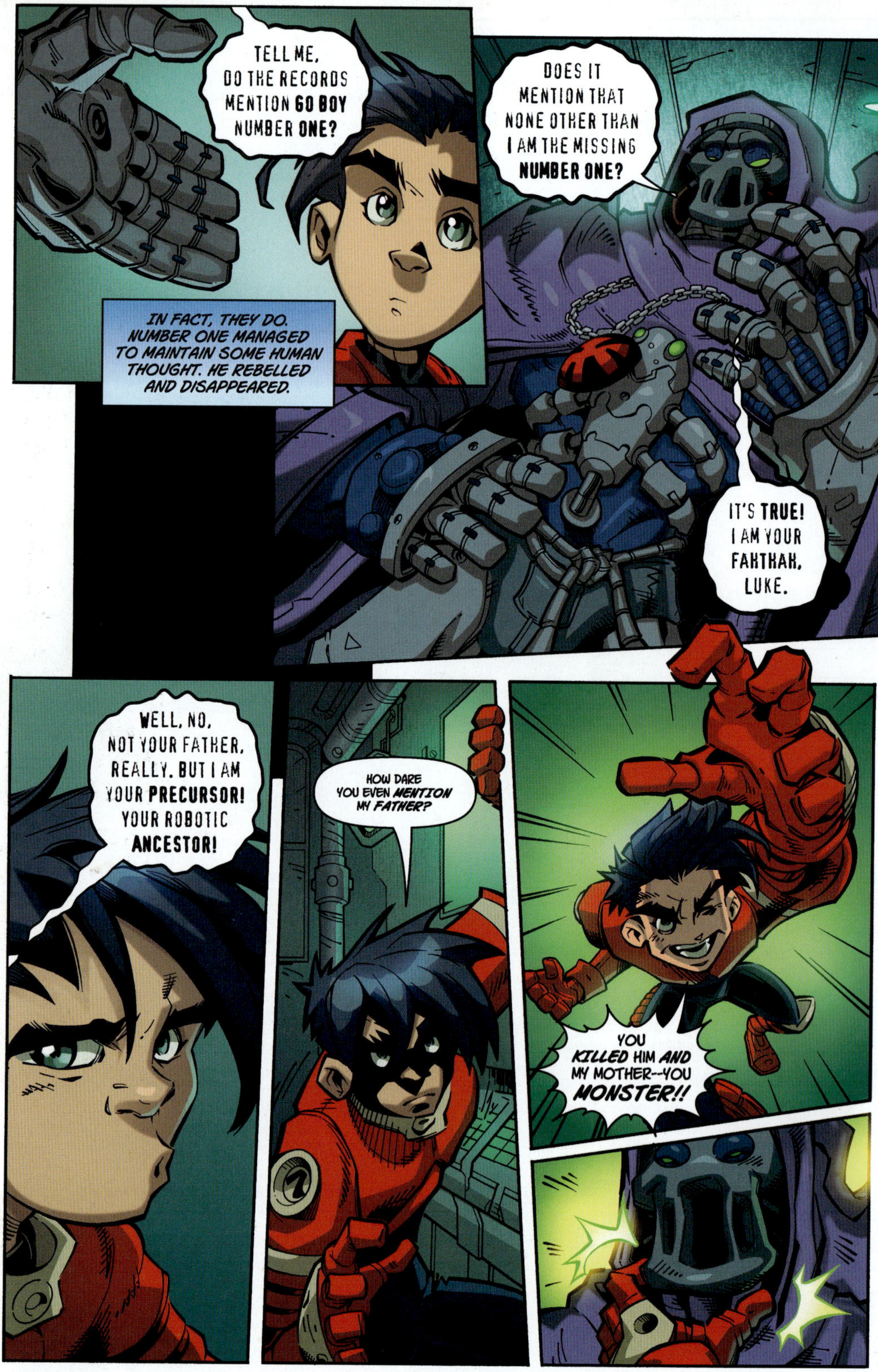
TELL ME, DO THE RECORDS MENTION GO BOY NUMBER ONE?
DOES IT MENTION THAT NONE OTHER THAN I AM THE MISSING NUMBER ONE?
IN FACT, THEY DO. NUMBER ONE MANAGED TO MAINTAIN SOME HUMAN THOUGHT. HE REBELLED AND DISAPPEARED.
IT'S TRUE! I AM YOUR FAHTHAH, LUKE.
WELL, NO, NOT YOUR FATHER, REALLY. BUT I AM YOUR PRECURSOR! YOUR ROBOTIC ANCESTOR!
HOW DARE YOU EVEN MENTION MY FATHER?
YOU KILLED HIM AND MY MOTHER--YOU MONSTER!!

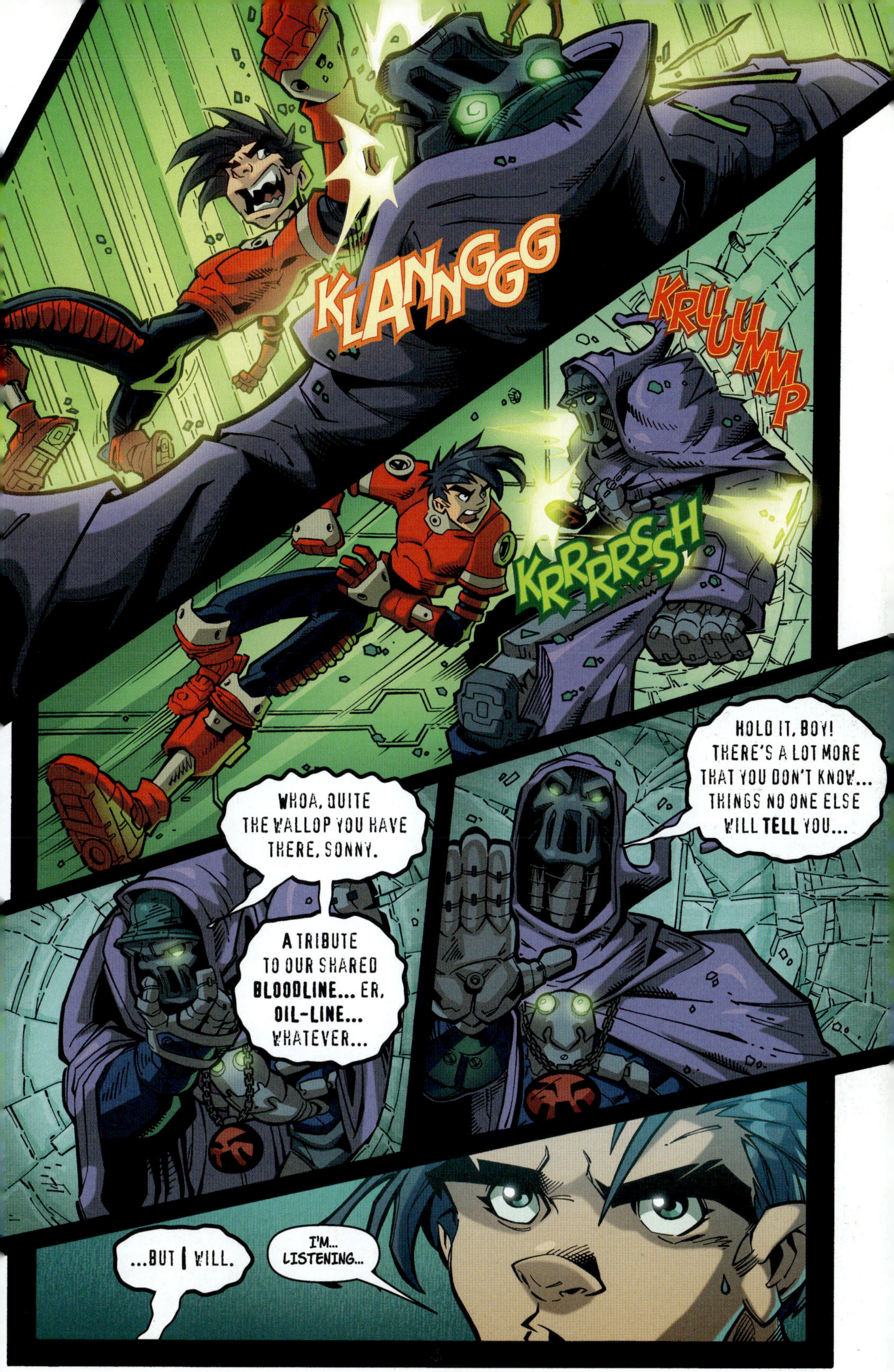
KLANNGGG
KRUUUMMP
KRRRRSSH
WHOA, QUITE THE WALLOP YOU HAVE THERE, SONNY.
A TRIBUTE TO OUR SHARED BLOODLINE... ER, OIL-LINE... WHATEVER...
HOLD IT, BOY! THERE'S A LOT MORE THAT YOU DON'T KNOW... THINGS NO ONE ELSE WILL TELL YOU...
...BUT I WILL.
I'M... LISTENING...

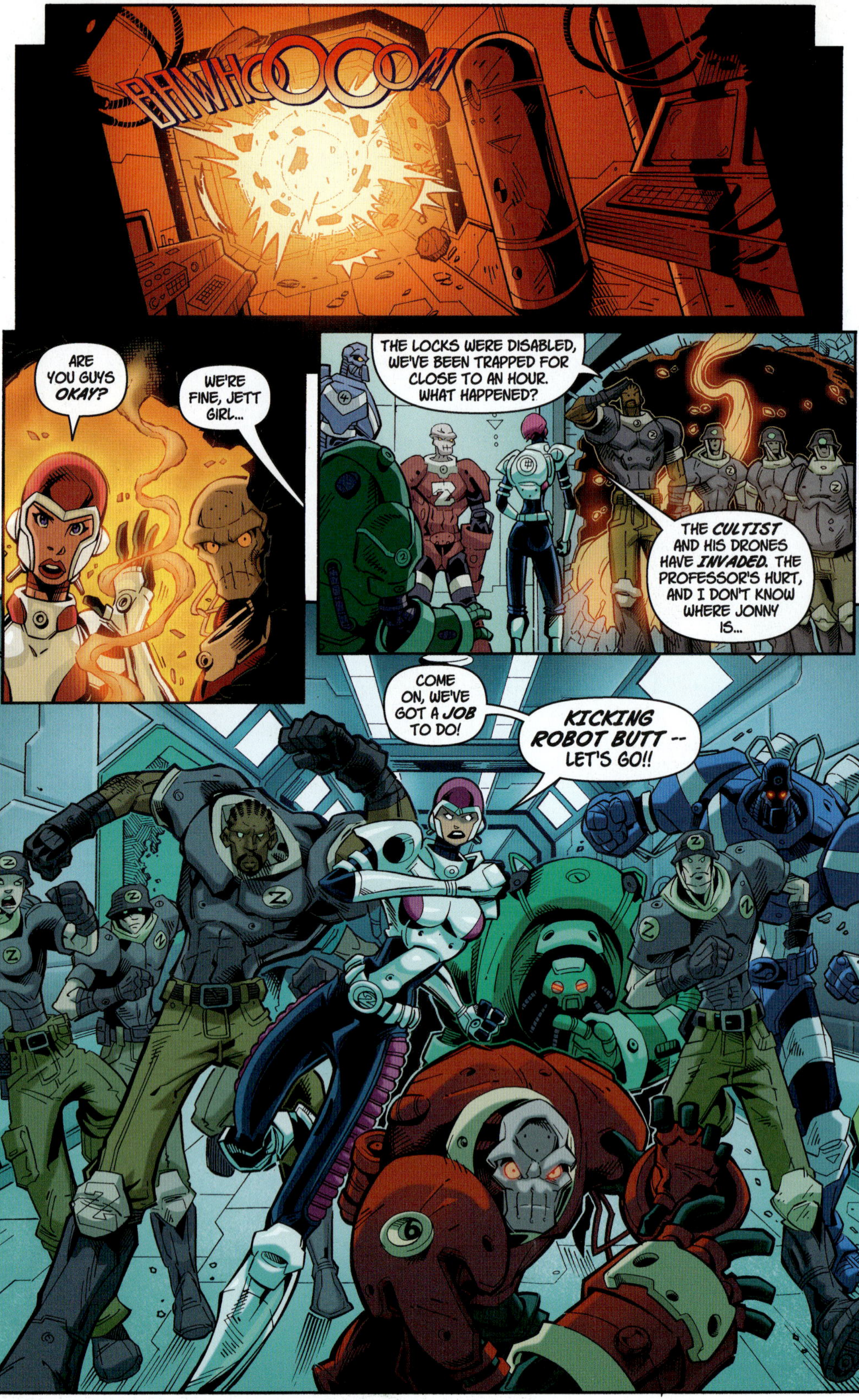
BAWHOOOOOM
ARE YOU GUYS OKAY?
WE'RE FINE, JETT GIRL...
THE LOCKS WERE DISABLED, WE'VE BEEN TRAPPED FOR CLOSE TO AN HOUR. WHAT HAPPENED?
THE CULTIST AND HIS DRONES HAVE INVADED. THE PROFESSOR'S HURT, AND I DON'T KNOW WHERE JONNY IS...
COME ON, WE'VE GOT A JOB TO DO!
KICKING ROBOT BUTT -- LET'S GO!!

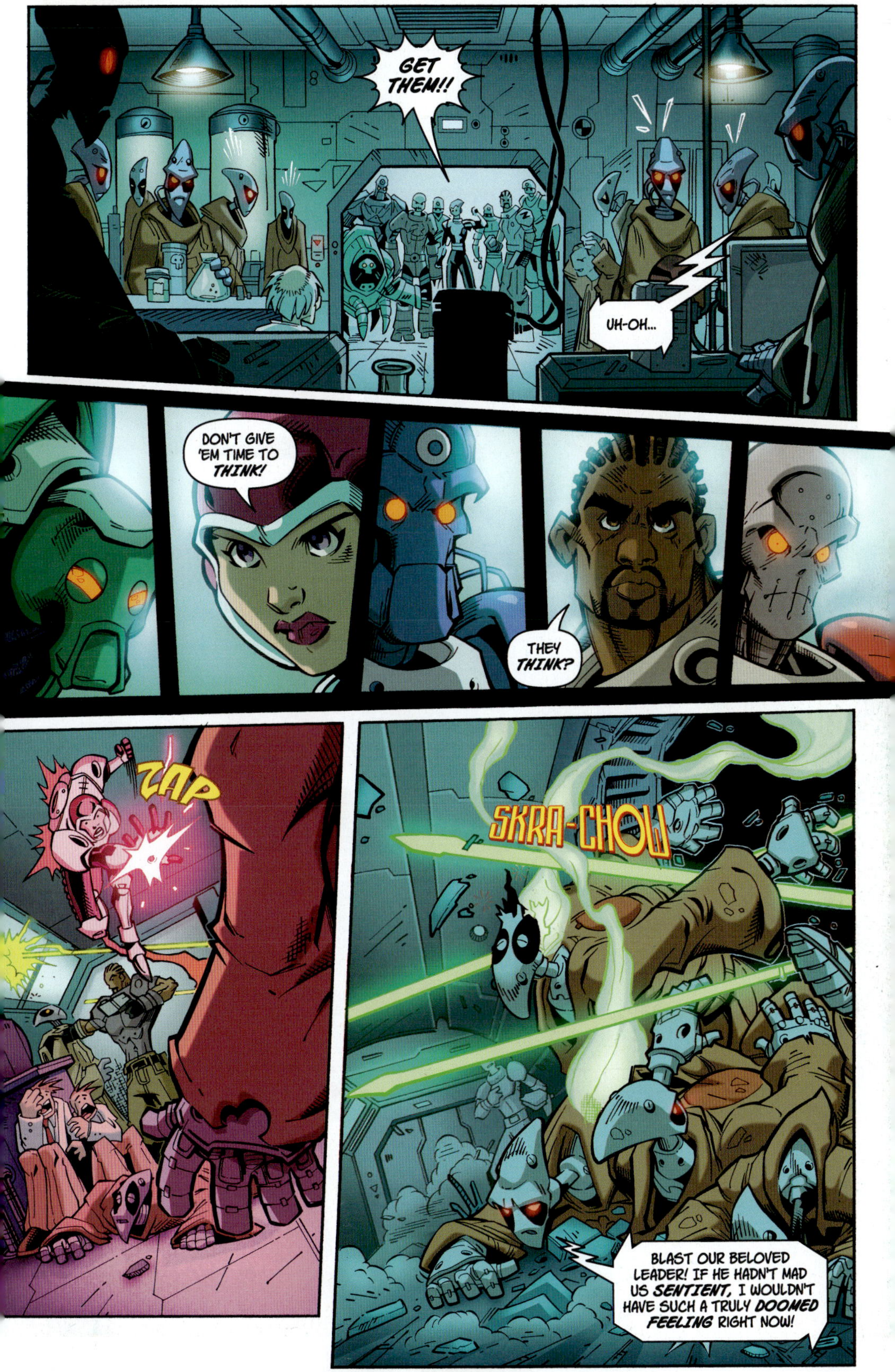
GET THEM!!
UH-OH...
DON'T GIVE 'EM TIME TO THINK!
THEY THINK?
ZAP
SKRA-CHOW
BLAST OUR BELOVED LEADER! IF HE HADN'T MAD US SENTIENT, I WOULDN'T HAVE SUCH A TRULY DOOMED FEELING RIGHT NOW!

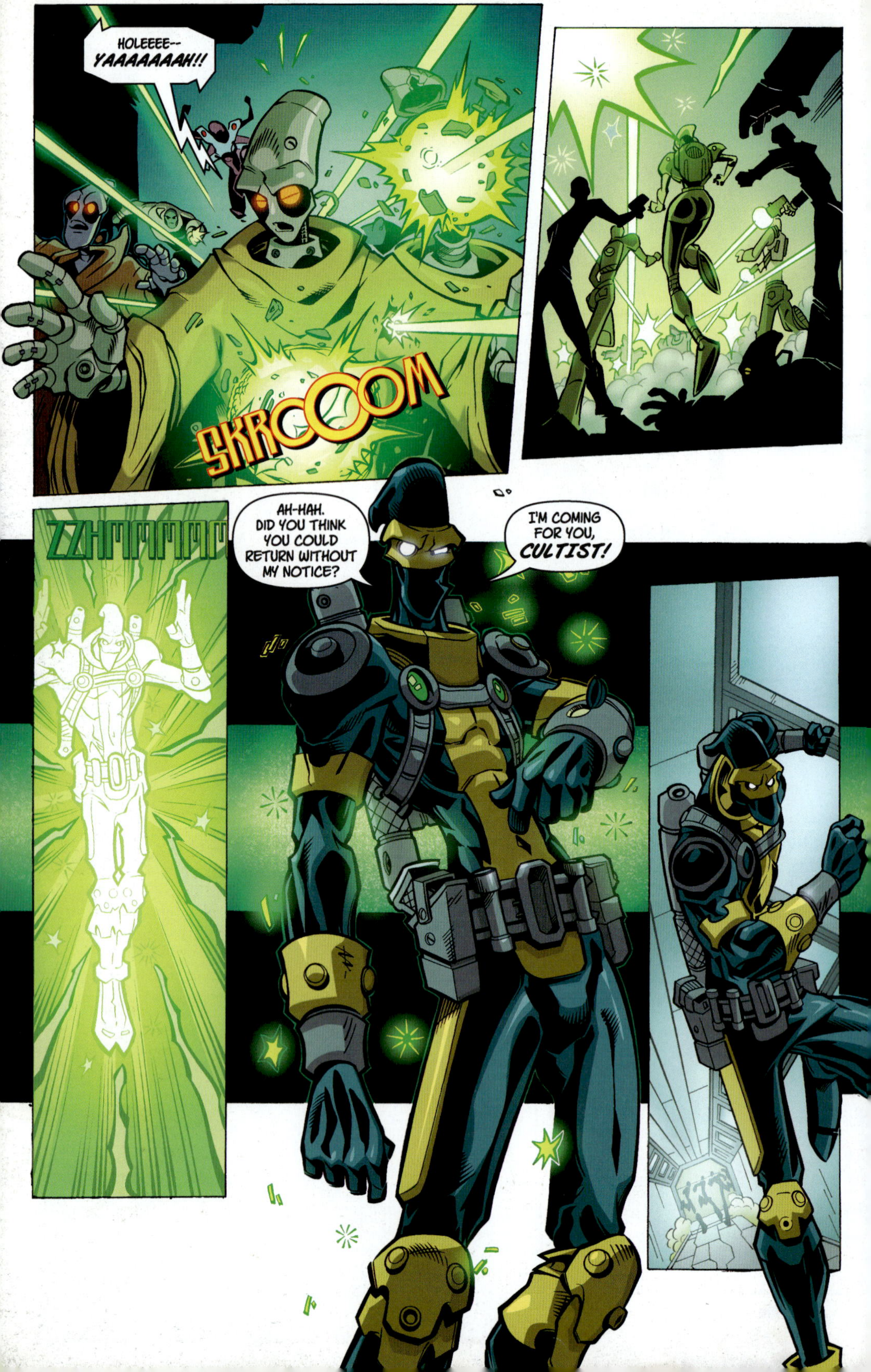
HOLEEEE--
YAAAAAAAH!!
SKRCOOOM
ZZHMMMMM
AH-HAH.
DID YOU THINK YOU COULD RETURN WITHOUT MY NOTICE?
I'M COMING FOR YOU, CULTIST!

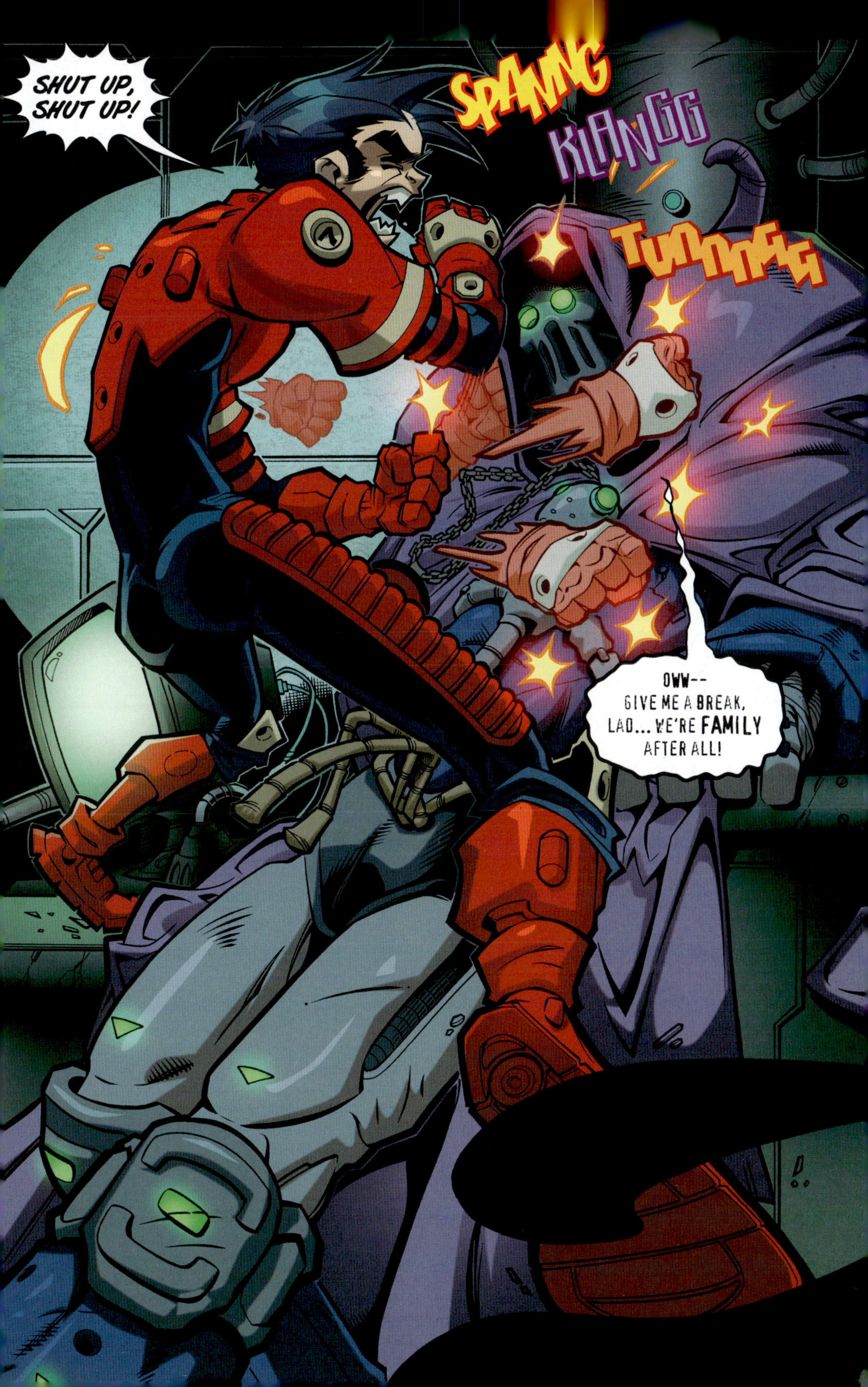
SHUT UP, SHUT UP!
SPANNG
KLANGG
TUNNGG
OWW-- GIVE ME A BREAK, LAD... WE'RE FAMILY AFTER ALL!

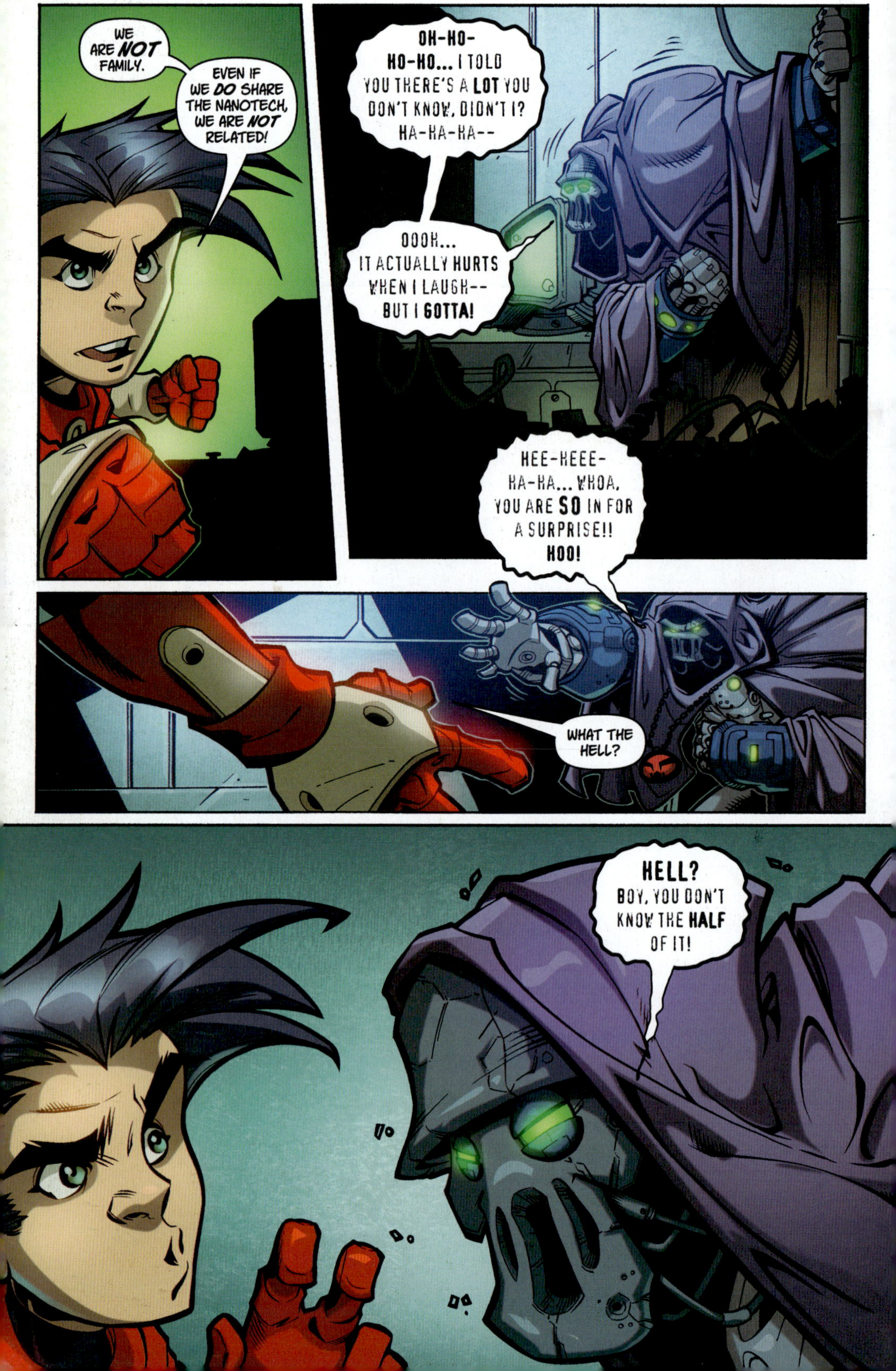
WE ARE NOT FAMILY.
EVEN IF WE DO SHARE THE NANOTECH, WE ARE NOT RELATED!
OH-HO-HO-HO... I TOLD YOU THERE'S A LOT YOU DON'T KNOW, DIDN'T I? HA-HA-HA--
OOOH... IT ACTUALLY HURTS WHEN I LAUGH-- BUT I GOTTA!
HEE-HEEE-HA-HA... WHOA, YOU ARE SO IN FOR A SURPRISE!! HOO!
WHAT THE HELL?
HELL? BOY, YOU DON'T KNOW THE HALF OF IT!

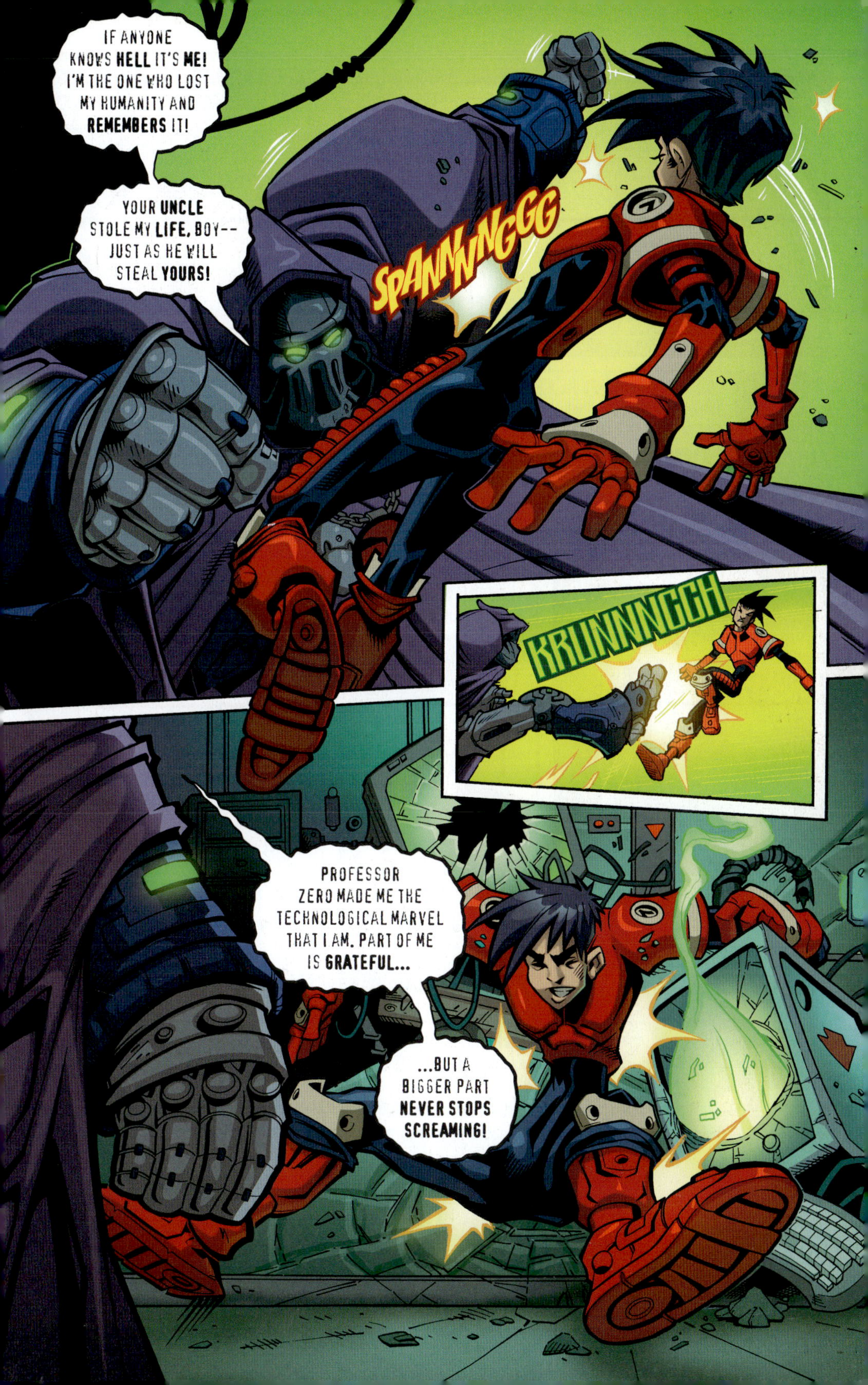
IF ANYONE KNOWS HELL IT'S ME! I'M THE ONE WHO LOST MY HUMANITY AND REMEMBERS IT!
YOUR UNCLE STOLE MY LIFE, BOY-- JUST AS HE WILL STEAL YOURS!
SPANNNNNGGG
KRUNNNNGGH
PROFESSOR ZERO MADE ME THE TECHNOLOGICAL MARVEL THAT I AM. PART OF ME IS GRATEFUL...
...BUT A BIGGER PART NEVER STOPS SCREAMING!

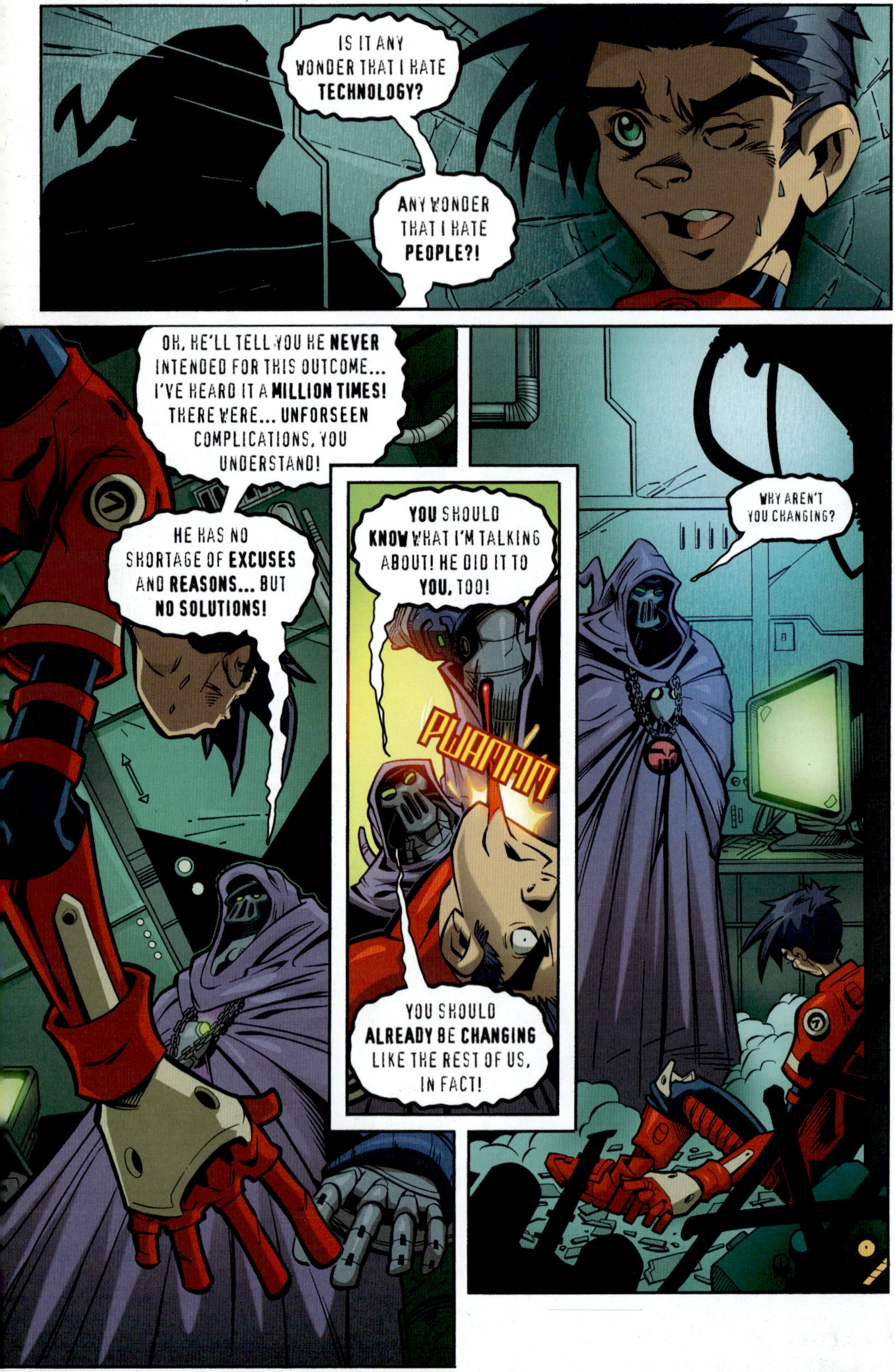
IS IT ANY WONDER THAT I HATE TECHNOLOGY?
ANY WONDER THAT I HATE PEOPLE?!
OH, HE'LL TELL YOU HE NEVER INTENDED FOR THIS OUTCOME... I'VE HEARD IT A MILLION TIMES! THERE WERE... UNFORSEEN COMPLICATIONS, YOU UNDERSTAND!
HE HAS NO SHORTAGE OF EXCUSES AND REASONS... BUT NO SOLUTIONS!
YOU SHOULD KNOW WHAT I'M TALKING ABOUT! HE DID IT TO YOU, TOO!
PWAMAM
YOU SHOULD ALREADY BE CHANGING LIKE THE REST OF US, IN FACT!
WHY AREN'T YOU CHANGING?

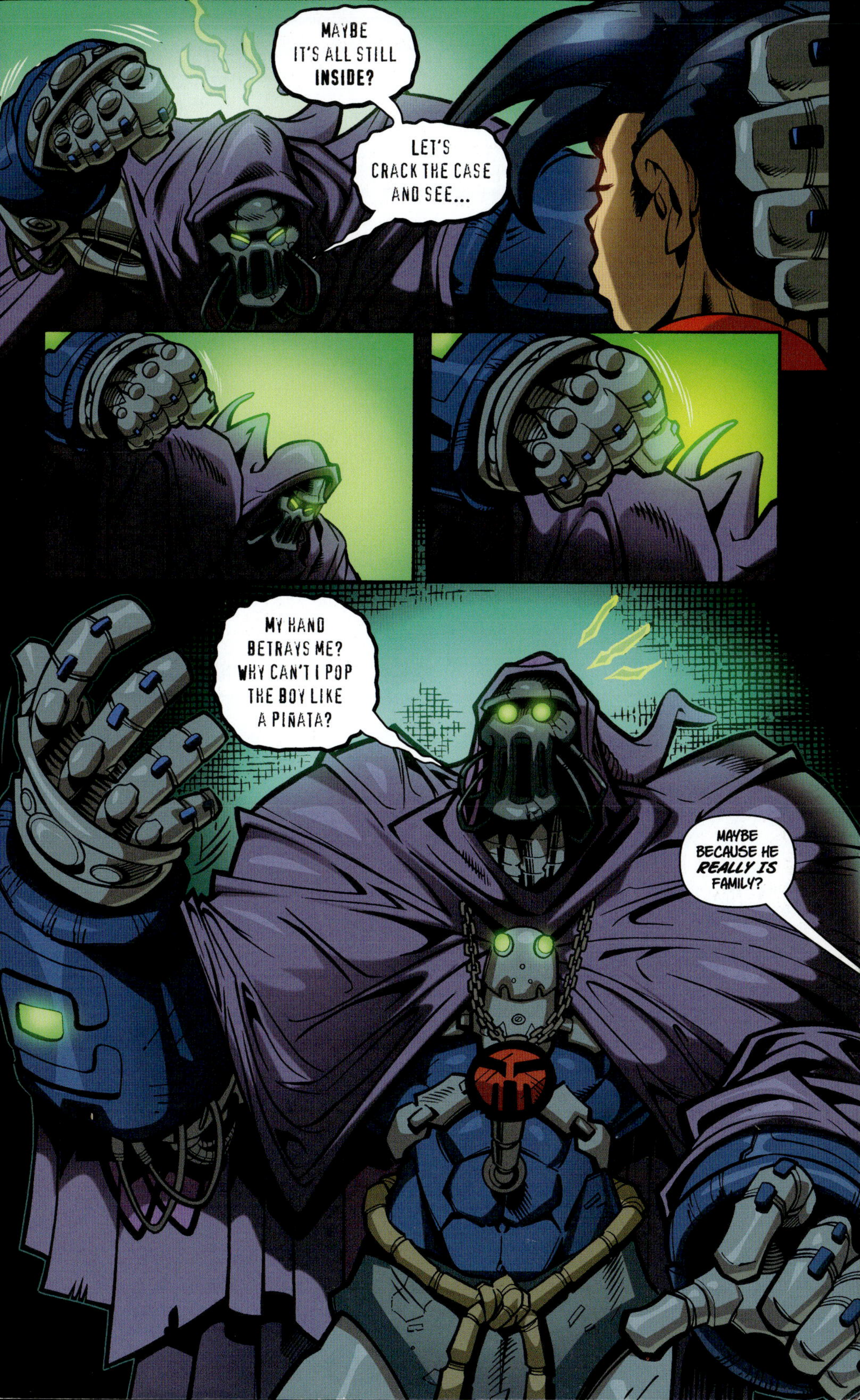
MAYBE IT'S ALL STILL INSIDE?
LET'S CRACK THE CASE AND SEE...
MY HAND BETRAYS ME? WHY CAN'T I POP THE BOY LIKE A PIÑATA?
MAYBE BECAUSE HE REALLY IS FAMILY?

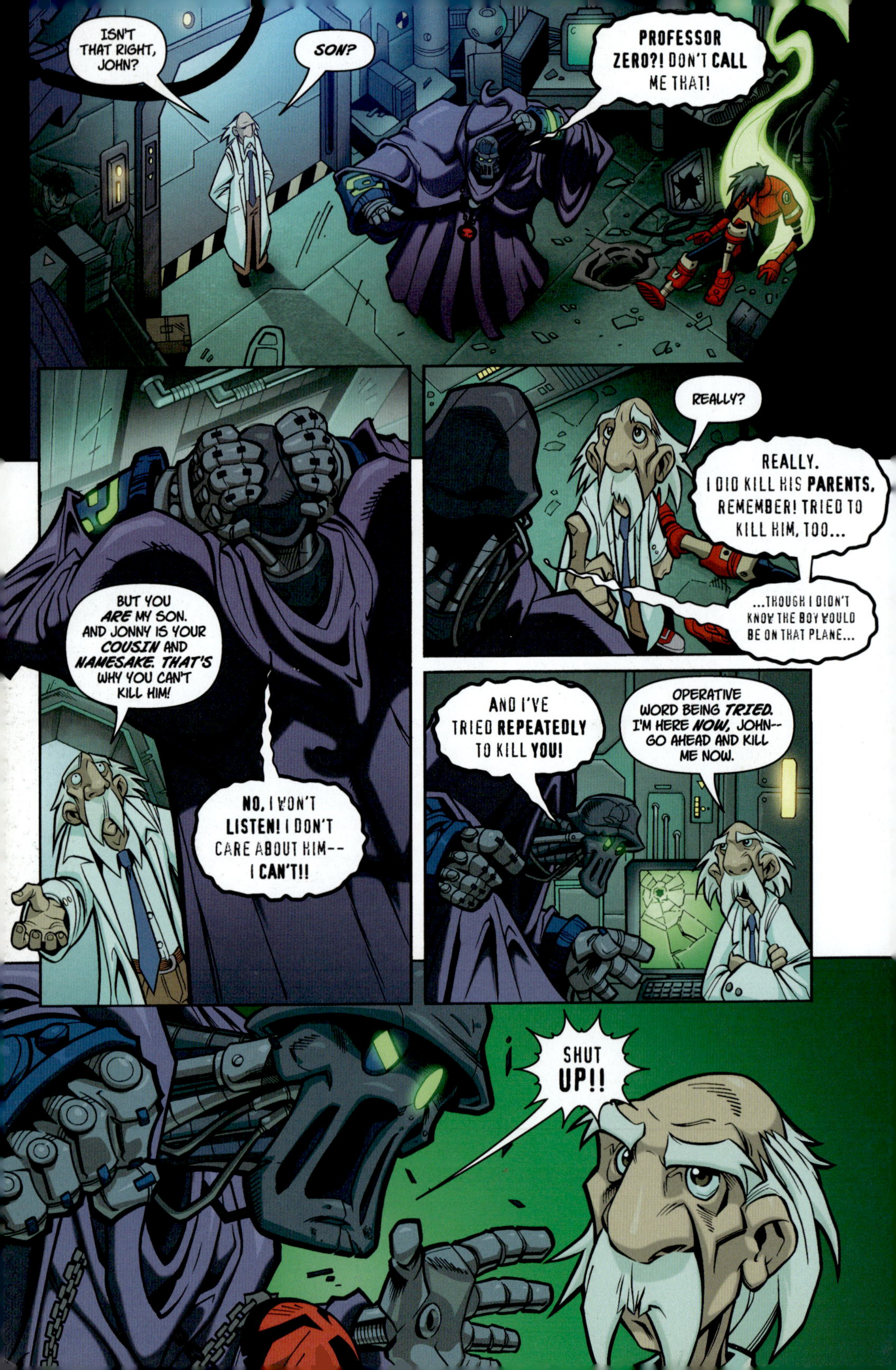
ISN'T THAT RIGHT, JOHN?
SON?
PROFESSOR ZERO?! DON'T CALL ME THAT!
BUT YOU ARE MY SON. AND JONNY IS YOUR COUSIN AND NAMESAKE. THAT'S WHY YOU CAN'T KILL HIM!
NO, I WON'T LISTEN! I DON'T CARE ABOUT HIM-- I CAN'T!!
REALLY?
REALLY. I DID KILL HIS PARENTS, REMEMBER! TRIED TO KILL HIM, TOO...
...THOUGH I DIDN'T KNOW THE BOY WOULD BE ON THAT PLANE...
AND I'VE TRIED REPEATEDLY TO KILL YOU!
OPERATIVE WORD BEING TRIED. I'M HERE NOW, JOHN-- GO AHEAD AND KILL ME NOW.
SHUT UP!!

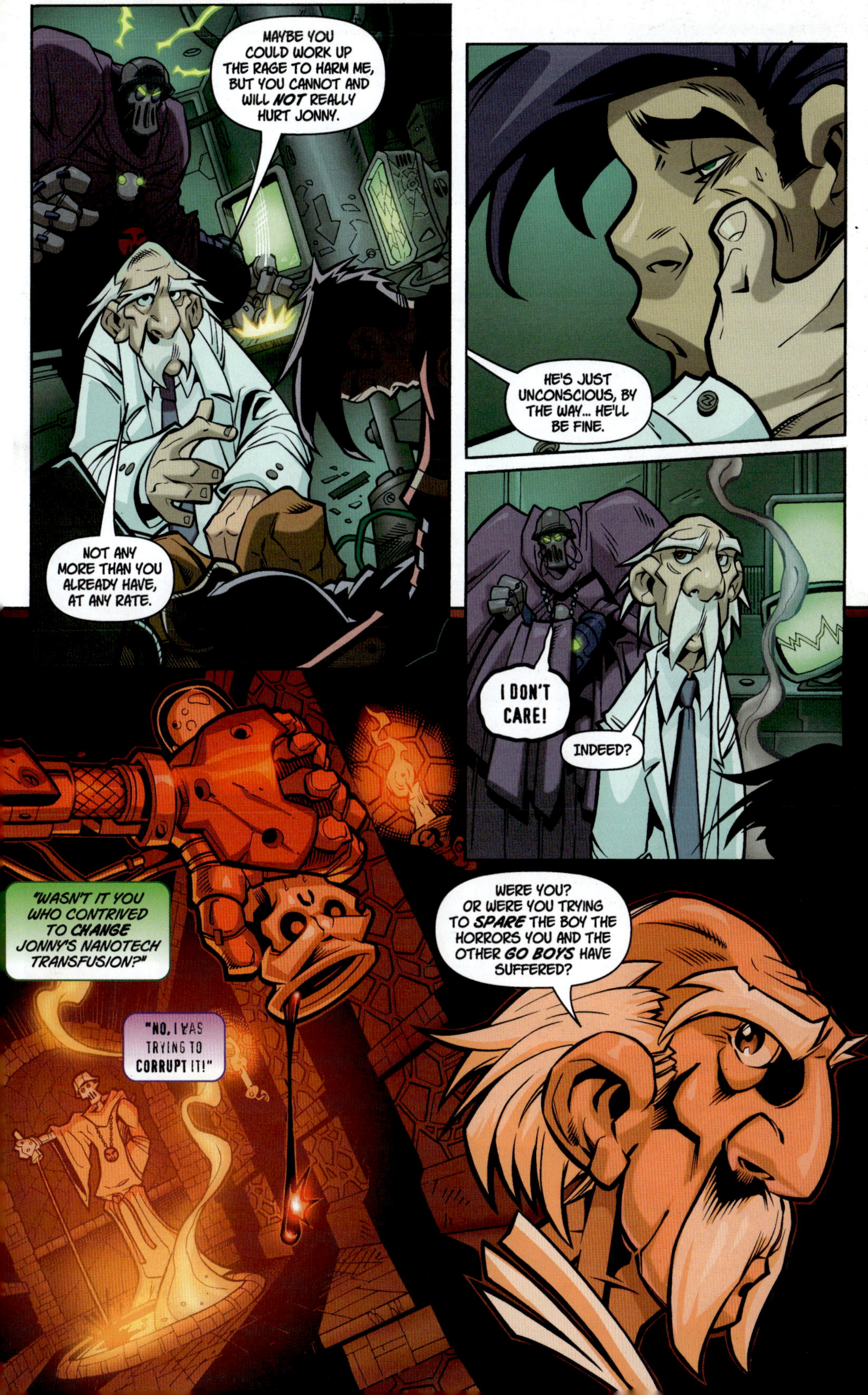
MAYBE YOU COULD WORK UP THE RAGE TO HARM ME, BUT YOU CANNOT AND WILL NOT REALLY HURT JONNY.
NOT ANY MORE THAN YOU ALREADY HAVE, AT ANY RATE.
HE'S JUST UNCONSCIOUS, BY THE WAY... HE'LL BE FINE.
I DON'T CARE!
INDEED?
"WASN'T IT YOU WHO CONTRIVED TO CHANGE JONNY'S NANOTECH TRANSFUSION?"
"NO, I WAS TRYING TO CORRUPT IT!"
WERE YOU? OR WERE YOU TRYING TO SPARE THE BOY THE HORRORS YOU AND THE OTHER GO BOYS HAVE SUFFERED?

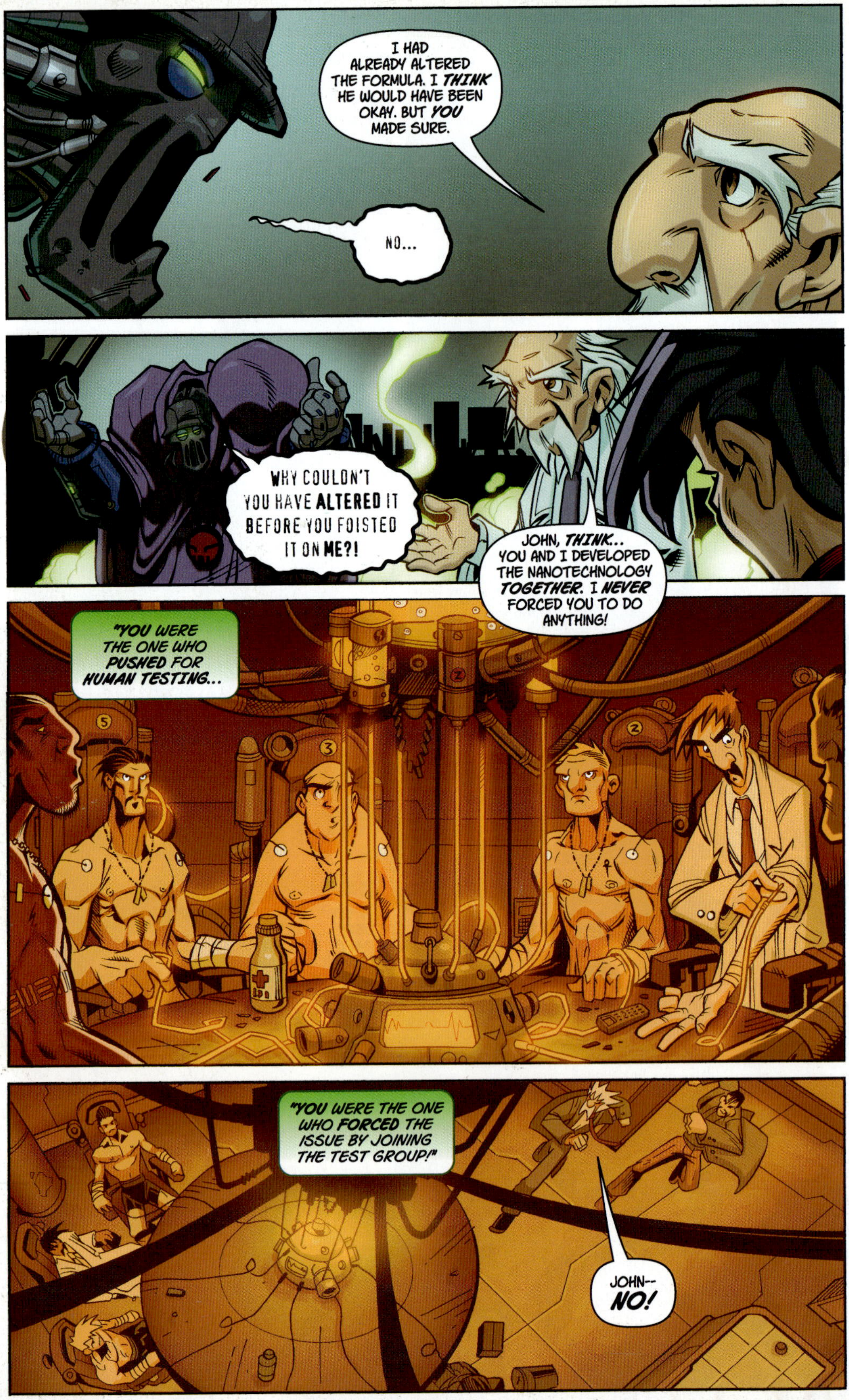
I HAD ALREADY ALTERED THE FORMULA. I *THINK* HE WOULD HAVE BEEN OKAY. BUT *YOU* MADE SURE.
NO...
WHY COULDN'T YOU HAVE **ALTERED** IT BEFORE YOU FOISTED IT ON **ME**?!
JOHN, *THINK*... YOU AND I DEVELOPED THE NANOTECHNOLOGY *TOGETHER*. I *NEVER* FORCED YOU TO DO ANYTHING!
"YOU WERE THE ONE WHO *PUSHED* FOR *HUMAN TESTING*...
"YOU WERE THE ONE WHO *FORCED* THE ISSUE BY JOINING THE TEST GROUP!"
JOHN-- *NO!*

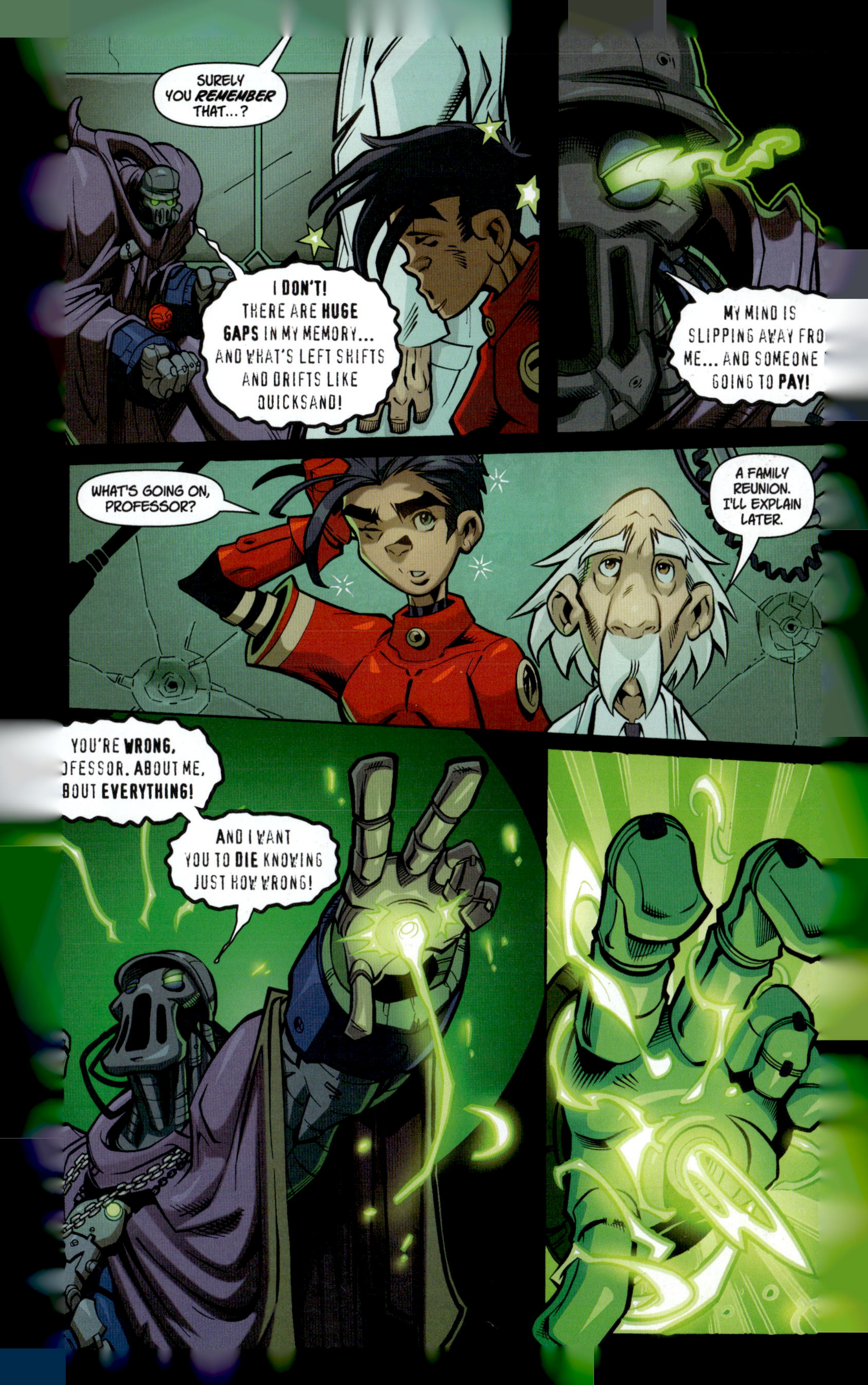
SURELY YOU REMEMBER THAT...?
I DON'T! THERE ARE HUGE GAPS IN MY MEMORY... AND WHAT'S LEFT SHIFTS AND DRIFTS LIKE QUICKSAND!
MY MIND IS SLIPPING AWAY FRO ME... AND SOMEONE GOING TO PAY!
WHAT'S GOING ON, PROFESSOR?
A FAMILY REUNION. I'LL EXPLAIN LATER.
YOU'RE WRONG, OFESSOR. ABOUT ME, BOUT EVERYTHING!
AND I WANT YOU TO DIE KNOWING JUST HOW WRONG!

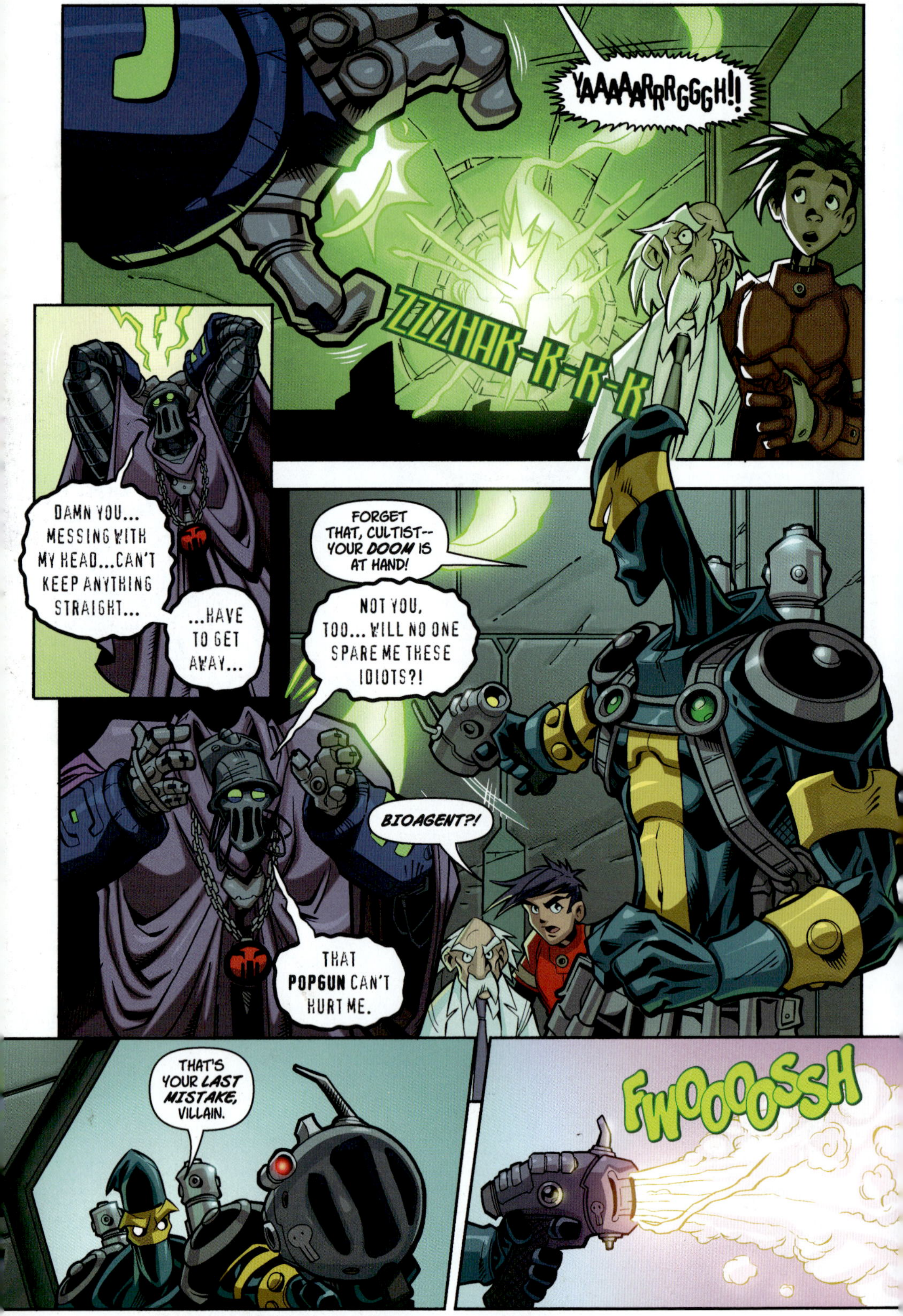

YAAAAARRRGGGH!!
ZZZHAK-K-K-K
DAMN YOU... MESSING WITH MY HEAD...CAN'T KEEP ANYTHING STRAIGHT...
...HAVE TO GET AWAY...
FORGET THAT, CULTIST-- YOUR DOOM IS AT HAND!
NOT YOU, TOO... WILL NO ONE SPARE ME THESE IDIOTS?!
BIOAGENT?!
THAT POPGUN CAN'T HURT ME.
THAT'S YOUR LAST MISTAKE, VILLAIN.
FWOOOOSSH

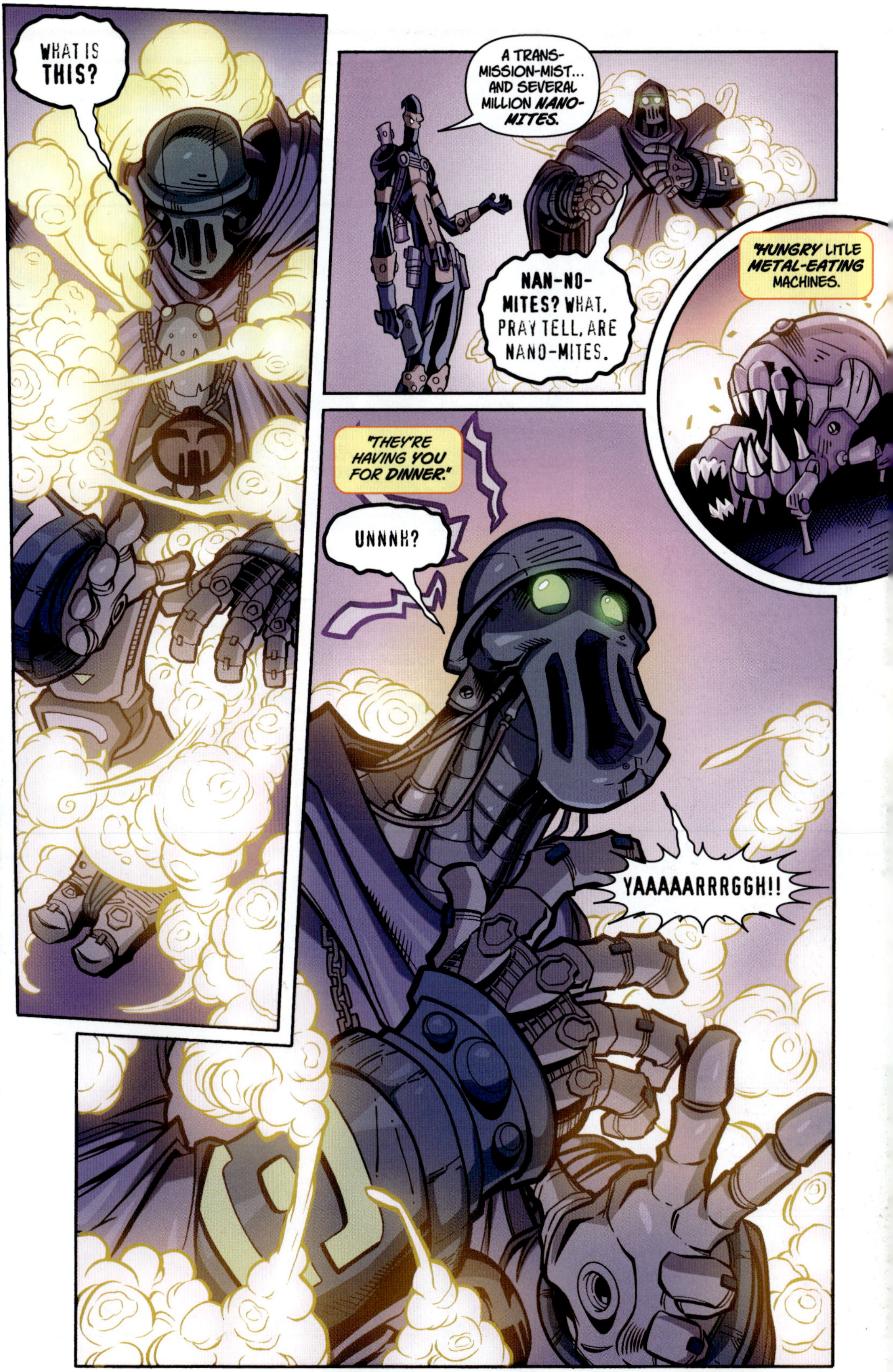

WHAT IS THIS?
A TRANS-MISSION-MIST... AND SEVERAL MILLION NANO-MITES.
NAN-NO-MITES? WHAT, PRAY TELL, ARE NANO-MITES.
"HUNGRY LITTLE METAL-EATING MACHINES.
"THEY'RE HAVING YOU FOR DINNER."
UNNNH?
YAAAAARRRGGH!!

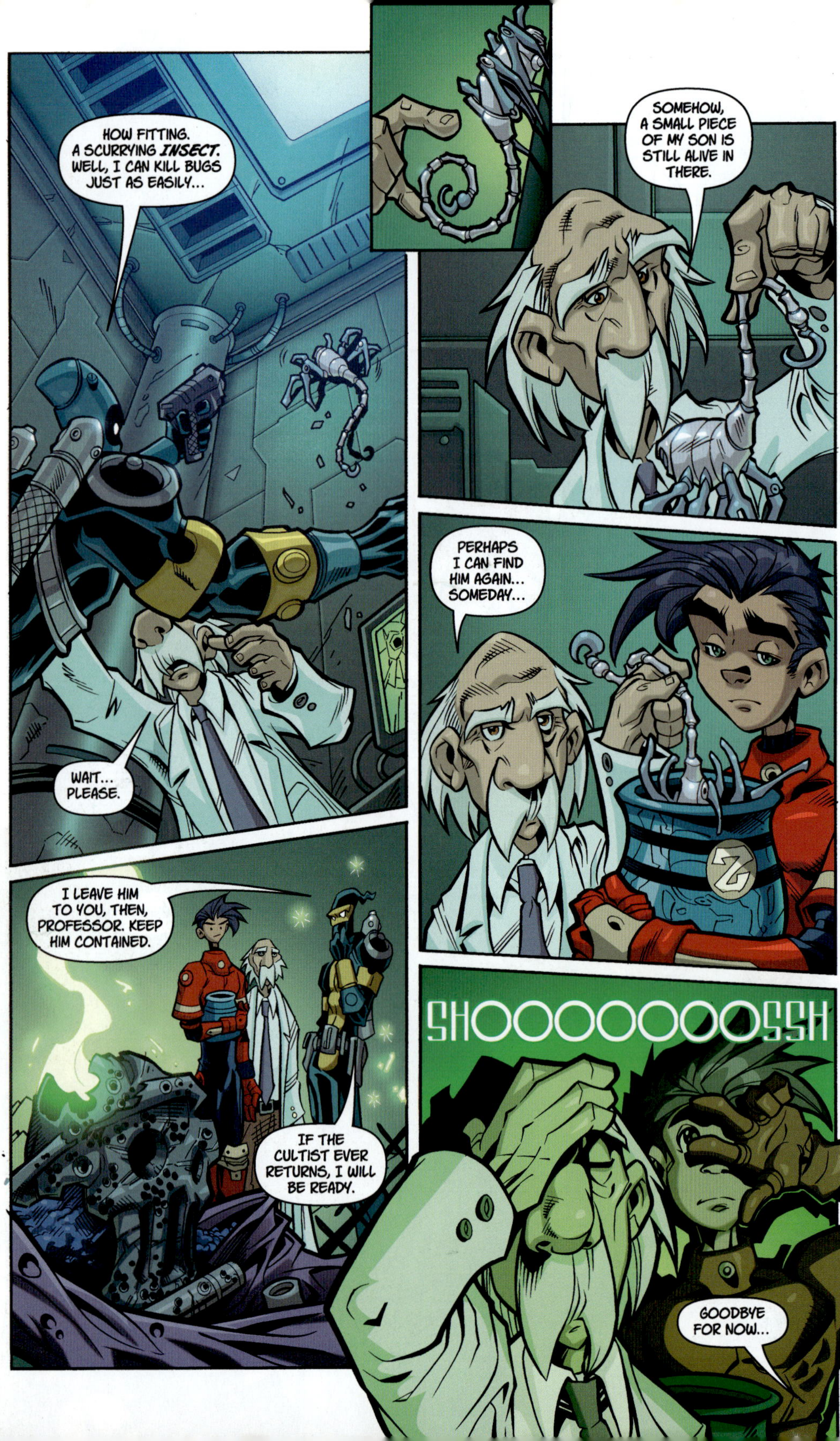
HOW FITTING. A SCURRYING *INSECT*. WELL, I CAN KILL BUGS JUST AS EASILY...
WAIT... PLEASE.
SOMEHOW, A SMALL PIECE OF MY SON IS STILL ALIVE IN THERE.
PERHAPS I CAN FIND HIM AGAIN... SOMEDAY...
I LEAVE HIM TO YOU, THEN, PROFESSOR. KEEP HIM CONTAINED.
IF THE CULTIST EVER RETURNS, I WILL BE READY.
SHOOOOOOOOSSH
GOODBYE FOR NOW...

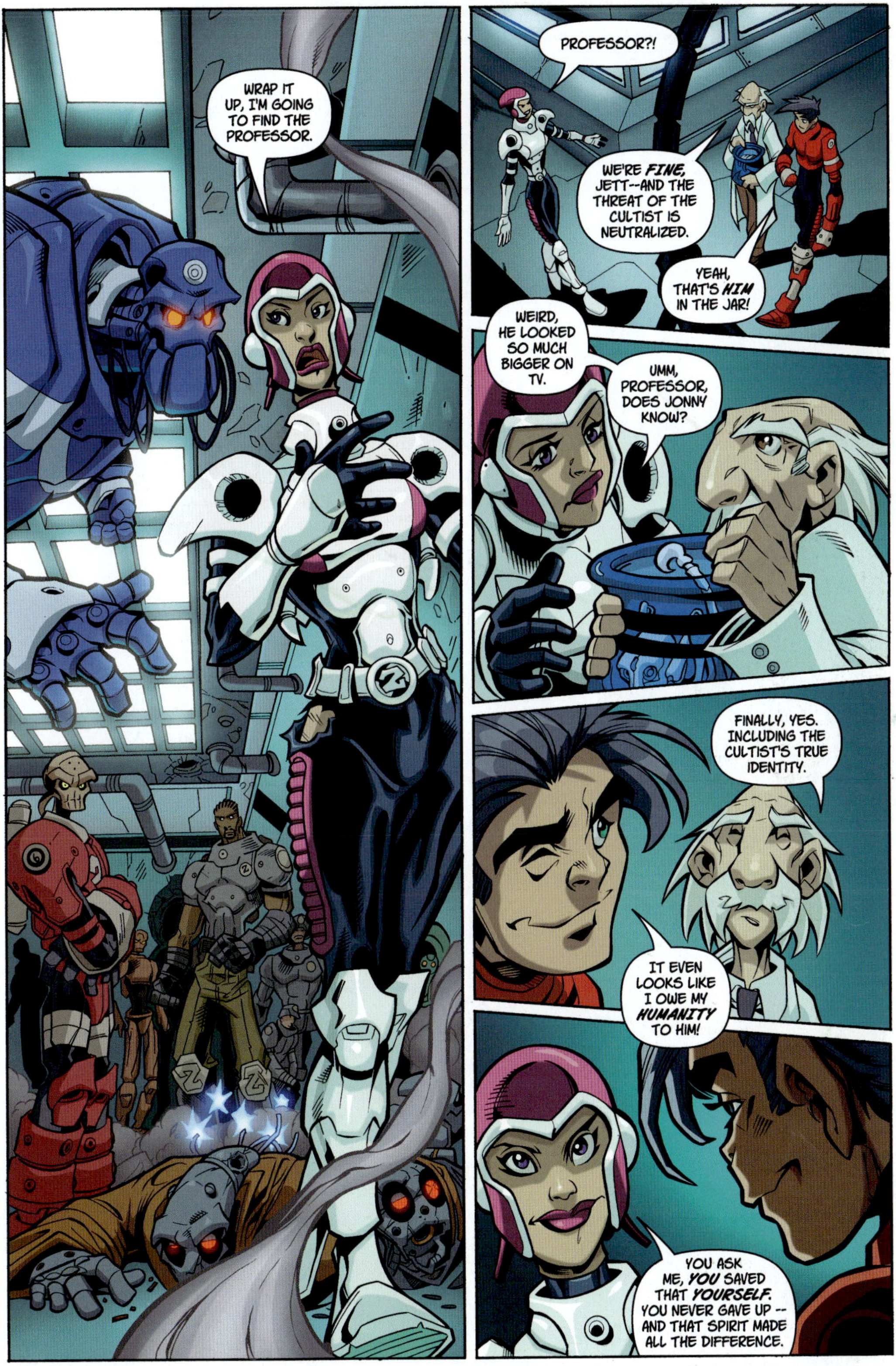
WRAP IT UP, I'M GOING TO FIND THE PROFESSOR.
PROFESSOR?!
WE'RE *FINE*, JETT--AND THE THREAT OF THE CULTIST IS NEUTRALIZED.
YEAH, THAT'S *HIM* IN THE JAR!
WEIRD, HE LOOKED SO MUCH BIGGER ON TV.
UMM, PROFESSOR, DOES JONNY KNOW?
FINALLY, YES. INCLUDING THE CULTIST'S TRUE IDENTITY.
IT EVEN LOOKS LIKE I OWE MY *HUMANITY* TO HIM!
YOU ASK ME, *YOU* SAVED THAT *YOURSELF*. YOU NEVER GAVE UP -- AND THAT SPIRIT MADE ALL THE DIFFERENCE.

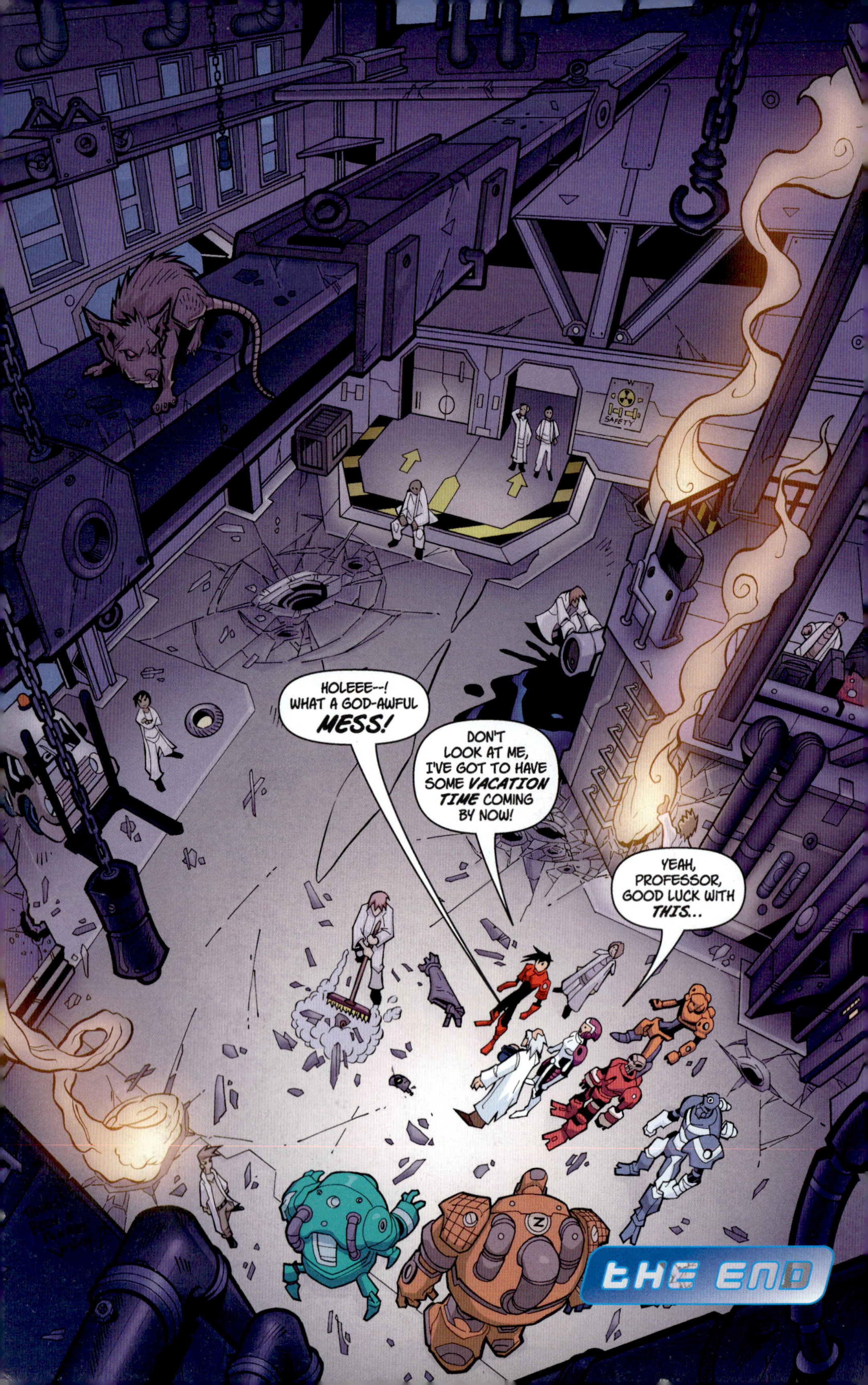
HOLEEE--! WHAT A GOD-AWFUL MESS!
DON'T LOOK AT ME, I'VE GOT TO HAVE SOME VACATION TIME COMING BY NOW!
YEAH, PROFESSOR, GOOD LUCK WITH THIS...
THE END

SKETCH GALLERY

ART BY JON SOMMARIVA

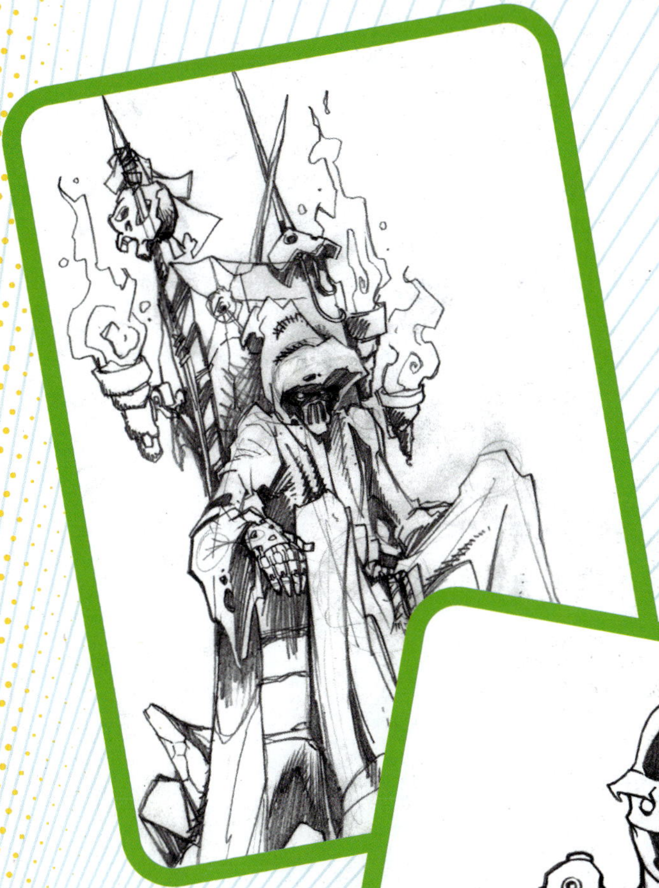

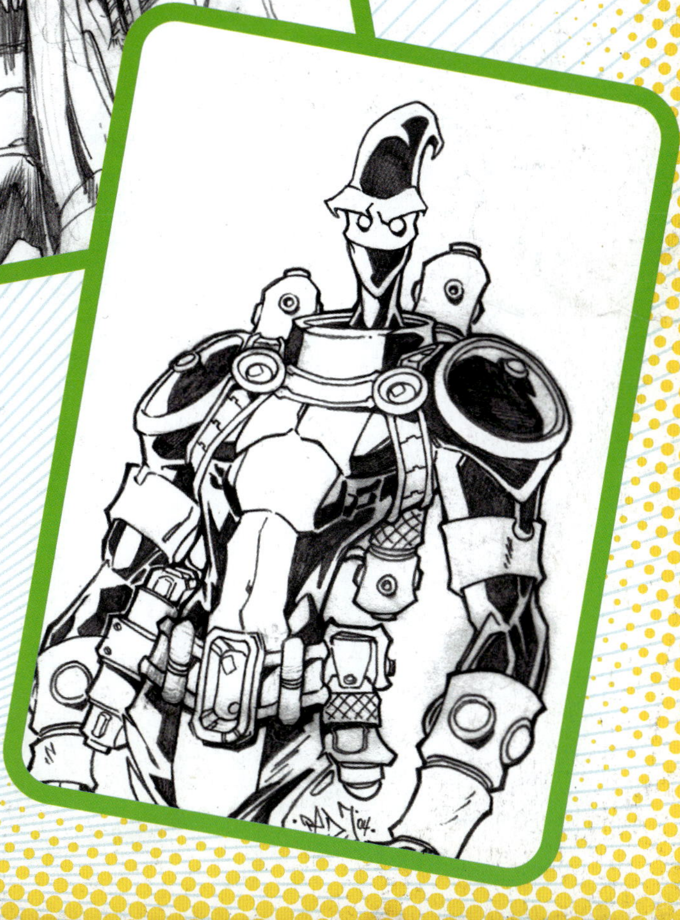

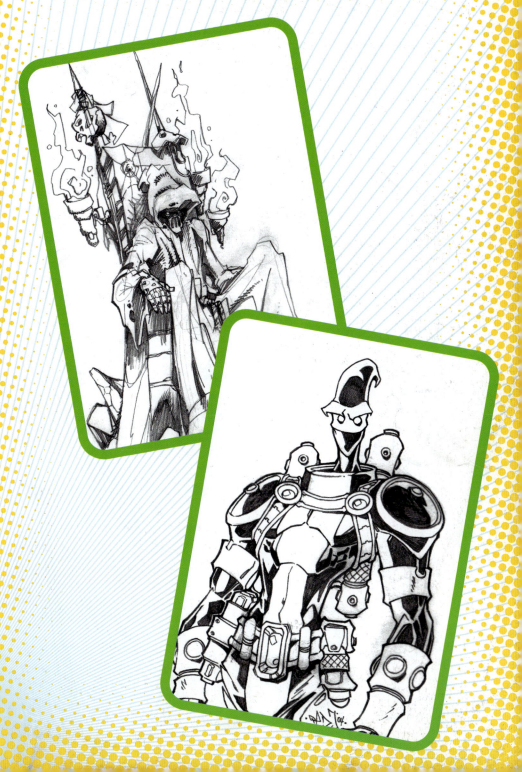

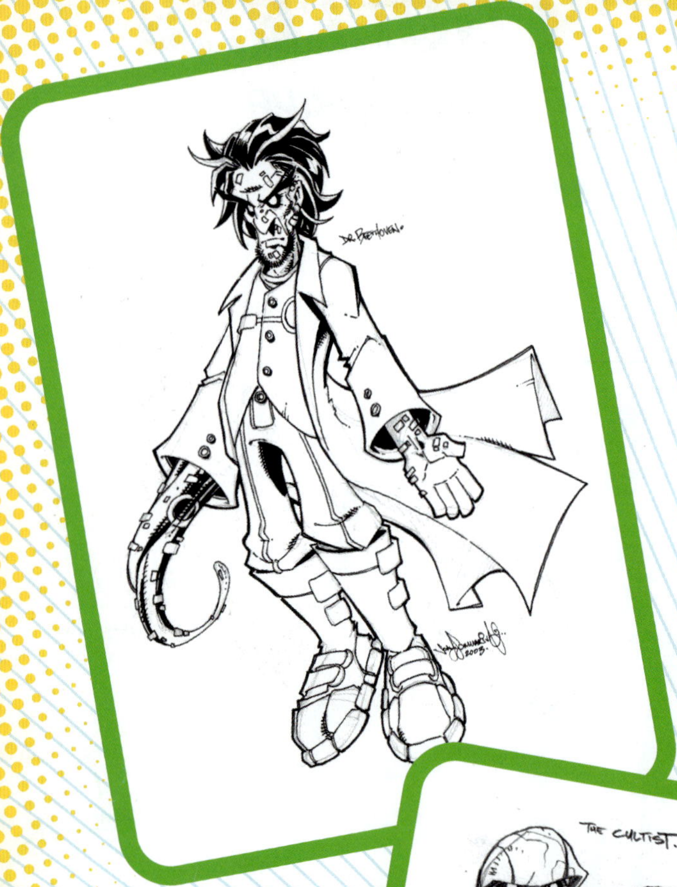
DR. BEETHOVEN.

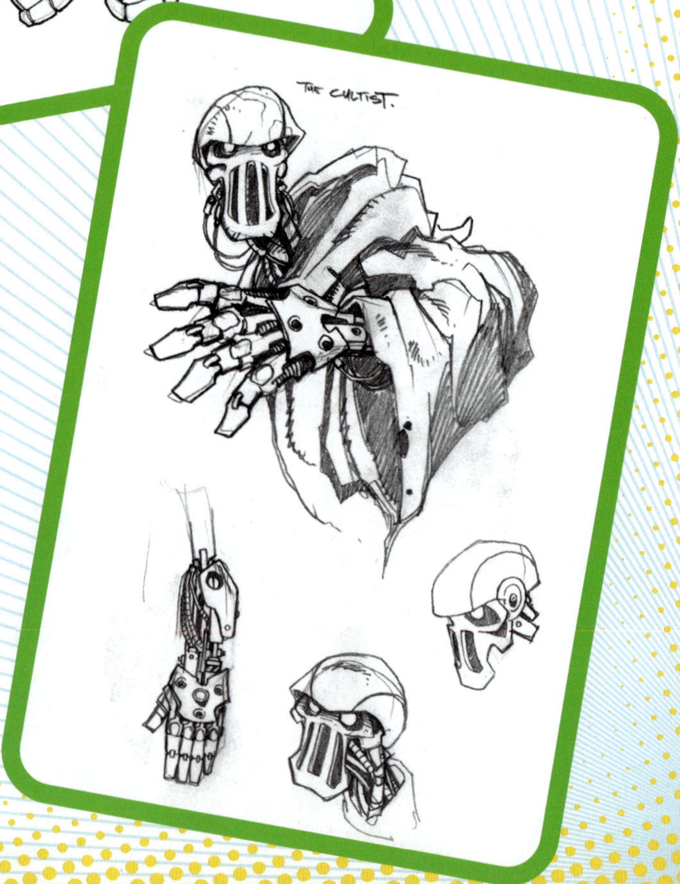
THE CULTIST.

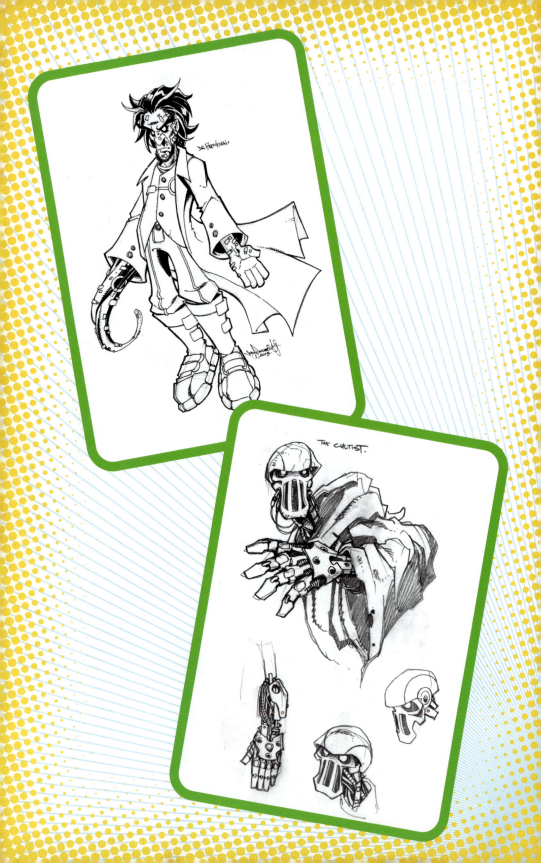